THIRSTING FOR MORE

THIRSTING FOR MORE
A Buddhist Approach to Craving
Kuladipa

THIRSTING FOR MORE: A BUDDHIST APPROACH TO CRAVING

Copyright © 2024 Kuladipa

First Edition, November 2024

All rights reserved.

ISBN 9798343693492

Cover art © Steve Johnson on Unsplash

All rights reserved. No part of this publication may be reproduced or utilised in any form or by any means, electronic or mechanical, including photocopying, microfilm, recording, or by any information storage and retrieval system, or used in another book, without written permission from the author.

Published by *Triratna InHouse Publications*
www.*triratna-inhouse-publications.org*

TRIRATNA
INHOUSE
PUBLICATIONS

Contents

Introduction: EXPLORING 11

PART ONE: THE PROBLEM

Chapter 1: INDULGING 24

Chapter 2: THIRSTING 47

Chapter 3: DELUDING 64

Chapter 4: FLEEING 84

Chapter 5: CLINGING 105

PART TWO: THE SOLUTION

Chapter 6: MEDICATING 124

Chapter 7: RELEASING 142

Chapter 8: PURIFYING 166

Chapter 9: DRIVING 183

Chapter 10: EXPANDING 207

WITH GRATITUDE 220

REFERENCES 222

To Maggie

with all my love

for her loyalty, honesty, elegance and fun

'One of the Buddha's main messages was that the pleasures we seek evaporate quickly and leave us thirsting for more'

Why Buddhism is True

Robert Wright

'To some extent, we all have temporal pleasure, but what we really need is eternal peace.'

The Essence of Tibetan Buddhism

Lama Thubten Yeshe

Introduction:

EXPLORING

We humans are a strange bunch.

We insist on doing things which we know deep down will make us unhappy or cause us pain. We can recognize that what we are doing is unhelpful to us, goes against our better judgment, but we still do it nonetheless.

Some examples. At dinnertime we might eat far more than we really need to and end up with a terrible bellyache. We stay up late to watch just one more episode of the latest boxset on TV, and then perhaps just one more and, in the morning, we feel wretched at work due to lack of sleep. We get into a discussion with a family member over something relatively trivial which gets more and more heated, confrontational, and personal; we know really that this is going to be bad news for us both and will have repercussions that will take a lot of effort to sort out, but we just can't stop ourselves, we can't give way.

We grab at things to make us feel better, but they often make us feel worse. We try to satisfy our various appetites but end up feeling disappointed. Doesn't it seem perverse that what humans turn to in order to make them feel better are the very things that end up causing them more unhappiness. Why do we continually punish ourselves?

It can feel sometimes as though we are being compelled to act, that there's a force driving us that we are not really in control of, even a drive that is outside of ourselves. This compulsion, this drive, we can call craving.

According to Buddhism, this urge underlies our unhappiness. In this book I shall look at craving in its many forms, describe how it plays such a dominant role in our life, and explain how Buddhist practices can help us to come to terms with our cravings.

A whim, an obsession

Yes, we have basic physical needs – when we are hungry, to eat; when we are thirsty to drink; when we are excessively hot or cold, to keep our body at a safe and comfortable temperature. But there are also physical desires which are not usually needs, for example, 'I want chocolate'. Our cravings can range from primeval urges to little passing fancies. From an obsession to a whim.

There are so many words similar to craving that can describe wanting something. We may *long* for solitude, *wish* for harmony, *desire* to drink something bubbly, *yearn* for a break, *thirst* for a thrill, *lust* after a work colleague, *covet* our neighbour's car, *fancy* an ice cream, *pine* for how things used to be, *itch* for a change of surroundings, *dream* of paradise, *hanker* after recognition, *ache* for sunshine, *mope* for Manchego, *binge* on biscuits, *be desperate* for a smoke, or *be dying for* a ….. (you can fill in).

We may have an *urge* to be destructive, an *appetite* like a horse, a *yen* to be like Oprah Winfrey or the Dalai Lama, a *passion* to dance the light fandango, a *mania* for online gambling, an *addiction* to sugar, an *infatuation* for video games, or a *hunger* for adventure.

We may *clutch* at straws, *cleave* to financial security, *fasten* to people like us, *adhere* to a religious creed, *embrace* certainty, *engage* in self-harm, *attach* ourselves to left-wing/right-wing views, or *grasp* at our sense of identity.

But here a word about terminology. When I use the word craving, unless it is qualified in some way, it is to describe desires that are unhelpful and unhealthy for us, and for other people. Desire is in itself a neutral word; some desires are harmful, some are beneficial. Some 'craving' words then do not always have negative connotations. We may have a lust for life, a thirst for knowledge, or a longing for freedom from suffering. Desire then can be both a negative and a positive emotion; we shall explore this in more detail later in the book.

There are states of the craving human mind which long for something quite abstract. Laziness, which I'm sure we all recognize and experience from time to time, is a craving, a craving for sensual comfort perhaps or a desire to avoid something difficult. Conceit, comparing ourselves to others is a craving, a craving perhaps to be 'superior'. Envy, a craving to have a quality or possession that somebody else has. Avarice, a craving to possess things for their own sake rather than to use and enjoy them.

Concealment and deceit, a craving to hide from others things which might make us look bad in the eyes of others.

We frequently want our world to be other than as it is now. We find ourselves bumping along on the 'if only' train – if only my body wasn't like this (fat, thin, old, infirm); if only the rain would stop, I'm aching for sunshine. If only my football team would win this week, for a change. If only I didn't have all that mental chattering going on in my head all the time, it's driving me mad.

And then there is technology; the cyberworld, something that is seemingly indispensable in our lives, but also frequently the bane of our existence. We can call it 'screen craving'. Everywhere we look we'll encounter perhaps the most generalised, predominant form of craving in today's world – the desire to look at a screen. For years I didn't possess a smartphone. I knew what compulsive viewing the digital realm can be, even when you were not carrying it around in your pocket all the time. But when I eventually succumbed, not that long ago, and bought myself a super-duper shiny new smartphone, I soon realized what an addictive little critter it can be. And I know that I'm not the only one.

Craving then appears to be a problem in our lives. When one craves one is not at ease; this we will explore in Chapter 7. As we have seen, cravings often lead to disappointment. Even if we get what we desire, there is the frustration that it will not last forever. That beautiful linen shirt that I've been looking at longingly online, but which fades and loses its appeal after the first wash.

The source of our dissatisfaction

In the *dharma*, the teachings of the Buddha, craving plays a central role. An understanding of what craving is, and how we relate to it, is fundamental to Buddhist practice. In brief, the Buddha saw that craving (he used the word for 'thirst') is the primary cause of the dissatisfaction and sometimes distress that we experience in life. He then went on to explain that craving can be approached in such a way that it no longer compels us, and he described a path that we could follow to achieve freedom from this compulsion. He also proposed categories of craving. All of these teachings we will start to explore in Chapter 2.

Buddhism says that craving is a 'poison', but that it is just one of the poisons, the *kleśa*, that afflict us.[1] Additionally, there are ill-will and delusion. Ill-will refers to hatred, aversion, resentment, and anger, directed towards others and also ourselves. Apart from a craving to possess, consume, grab hold of, cling to something, there are also what we can call negative cravings; a craving to avoid or get rid of, a desire to push things away; things or people we don't like or don't want to have in our experience. And we can see then that this is just another form of craving. A desire not to engage with the unpleasant. Ill-will is just craving pointed in another direction. One is a running away to, the other a running away from. Hatred, aversion, ill-will, anger are in a sense frustrated craving.

Craving and delusion are also closely connected, as we shall examine particularly in Chapter 3. The most obvious way in which they relate to each other is that we delude ourselves about the amount of pleasure we may get from indulging our cravings. We over-emphasize the positive aspects and under-emphasize the negatives. Here's what the Buddhist teacher and writer Subhuti has to say. 'Let's take a simple example such as alcohol. We see a bottle of wine or whiskey, and in our mind arises the idea of happy forgetfulness, that pleasant mood of easy relaxation in which we don't worry about what we say or do, and all our cares have evaporated. At the same time, we choose to ignore the fact that we are going to wake up the next morning with a splitting headache and realize with a groan that we have made fools of ourselves, at the very least. In this way, we exaggerate the pleasure-power of alcohol, and deny its pain-power.'[2]

Clearly some of us suffer more than others from the effects of craving. For one person a velleity[3], for another a destructive addiction. What one person may crave and see as problematic, another person may see as very minor. I remember once being in a group of fellow Buddhists who met weekly to support and encourage each other. One of us shared that he'd been having a lot of lustful fantasies recently. Others treated it very lightly and said that this happens with them all the time and he shouldn't bother about it too much. However, for him it was a real issue that was disturbing his peace of mind and he needed to address it for that reason.

But craving is there for all of us in one form or another, and to all of us it brings at the very least dissatisfaction into our lives. As Jon Kabat-Zinn, the well-known proponent of mindful approaches to mental well-being, puts it, we have 'life-constraining addictions, small and large'.[4] A particular craving may unsettle you, send you off kilter, and disturb whatever equilibrium you have in your life.

Becoming compulsive

As we shall return to in Chapter 4, some cravings are by their very nature harmful. For example, all kinds of addiction, to heroin, to alcohol, to online gambling. They are naturally intoxicating and damage our physical and mental well-being. Others are only harmful if we cling to them in a compulsive manner. For instance, we may have a strong desire to be alone, which in itself is not a problem and may be very beneficial to our mental health. But if it develops into agoraphobia, an inability to go out of the house, a dread to mix with others that becomes neurotic, then clearly this is going to cause us great difficulties.

It is those desires which are excessive and uncontrolled which damage, inhibit and blind us. Working out, going to the gym, can be a very healthy activity to maintain one's fitness, but it can also become compulsive and take over our lives. To be the best that one can at one's job is praiseworthy, but if 'achiever-fever' sets in it can cause much stress to us and those around us. A desire for order in one's life may be a good habit to develop, but a longing for everything to be always neatly and tidily organized, to be always in charge of every little detail, can become obsessional and drive one crazy. Our cravings may become a big deal for us; they can dominate our lives.

Craving, in the many ways it manifests itself, tends to be our favourite pastime as human beings. It is a trait that we are on first-name terms with. We spend our time craving in all sorts of subtle ways, often in ways which we are unaware of. And we shouldn't feel bad about ourselves because we think we should be in control of these urges when we're not. Longings, urges, are ubiquitous in our consciousness. Part of being human is to experience cravings. We live to crave. We are not alone in this respect, and it can help to realize this; it is part of our common humanity, what we share with all other humans.

But despite the fact that humans all experience these strong desires, we find no easy ways to deal with them. Most of the time we just *want* something. What are you wanting right now? Something that is unhelpful to you and unhealthy, or something that is beneficial to you and others?

Buddhists are not exempt from craving. Sometimes, as a 'good Buddhist' who practices non-attachment, I can't help but feel perplexed (and ashamed) at being a prisoner to my cravings and feel what an idiot I can be at times, to be slavishly following my mouth-watering appetites. That cheesecake certainly looks good to me, in fact almost irresistible, but I know if I have one slice then I'll have to have another, and from past experience two slices will make me feel a bit sick.

Actually, on second thoughts, having given myself a bit of space to think about it, I don't think I will indulge thank you very much; not this time anyway. Giving your mind a bit of space, a gap between the urge when it arises to consume the 'cheesecake', and the actual grasping for it, this is a Buddhist practice of mindfulness, of watching the workings of the mind rather than slavishly giving in to them. We will find out more about this in Chapters 2 and 7.

Taking the time to address our craving

If craving is a hindrance in our lives and a barrier to our contentment and fulfilment, then we need to take the time to address it. Problems do not go away of their own accord; they have to be worked through or else they become an obstruction to our well-being. But, although the question of our craving is a predicament that we all need to deal with, this doesn't mean that we need to lead a life of self-flagellation, punishing ourselves for every passing fancy, as though this was the only way to achieve happiness. Quite the opposite. When we find ways of addressing and giving up these tricky longings and urges, we can experience real joy and a sense of liberation that we may never have experienced before.

We know how difficult it is to give up habits, habits that may have developed over many many years, even when we know they are not doing us any favours. But although there are unhelpful and unhealthy longings, habitual cravings that can plague us and haunt us, there are also helpful and healthy longings which lead us to contentment and fulfilment. As we shall see later, desire, or at least certain types of desire, far from being a hindrance to our happiness, are in fact central to it. What desire could be more excellent than the desire for all living beings to be happy?

And here we arrive at the great paradox. Desire makes us unhappy, leaves us unfulfilled, and yet we cannot live without it. It is our enemy, but at the same time our friend.

The good news is that we can come to terms with our powerful cravings without resorting to thoughts like "I'll go mad if I can't have my fix of nicotine" or "What am I going to do when I experience anxiety if I can't have a drink?". Giving in to craving doesn't reduce stress. It gives the impression of an immediate relief of tension, but the relief is just temporary, it never solves the stress, and can actually make it worse.

People subject to strong cravings tend to be more stressed than those who are not; habitual craving is itself stressful. But, using Buddhist teachings, we can address and deal with these stresses. We can live a life which is not frustrating and constraining, but rather rich and rewarding. 'We each possess within ourselves' writes the Tibetan teacher Lama Thubten Yeshe, 'not only the answer to our own problems but the potential to live our lives on a much higher level than we currently imagine possible.'[5]

What this book is about

If you're not bothered about your cravings, as I have described them here, and are happy indulging them, gratifying them, then these writings are probably not for you. If, however, you see craving as an issue in your life that is causing you unhappiness, unease or makes you feel bad about yourself, and you want to do something about it, then read on. My hope is that these writings will have something to say to those of us who are struggling to deal with longings, urges and compulsions which are having a negative impact on our lives, as well as to Buddhists and others who are interested in exploring the phenomenon of craving more deeply.

To get something out of these writings, it does not matter whether you consider yourself a Buddhist or not. I do, but you may not. What is important is what you value in life. The Buddha's message is there for all. These writings are an attempt to use the Buddha's teaching to explore craving; what craving is, and how to address it. You don't have to be a monk or a nun in a monastery to apply the Buddha's *dharma* to your life. Here in the 21st century, wherever we live, whatever work we do or don't do, the *dharma* is available to us all. This is a book for those of you who want more than just a temporary reprieve from your difficulties, from your itches and pinings; a glass or two of wine might achieve that. Buddhism says that there is a different way of looking at life, a way that leads to freedom and contentment. And it is for those who seek this freedom that these writings are aimed.

For me this is also a personal exploration. Craving is my preferred pastime too. Underlying these writings is how one person has benefitted from Buddhist practice in order to address his cravings. I first encountered Buddhism as a teenager through reading a Sunday newspaper supplement during a tea break while working as a hospital porter. So drawn was I to what I read that, within a matter of weeks, I was on my way to India on a pilgrimage to try to find a Buddhist guru who could teach me more. Unfortunately, the teacher didn't materialize at that time, and it was only many years later, seeking a solution and meaning to my crazy mixed-up life, that I re-engaged with Buddhism. I haven't looked back since, and my life has changed immeasurably, for the better.

The eighth century Indian Buddhist Śāntideva said at the beginning of his famous work, the *Bodhicaryāvatāra*, that he was writing in order to perfume his mind. I take this to mean that the process of writing brings insight. It certainly has for me, and I hope for you the reader this book will bring some insight too.

I am a member of the Triratna Buddhist Order, and Triratna is a worldwide movement which seeks to draw from many different Buddhist traditions and present the *dharma* in a way that is accessible to all. In the spirit of Triratna, I have tried to be eclectic. Since Buddhism does not have one authoritative formal creed, but rather a set of principles which have been interpreted and developed in different ways over the centuries, numerous Buddhist traditions have arisen promoting different aspects of the *dharma*. In these writings I have followed the example of Sangharakshita, the founder and principal teacher of Triratna, with a wide-ranging approach to examining craving. My aim has been purposely to bring together, and quote extensively from, the thoughts and ideas of a variety of Buddhist teachers from a broad range of Buddhist traditions. In addition, I would like to think that this book can also be seen as an introduction to some of the main teachings of Buddhism through exploring the theme of craving. No prior knowledge of Buddhism is required to get something from this book, as Buddhist terms are explained as they arise.

These writings are an exploration then, a search for what this thing called craving actually is, how it manifests itself in many different ways and, principally, what Buddhism says we can do about it. *Thirsting for More* is not primarily a scholarly work, a book aimed at those with an intellectual or philosophical bent, but rather I aim to simplify and clarify Buddhist approaches to desire. The hope is that, by taking an emotion that everyone experiences constantly and can relate to directly, you the reader will be drawn into wanting to find out more about how Buddhism can address issues which plague our lives. Although this introduction is entitled Exploring, in fact the whole of these writings is an exploration into what craving is and how we can address it in our lives. Some themes will reoccur in different places as I try to explore them from different perspectives.

These writings are based on the teachings of the Buddha. Those teachings, as they have been passed on through succeeding generations across twenty-five centuries, are not so much about transferring on a body of information. Rather they are about communicating the teachings in such a way that they relate to people's own experiences, helping and encouraging them to reflect on the teachings, and apply them to their day-to-day life. The writings presented here are done so in that vein.

What is extraordinary is that teachings, expounded by the Buddha so long ago in a totally different culture to that in which most of us live today, should have so much relevance right now to us, the world in which we live, and the problems around craving which we all face. The *dharma* of the Buddha is timeless. How does it seem possible that a teacher from two and a half millennia ago can speak directly to us about reducing our dependence on a smartphone? But he does. We would all like to stop screwing up. Buddhism provides us with a set of guidelines, not commandments, on how to live our lives without screwing up. It has the immediate goal of reducing our unease, and the ultimate goal of eliminating it. And throughout the centuries, as the Buddhist writer David Brazier points out, the 'Buddha's message of compassion has been a wonderful inspiration to millions of people.'[6]

Buddhism is a spiritual path. The word spiritual can often throw people, it may seem too airy-fairy, idealistic, impractical or concerned with weird rituals and beliefs. Or it may conjure up memories of a religion that one has long since abandoned or indeed never related to. In fact, the spiritual path is really about developing those qualities of the human spirit that bring about happiness for ourselves and others. Qualities such as kindness, love, generosity, tolerance, forgiveness, gratitude, contentment, compassion, equanimity and transcendence. And freedom from the emotions that restrict the great potential that we have - emotions such as craving. Until we address our cravings we cannot progress spiritually, our well-being can only be partial. In fact, a spiritual path is a continual revisiting and readdressing of those things, thoughts and emotions which we find difficult. Do Buddhists long for anything? Yes, most definitely. We long 'to experience a type of peace and happiness that is stable and reliable, unruffled by changing circumstances and uninfluenced by the passage of time.'[7] This is the theme of *Part Two* of the book.

At the end of each chapter there are questions for the reader to reflect upon. Reflection is an essential part of the road to wisdom[8]. Through reflecting we examine our own cravings and how they manifest themselves in us.

The structure of Thirsting for More

Buddhism is about 'doing'. It is a practice, or a set of practices that we do, not just a bunch of theoretical musings; practices such as meditation, study and reflection, behaving ethically and altruistically, and deep friendship. This is why the titles of the chapters in these writings are all verbs, 'doing' words - Thirsting, Clinging, Releasing, Expanding. They represent processes rather than static ideas. Life we can say is a verb rather than a noun. This in fact is how Buddhism sees the world, as a system of becoming rather than a system of being.

Like other Buddhist authors before me, I use the medical metaphor of the Four Noble Truths for the structure of these writings - the existence of the illness; the cause or its origin; the prognosis or its ceasing; and the medicine or the means to its ceasing.

The chapters in *Part One:The Problem* diagnose the 'illness' we are all subject to, and describe the cause and the symptoms of that illness. Chapter 1 *Indulging* looks at the most basic craving, the 'craving for sensual pleasure' in its many forms. In chapter 2 *Thirsting* there follows a survey of why and how craving is central to Buddhism. Fundamental to our craving is that it is based on misconceptions, and chapter 3 *Deluding* explores how we deceive ourselves and impute unrealistic qualities to our objects of desire. Chapter 4 *Fleeing* looks in detail at the Buddhist term 'craving for non-existence', which we can summarise as the desire to avoid difficult experience. *Part One* finishes with Chapter 5 *Clinging*, an examination of the 'thirst' which is at the heart of all our craving, namely the 'craving for existence', for the reinforcing, satisfying, promotion and protecting of our 'self'.

But it is not enough to diagnose and describe the unease or pain that our cravings create for us. That would be akin to moaning on about the noisy next-door neighbour or the leaking roof, but not proposing to do anything about it, not trying to come up with possible solutions. And so, *Part Two:The Solution* is about the medicine, the treatment that Buddhist teachings offer us.

Chapter 6 *Medicating* sets the scene by proposing that craving is not something we can just ignore or bury, but need to attend to, and presents an outline of different practices which are amplified in the remaining chapters. Chapter 7 *Releasing* examines how we can turn away from a life based on clinging onto objects and ideas which are ultimately unsatisfying. Chapter 8 *Purifying* begins to take us deeper into Buddhist practice and shows that we can refine our perception and develop insight into the insubstantial nature of our cravings. In Chapter 9 *Driving* we explore how we are able to integrate and incorporate our scattered dispersed energies and transform them into the desire that we need in order to make progress on the path towards fulfilling our potential. In the end, as Chapter 10 *Expanding* describes, we can move beyond our everyday life of self-centered craving to one of generosity and love; from a self-mode to an expansive mode.

Part One then mostly describes, *Part Two* mostly prescribes. I invite you to explore with me this most basic of our emotions, this most fundamental aspect of being human, this most devastating of our afflictions, and this most powerful energy for liberating us.

PART ONE: THE PROBLEM

Chapter 1:

INDULGING

For us to really understand the hold that our desires have upon us, we firstly need to look at the *process* of craving in more detail, to see how it operates and how it manifests itself. We need to recognize craving in ourselves. In this chapter we will explore the role our senses play in the arising of craving and how we respond to whatever stimulates our desires. We'll look at the ways in which we seek excitement, how forces at play in our everyday lives provoke our appetites, and how our urges may lead us to bypass whatever values we may hold.

The thirst for sensual pleasure

The basic human urge for something, the basic craving, is the desire which arises through the six senses; as well as the five traditional Western senses, in Buddhism the mind is also categorised as a sense. This craving is sensual desire. It is a craving for sense objects which provide a pleasant feeling; a craving for the sensory pleasure itself; a craving for happiness incited by a smell, a taste, a touch, a sight, a sound, a mental image. If coffee, for example, is your favourite drug, you could be hooked by the smell of coffee; by the imagined taste of it; by the feel of coffee beans between your fingers; by the sight of a cup of it in a cafe; by the sound of a coffee machine; or by the thought of the caffeine buzz.

Every one of our senses thirsts for its own particular satisfaction. To *see* attractive colours and forms, and turn the eyes away from the ugly; to *hear* harmonious sounds, and to shut out jangling cacophony; to *smell* pleasant fragrances, and close off obnoxious stench; to *taste* flavoursome food and drink, and to spit out the unappetizing; to *touch* that which is pleasing to our skin, and to avoid contact with that which stings; to *conjure up in our mind* agreeable thoughts and images, and to block out that which pains. We live in a state of desire. This longing for stimulation of the senses runs so deep, is so embedded within us, that the deliberate deprivation of sensory stimulation has been used as a form of torture.

The Buddhist term for sensual desire is *kāma-taṇhā,* which can be translated from the Pali[9] as a 'thirst for sensual pleasure'. Thirst, *taṇhā,* is quite a poetic or imaginative word for craving.[10] But it conveys the power that the word craving can connote, that craving is an intense desire for an experience, an extremely strong force. In the same way, we talk of 'starving' not only for food, but also starving in a metaphorical sense, for instance, starving for intimacy. Even the etymology of the English word craving - it comes from an Old Norse word which means 'demand' - implies something that is compelling. Our craving demands to be satisfied.

Gratifying our appetites is most commonly experienced as a relief of tension. We indulge in our habits to try to soothe ourselves. As J.P. Donleavy writes about his protagonist after he experiences an orgasm, 'for the next silent minute he was the sanest man on earth, bled of his seed, rid of his mind.'[11] The pleasure we get from indulging our craving is not from the object itself, but rather it is relief from the tension, the unease, caused by the craving in the first place; that is say, release from the pain of craving.

As we have already seen, craving generally is seen as a 'poison' in Buddhism, something that pollutes us, harms us and even can kill us. And we regularly consume poison but frequently don't seem to care about it; in Chapter 4 I discuss further the phenomenon of 'I-don't-care-ism'. We put into our bodies things which some of us might consider as noxious or harmful, yet we persist in their consumption. Interestingly, there is what I think of as a rather old-fashioned expression "What's your poison?" for "What alcohol do you drink?". As Allen Carr writes in relation to smoking, but equally applicable to our drinking and eating habits, 'All creatures on this planet instinctively know the difference between food and poison.'[12] Why do we consume things then which are 'poisonous' to us rather than nourishing?

Creature comforts

If I think of my sensual cravings today, I'd probably come up with - caffeine; a sweet treat; sleep; to sit down; to avoid exercise; a fizzy drink. That might indicate to you that I'm feeling a bit weary and need something to buck me up. And you'd probably be correct. They all also point to a need for physical comfort, for things that are comforting. Those of us who live through lengthy cold winters long for warmth – for hot drinks, cosy armchairs, sitting close to a radiator or fire, curling up.

Sometimes the desire for sensual comfort and warmth can express itself as the desire to cuddle up to another sentient being, human or pet.

At the root of seeking physical comfort may be something instinctual, primaeval, going back to needing the protection of caves, protection from wild animals and the elements. We talk about our need for 'creature comforts', which also seems to hark back to the early history of humankind.

The craving for comfort is strong within us. It implies ease, reassurance, security. The need for security is very powerful in humans, the need to find some kind of stable footing. Latching onto a whole variety of objects, emotions and ideas, including wealth, love and power, is a way in which we hope and believe that we will find security and reassurance. And they may give us relative security for a while; but Buddhism makes clear that such security is transient and in essence ultimately unsatisfying. A much more profound security can be achieved when we don't rely on things external to us. We have everything that we need within us.

We can be surprised at how over-riding this need for comfort is. Some years ago, I spent a month up in the mountains in Spain on a retreat where I was ordained with eleven other men into the Triratna Buddhist Order. The location of the retreat centre was stunning, there was something mythological about the occasion, the sense of brotherhood amongst us was deep, and there was a feeling of transition into a new life. But for much of the time, particularly early on, I was not completely in that place. Living with an earth toilet, a concrete bed-base, the consequent lack of sleep and restricted opportunities to shower, the lack of my creature comforts dominated my days. I guess my comparatively comfortable lifestyle had made me soft, even at such an important event in my spiritual life.

This is just one example, but I wonder whether our longing for comfort can cheat us out of a real deep experience of life's myriad facets. Some of us rise to the challenge of experiencing physical discomfort, are happy to go camping in wet and windy weather and don't let it bother us. Others of us don't but are maybe missing out on something.

The phrase 'comfort eating' is familiar to us. Possibly the word craving initially conjures up the idea of food for you. When I look up 'craving' in a search engine, most of the results relate to food. A while back, my little granddaughter had a thing about ice-cream, she wanted it all the time, and she would just say the word ice-cream over and over again, inserted into nonsense sentences. Like "Nanny ice-cream loves me and ice-cream, my ice-cream tastes like ice-cream, Mummy Daddy ice-cream says yummy, more more ice-cream love love......." etc etc. It's as though for a while her whole world consisted of nothing else, she was fixated on this one thing.

Our fixation on objects that on the face of it promise comfort may not be as obsessional as my granddaughter's, but the compulsion to eat when we don't really need to is an example of the strong pull of craving in the face of our better judgement.

Pizza is a pretty common food to crave. Some of them are huge and half of one is usually sufficient to fill your stomach. But can you just stop at a half-pizza? Frequently not, and you may gorge yourself because the pizza is sitting there, until you feel uncomfortable and wish you could turn back the clock to half-time. Comfort eating often leads to discomfort, in the belly, and later in the mind, "Why did I do that?" It's as though we get captivated by what appears to be a solace for us and can't see the wood for the trees, as we shall see in Chapter 3.

We only need to look at the growing spread of obesity in our modern societies, and the negative consequences it has for our health, to see how this plays out. Chocolate is a favourite one, both to consume and to exemplify food compulsion. David Webster talks about 'the pseudo-biological craving for chocolate'[13] to indicate that there is a difference, not always easy to ascertain, between real hunger and comfort eating. One is about the need to maintain our lives, the other is potentially damaging to our lives.

We may entertain the belief that desire is an important human experience that is natural, which leads to happiness and pleasure. This however is only partly true. As we shall see later, it depends upon the type of desire we are talking about. 'Buddhism is not saying we should not have desire', writes Traleg Kyabgon Rinpoche. 'It does mean that we should be alert to the danger of unchecked desire, as it can become excessive. If we do not put some kind of restraint on our excesses, all our experiences will lack fulfillment and lead to frustration and disappointment.'[14] For now, we can say that Buddhism shows us a way to go beyond the realm of sense desire, to a way of living where we accept that we have desires, but learn to live with them, to refine them and to transform them. We can mindfully acknowledge our cravings without indulging them and without dissipating our precious energies.

Intoxicants that cloud the mind

Most Buddhists have a set of five ethical precepts, training principles which we commit to follow.[15] In the fifth precept we 'undertake the training principle of abstaining from intoxicants', sometimes extended to 'abstaining from intoxicants that cloud the mind'. The antidote to taking intoxicants, the positive precept in my Triratna Buddhist Community, is 'with mindfulness clear and radiant, I purify my mind'. Dealing effectively with intoxicants, with excessive alcohol consumption for example, with the poison of craving, requires awareness, as we shall see in Chapter 7.

I mentioned 'screen craving' in the previous chapter. Let's look at possibly the most craving-inducing intoxicating thing (apart from sex maybe) that we have ever seen on this planet: the smartphone. Dependence on one's smartphone is so obvious that it barely needs detailing – in the street, on the bus, in the cafe, wherever you are, people are glued to their magic piece of technology, clinging to their object of desire like a parent to their child – unable to let go for too long for fear of missing a message, seeking yet more dubious 'information', infatuated by the buzz of discovery. Obsessively checking emails or messages in the hope that someone is going to contact you – a tentative girlfriend/boyfriend maybe, affirmation from somebody you haven't heard from for a while, a friend you texted half an hour ago who hasn't replied yet, or just a message from anyone about anything. Unable really to get on with anything else because the longing for a message is constantly playing at the back, or even the front, of your mind. In the meantime, you're maybe ruminating on the thought that people don't care about you. And then when the longed-for message eventually arrives, there's the disappointment at the arrival of mere spam.

We find it so hard to leave our phones alone. Many of us binge screen-watch and are addicted to this little object of desire, whether we are prepared to admit it or not. Constantly messaging, googling, videoing, selfie-ing, checking, scrolling, prying, escaping. In my local swimming pool even, the jacuzzi is full of people consulting their machines; not even there is an interlude of non-input to be had.

There's just always something to look up, to check up on, with a smartphone. The smartphone is the new 'now'. Being in the present is being on my smartphone. We need our fix, it cannot wait. In a metaphor from Dr Anna Lembke, 'the smartphone is the modern-day hypodermic needle, delivering digital dopamine 24/7 for a wired generation'[16]. What would a visitor to our world from even thirty years ago make of this obsession?

In a revealing article about her obsession with her smartphone, Michelle Drouin writes, 'I'm actually in a relationship with my phone. Through its lights, sounds and vibrations, my phone makes bids for attention, and I respond. Much like the way I respond to others in my life who make these bids (e.g., my husband and children), I turn to it, attend to it and seek to resolve the issue that prompted the alert. …. But it's not only responsiveness that has solidified our relationship. I carefully wipe its screen to remove smudges (social grooming). I carry it with me everywhere I go in either my purse, hand or pocket (skin-to-screen bonding). I get nervous if I cannot find it (separation anxiety). We are bonded, and I am smitten.'[17] Does this ring a bell with you?

The case-study of the smartphone reveals to us that we can be very aware of a craving, of an attachment, we can know that we are 'bonded' and 'smitten', but that we are not prepared to do anything about it. Or very little. The smartphone is central to our modern-day lives. How can I do without it?

To be sure, there is some very interesting and useful stuff out there in the cyberworld, we just need to be selective in how we respond to all that information. Otherwise we can drown in it. Making choices is key, and Buddhist teachings can help us make the right decisions, skilful decisions that are benefit to us and others, decisions based on awareness (mindfulness) and the consequences of our actions (*karma*).

Screen news browsing can become compulsive. "I need to get the most recent news, I've only looked at it a couple of times so far today". We can watch the news as a distraction; all-day-and-night news has become entertainment, to feed or cultivate a need for new 'information'. Most news is bad news, and it can induce anxiety, helplessness and desensitization. All news is an oversimplification; we need in fact to watch it with a degree of detachment and questioning.[18]

There can be a real impatience linked to craving, an unwillingness, or even inability to put off, or give in to, the immediate gratification of our urges. The need to indulge our cravings is incredibly powerful; in sex of course, but also in our appetites for other things, for a drink, for a screen to look at, for revenge. We typically yearn for constant and immediate satisfying of our cravings, and we seem to be in need of continual gratification.

When we indulge a craving, that it is to say, when we give in to our craving, it is like a wound that we have been dying to scratch. And when we do give in to the urge and scratch the wound, it may give temporary respite, but we know that it will not help the wound to heal. In fact, it will actually delay the healing every time we scratch the wound. And the continual scratching may even encourage a nasty lasting scar to develop, or the wound may become infected and lead to further problems. The same applies when we continually give in and indulge a craving – the consequences can be harmful to our well-being, both short-term and long-term. Indulging a craving may soothe a wound but it cannot heal it.

The more often we give in to an urge to gamble online, say, the harder it is to resist next time, the more dependent we get upon this outlet for stressbusting, at a cost to our pocket, possibly our relationships with those close to us, and eventually our mental health. And ill-will often follows on from indulging our cravings - ill-will towards ourselves for being so stupid, weak, and mindless. This ill-will, or self-loathing, can then lead to further craving, as a strategy to make us feel better again. And so on and so on. Binge eating exemplifies this well. We may be disgusted with ourselves for over-eating and putting on weight, and then try to appease that disgust by comfort eating.

But we don't have to be disgusted with ourselves. We can learn to accept that these unhelpful desires arise within us, as they do within others, that we have this in common with all humans. And we can learn to be kind to ourselves as a result, acknowledge these cravings but realize that we have the ability, with awareness, to let them go, to not follow them slavishly, to see that there is a different, wiser way of responding, which will make us happier and be far more satisfying than any indulged craving can.

Gross and subtle urges

Of course, we don't just crave material objects. There are different types of intoxicants which cloud the mind, the literal ones such as alcohol and other drugs, and the more abstract ones. We can talk about gross cravings, such as money, food, sex, shopping, and gambling, and more subtle ones. I often feel the desire to know; to know anything and everything. Most of the time it's just facts I grasp for. The capital of Burkina Faso or the number of Test match wickets Jimmy Anderson totted up. The internet lends itself perfectly to be a tool to find out facts. The trouble is they are often just facts for their own sake, not there to be of any particular use or benefit to anyone. Why do I go to the trouble of looking up the biographical details of an actor I've been watching on TV? Just in case it might be useful one day, and I can tell someone impressively that he was born in Hove actually not Brighton? Really? When you get older you may think that you know all the answers, but the trouble is that nobody asks you the right questions.

There's a danger as well in not just wanting to know, but wanting to be the one that knows. Herein lies conceit, thinking you know, or wanting to know, more or better than others. Conceit is about comparing oneself with others, usually as someone superior. However, we may also compare ourselves with others as inferior to them, in all sorts of ways, not only mentally but indeed physically. As a result, we can develop an unhealthy envy or resentment. Images in adverts today of fashion models with seemingly perfect (although perhaps airbrushed) bodies can easily create dissatisfaction with our own bodies and perpetuate what is in reality unattainable for most of us.

Through the sixth sense of our mind, we can also experience pangs of regret, wishing that we hadn't done this or that in the past, wishing that things had been different. I am sometimes haunted by unkind things I said to my mother when I was a teenager; I would like to apologize to her, but it is too late now, as she died many years ago. This is a desire, like many, that cannot be directly acted upon.

We may crave to be liked, possibly because being liked will help us 'to get on' in life. If my boss likes me, I might be able to keep my job at the end of my temporary contract. The desire to be accepted is very powerful, and we can go to all sorts of lengths in bending, twisting and suppressing ourselves in order to try to make ourselves more agreeable to others, to fit in, to be part of the group, to be seen as 'cool'.

Moreover, we may long for dream-places, yearning after 'remote blue distances'[19] where all our troubles magically dissolve into nothingness; if only I could live on a beautiful tropical island, swimming and sun-bathing the whole day through. We can live out our secret desires through the medium of films and television, projecting our fantasies onto characters and plots to make up for the lack in our lives. Fictional stories are great for stimulating the imagination but beware of inhabiting an imaginary world all the time, it can lead to alienation and frustration.

Some of us have a compulsion to talk, to verbalise all that messiness that's going around and around in our minds. A character of Joseph Conrad's 'talked as thirsty men drink.'[20] It's beneficial to unload and share with others difficult issues that we are facing, but in my experience very many people long to talk almost exclusively about themselves, rather than to listen carefully to what somebody else is saying; conversations at these times often just develop into non-conversations, simply one-way traffic. We might better be guided by the Dalai Lama's dictum, 'When you talk you are only repeating something you already know. But, if you listen you may learn something new.'

Hopes are a form of craving as well. A hope maybe that there will be cakes at a meeting. A hope can be a rather weak or vague wish, "Hope you're well", "I hope to be rich one day", "We hope to have a holiday once COVID allows". It can be quite optimistic, the sort of desire that is an expectation for a particular thing to happen, a wanting for something to be the case, an intention to possibly do something, a desire for something to come about (usually positive, although we may hope that our enemy comes a cropper). It can also be delusory; "She is hoping against all odds that her relationship will work out".

Related to hopes are fantasies, wishing in our imaginations for impossible or improbable things, conjuring up fanciful images which have little basis in fulfilment. At a time when I was miserable and stressed in my job, I fantasised that I would turn up at my workplace one morning to find that the boiler had broken down, and so I could celebrate not having to work that day. Dwelling with our fantasies for short periods of time may not be too harmful, but living in a fantasy land can be very disorientating and disintegrating.

Stimulation seeking

As we shall see below, we seem to have an in-built desire for new and different things in our lives. This can manifest itself in the desire for changing our current experience, a craving for distraction from the sometimes uncomfortable present, a restlessness. Wanting excitement is restlessness. The urge for excitement can be a reaction to the ordinariness of everyday existence. It's as though there's a hollow in us, there's something missing, an abyss we need to pour something into; we will investigate this aspect further in Chapter 3.

The longing for excitement is a desire for a different mental state, but it is generally accompanied by a strong physical element, a tingling perhaps in the body, a rushing of the blood, a fluttering or pounding of the heart; just think of sexual attraction, or even doughnut attraction.

Sometimes we can equate this with 'really being alive'. We may kid ourselves into thinking that excitement is the same as happiness. We frequently equate desire for the excited state, the thrill, the buzz, with the desire to be happy. This excitement however is the opposite of calm and contentedness, which is a state of mind where we are satisfied with what we have, with what is happening right now.

We often feel we can find better stimulation or more interest elsewhere. What is boredom but looking for distraction from our present experience? We often find it difficult to stay with any one mental state for too long before we become restless and uncomfortable. 'I came there' writes one of my favourite authors, Stefan Zweig, describing a character who aimlessly and apathetically wanders from place to place, 'out of tedium, out of the painful emptiness of the heart that wells up like nausea, and at least tries to nourish itself on small external stimulations.'[21] This is a kind of impatience, and is the opposite, incidentally, of meditation practice, where we can develop the skill of sitting still and focussed for lengthy periods.

This restlessness is similar to the way in which we are unable to stay in one physical position for too long, for example, sitting in a chair or lying in bed. This appears to be a question of equilibrium. Perhaps equilibrium in life is a question of alternating periods of stillness and movement, rest and action, calm and stimulation; a middle way, maybe. [22] Too much of one or the other means we lead an unbalanced, lop-sided life. People who are busy all the time need periods of rest, of doing nothing, of space. People who have a tendency to inaction, sitting around all day, need to get up off their backside and get stuck into something.

There is the craving to possess and the craving for thrill. We can see that they are connected, for instance, in the purchase of some new tech – I want to have it and I'll get a buzz from it. There's the thrill of the acquiring, the exciting expectation, which often turns out just to be a cheap thrill, a shallow excitement. It frequently does not live up to what we were hoping for.

This urge for excitement is characterised by the mind being unfocussed and drifting. Buzz, buzz, buzzing from one honeypot to the next - the busy bee, but rarely the satisfied bee. I can't sit still; I need to be *doing* something. The well-known psychological condition of attention deficiency, particularly noticeable amongst schoolchildren and young people raised on a diet of screen nourishment, is a corollary of our restless pursuit of escape from boredom.[23] But not only with digital distraction; I can't settle when all I'm thinking of is chocolate. Craving can be both a retreat into an illusory world that promises pleasure, into what Buddhism calls a false refuge [24], and also a yearning for excitement, to counteract 'boredom'.

Whether you're a follower of sport or not, you can probably see that there can be an excitement, sometimes manic, which comes from watching sport. Many years ago, I had a season ticket to watch the football team I supported where I grew up. Worked up sometimes to a frenzy, I am not proud of some of the harsh language that came out of my mouth, directed at players and fans from the opposing team or the poor referee, urged on of course by the excitement of being part of a hugely biased crowd of fellow fans. Like many thousands of other football supporters on those Saturday afternoons, I deeply longed and cheered for 'my' team to win. Football fans want goals, and more goals, there are never enough (for your own team, of course). Years later I went to a match, a trip down memory lane, and could only get a ticket at the last moment, close to the supporters of the visiting team. In that somewhat neutral situation, for the first time I was really shocked by the level of vitriol and hate that was being hurled from the terraces, the fever-pitch obsession with victory. I don't think I've watched sport in the same prejudiced subjective way ever since. More recently I went 'cold turkey' altogether on spectating and following sport. I felt much freer and calmer.

There is disturbance in the mind when there's excitement about. Buddhism concerns itself with examining what leads to less disturbance. My mind may be disturbed by violence in a film whereas yours may not be. It's not the source of the excitement or disturbance that is the issue then, because we both react differently to it. It's not the external object that is the cause of mental disturbance, but rather how we respond to that source or stimulus. We shall look at this more in the following chapter.

The thirst for excitement is essentially a wish for a departure from the mundane. So, equally, is the thirst for a different kind of consciousness, one that is not plagued by irritating and haunting longings, a desire to be free, which is ultimately the reality of Buddhist enlightenment, that reality which transcends our everyday perception of how things normally are. This is the essence of Chapter 10. Our thirst for excitement is at base a quest for something much more fulfilling than what we are currently experiencing.

Excitement is inherent in the sexual urge, which of course is thrilling. Stefan Zweig described this excitement through one of his characters, 'He felt a kind of bridal expectation, sweet and sensuous yet vaguely mingled with anticipatory fear of its own fulfilment, with the mysterious shiver felt when something endlessly desired suddenly comes physically close to the astonished heart.'[25] The build-up to sexual consummation can be electrifying.

In some forms of craving, such as for sexual fulfilment, there is a ritual involved which is a major part of the process, and which itself is pleasurable. This is the chase, the hunt, the expectation, the waiting, the preparation. Incidentally, we can see this in other contexts as well; the taste of the bowl of tea at the end of the tea ceremony is not the be-all and end-all of the ceremony. The looking forward to a holiday over a period of months and the setting-off on the journey can be as exciting as the brief period spent away. The ritual of preparing the fix forms part of the drug addict's fix itself.

Of course, there's a huge variety in the extent to which we experience sexual longing. For some the urge is very strong, concupiscence, an infatuation or a compulsion, a force that seems to dominate our waking moments; others can go a long time without thinking about or needing sexual gratification; or it can be a fairly run-of-the-mill activity, even a routine for some, a need gratified when necessary and then forgotten about. Some of us need sex to stay sane, others don't. Some have made sex the centre of their life. This urge may change during different periods of our life and at different moments. But the sexual drive does not necessarily diminish with age - 'the one thing that stays young is craving', wrote the fifth-century Sanskrit poet Bhartrihari in this context.[26] The drive of course may still be there but not necessarily the capability or the opportunity.

In some Buddhist traditions, as in Christianity and other religions, monastics and other practitioners live a cloistered celibate life as a way of dealing with the temptations of sex. Buddhism however, generally speaking, does not moralise about sex, only in the sense that it encourages us to abstain from sexual behaviour which is harmful to others or ourselves;[27] this principle is a reflection of the Buddhist principle to treat all beings, including ourselves, with *Mettā*, with universal loving kindness.

But, instead of relating to other people with *Mettā* and empathise with them, we can easily objectify them, treat them as sexual objects. In general, we objectify the things that we crave; there is me on the one hand, and on the other hand the object that I crave. With sexual attraction, that duality can become exaggerated - a duality that is always present in any human relationship - between the person desiring and the person who is the object of the sexual fascination. At the extreme, there is no openness, no connection between us, we feel that we are apart from the other. There is a pull towards the object of the desire and this need has to be gratified, and this ironically is easier when we have no real intimate connection to the person. Eroticism thrives in the space between the self and the other, so craving depends on blurring the connection between subject and object.

This is explicit in the widespread use and normalisation of pornography, the power of which relies on a lack of empathy, a distance between the observer and the observed. We do not have to reflect long to realize that this demeaning, degrading relationship does not make us feel good about ourselves. Watching pornography may just seem like titillation, but we can titillate ourselves to death (or almost). We can rationalise this behaviour and say that we are doing no harm to anybody but ourselves. But there is an implicit exploitation and dehumanisation at the heart of pornography. The creators of pornography, overtly or not, exploit and dehumanise the person portrayed as well as the user; and the user, as well as being exploited by the creator, is implicit in the exploitation of the person portrayed.

Using the term 'eros', which we shall delve into in chapter 9, the French philosopher Alain Badiou widens the import of pornography, whilst stressing its pervasiveness and the way it depersonalises sex, taking it away from the intimate. 'Capitalism is aggravating the pornographication of society by making everything a commodity and putting it on display. Knowing no other use for sexuality, it profanes eros—into porn.'[28]

There is a lack of awareness in any compulsive craving. 'Buddhist practice involves the cultivation of awareness,' writes Sangharakshita, 'but sexual craving, on account of its blind instinctual nature, takes us in the opposite direction.'[29] Erotic desire burns, in an almost inexplicable way, desire that can be unbridled. Buddhism is not saying there is anything wrong with the sexual urge in itself, it is all about how we address it. And as we shall see in Part II of this book, the various Buddhist traditions have different strategies for doing just that.

The romantic relationship

Alongside our sexual desires goes the longing for romance. We can become addicted to the intensity of romantic love, searching and pining for more intensity. And we can come down with a bang if it disappoints. We may be thinking obsessively about the person who we wish to be romantically involved with. There can be a need to be desired, craving affirmation through a romantic partner, and that person's attitudes can shape our response towards them. Or what is lacking in us we search for in another, projecting onto them qualities that we ourselves desire. When our romantic partner is not present, we can feel a chasm in our lives.

There is a dependence, which in itself is a general feature of obsessive craving. In a similar way to how our cravings for material consumer goods are manipulated for commercial purposes, as we shall examine below, in the West romantic love and sexual desire are fetishized, in the sense that a massive amount of importance is given to them, and interest engendered for them, in our cultures, across our media. A perfume named Obsession, with everything that implies, is just one example of this. The fascination with the romantic lives and sexual partners of media celebrities is another. Advertising, social media, film and television all play a part in the social and cultural construction of sexual and romantic desire. It is no wonder that we often have unhelpful idealised expectations of romantic love.

However, there is a lot more than dependence, obsession and projection to be said about romantic relationships. The Buddhist scholar Silavadin has written a very interesting article[30] about intimate relationships which runs counter to the idea that the ideal Buddhist life is a celibate one, free of sexual and romantic ties. He describes the dangers that come with celibacy, as in the abuse uncovered within the Roman Catholic church, as well as in many religious traditions. Celibacy may suit some, but it has its dangers. Evidently, much can be said about the value or not of suppressing or denying sexual drives, and we shall examine specifically the suppression of desires in Chapters 6 and 9.

However, in an intimate relationship, Silavadin writes, 'you surrender your temporal, imperfect being to the gaze of the other, and you trust that this person will also look at you as a person, and not just as a body and an exemplar of the species…. this process of knowing and being known creates an intimate circle.' Thus the intimacy of being in a healthy sexual, romantic relationship can foster giving, sharing, mutual respect, acknowledging, empathy, seeing the world through another's eyes, trust and surrendering one's 'self', all virtues to be valued. Being naked to another, literally or not, allows us to bring to light and let the other in on things which hitherto we may have wished to remain hidden as seemingly shameful. In this manner we can go beyond seeing ourselves as private persons. Silavadin points out, 'knowing and being known by your partner…has a healing effect on your personality, and this is of course the basis for the Buddhist path.'

The Buddhist teacher Rob Burbea agreed. He believed that we do not need to disassociate romantic or sexual love from the all-embracing love of the Buddha: 'I feel that one can experience the love for a particular human being as almost something impersonal, coursing through one, as one part of a force or energy that runs through all human beings…so awake to the beauty of the world within and around us, connected to all those who are in love now, or who have, throughout history, ever been in love.'[31] Here there is the possibility of a union of the spiritual and the flesh. Although a closeness may be found with family and friends, and especially within a spiritual community of friends, the sexual aspect adds a different layer of intimacy. The emphasis here of course has to be on a *healthy* sexual, romantic relationship, that functions more or less beneficially for both partners, and allows freedom within mutual love.

In every type of relationship - whether it be long-term or short-term, marriage, promiscuity, monogamy, chastity (a non-relationship) - there are neurotic and non-neurotic possibilities. A neurotic relationship implies craving, imbalance, and frustration. The non-neurotic relationship implies contentment and tenderness. Buddhist practice has developed and incorporated many original aspects over twenty-five centuries. The argument of Silavadin and Burbea that an intimate sexual, romantic relationship can indeed be a Buddhist practice is I feel a valid one.

Stepping over the line

As with sexual longing, the ache to indulge our cravings can be so powerful that it may lead us to disregard whatever moral values we have. We succumb to desires which we would normally consider taboo; wishing bad things to happen to a friend, for instance; sending a malicious tweet; or defying our vegetarian principles by scoffing a bacon sandwich. We often perceive our behaviour as unavoidable, "I can't do anything about it, I can't help it". This is the pleasure principle, only following what we desire and disregarding the consequences. The intellect tells us it's wrong, our emotions tell us it's OK. Blinded by desire, with no concern for what's rational, no concern for our own wellbeing, driven to gratify our sensual desires. This is the battle between our Apollonian nature, the constraint and inhibition of our desires, and our Dionysian nature of uninhibited release and lust. The compulsive craver leads a double life. We all face this battle one way or another.

When there is a choice between doing what we feel like doing and doing what we know we 'should' do, and there always is that choice, we frequently take the easier first option. After all, we are free individuals, aren't we? Why shouldn't we? We feel that we can't resist something or somebody, they are irresistible. But at the same time, we feel a resistance to behaving in a way which rationally makes more sense. For example, those of us who meditate, and know how beneficial it is for our wellbeing and spiritual development, often experience nevertheless a resistance to sitting down to meditate, an aversion to doing something which requires effort.

We know that we are less likely to indulge our gross cravings when we know somebody else is looking. There is this concealed aspect of craving – concealing from others, concealing from ourselves. We often indulge ourselves in secrecy. I may say to others, "I am not a TV watcher, you know, I think it's mostly a waste of time, there's nothing but rubbish on, and it's not good for me to spend hours in front of a screen." But, to myself I say, "I'll just watch a couple of programmes tonight, like I did last night, and if I do tomorrow tonight again, well I can get back into good habits next week, or maybe the week after. Nobody will know anyway, apart from me."

There are some types of behaviour which are always concealed. Desmond Morris reckoned that almost the entire population indulges in voyeurism of one sort or another - observing others engaging in some form of intimate behaviour without their knowledge[32]. Some of us love to gossip, always behind other people's backs. We may encounter gossip in workplaces which is sometimes dressed up by managers in the misleading garb of 'organisational intelligence'. We conceal because we don't want others to see what we're doing. We wouldn't want our minds to be open for others to see our thoughts, we wouldn't want our actions to be there for everyone to observe.

Subhuti talks about the 'morality of the private moment'.[33] In private, we can easily feel that because nobody can see us it does not matter what we get up to. But it does matter; actions whether private or public, in thought word or deed, will have an effect, upon us and our relationship with the world, sometimes small sometimes great. We cannot escape *karma* – as we shall see below - the consequences of our actions major or minor, even when there is nobody looking at what we are doing.

Being secretive about our desires also means that we are not able to integrate all of ourselves, not able to come to terms with those parts of us that we are ashamed of. And so we can experience guilt. Mark Epstein tells us that this is 'the usual way of approaching desire in our culture, which is to indulge it either mindlessly or guiltily.'[34] Or both mindlessly *and* guiltily.

Or we may feel no guilt at all. Some of us are able to selectively engage and disengage our moral standards – a 'good' husband can be a guiltless cheat. The Viennese author Arthur Schnitzler gives one such example, 'the thought of leading a kind of double life, of being at once a hard-working reliable progressive doctor, a decent husband, family man and father, and at the same time a profligate, seducer and cynic who played with men and women as his whim dictated – this prospect seemed to him at that moment peculiarly agreeable'.[35] Our desires may lead us to cheat on our partner, and then get tangled up in knots of deceit and lies. Satisfying our passions then brings us into conflict with others. Indulging in some desires can be a risky business, for example, doing a deal down a dark alley with someone you don't know who tells you the pills you're buying are Ecstasy. Craving, like a giant vacuum cleaner, can suck us into places where we don't really want to be.

One of the most famous and vivid expositions in Buddhism of how harmful are craving and its connected mental states (and also how we can turn away from them and free ourselves) is *The Fire Sermon*[36]. All of our senses, including our mind, are burning with craving, says the text. 'All things are on fire…with the fire of passion, say I, with the fire of hatred, with the fire of infatuation' We can imagine the friction of two sticks being rubbed together, one stick the sense faculty and the other the object sensed. The fever of passion is the fire that comes about through this contact, the fire that longs for fuel.

We consume therefore we are happy

A dominant facet of the lives that many of us lead today is our seeming compulsion to consume. This is consumerism, in the sense of a preoccupation with acquiring goods and services in increasing amounts. There is so much that has been written and said about the power of consumerism in the societies that we now live in.[37] I don't intend to add too much to those discussions, but I feel that no exploration of craving in the early 21st century would be adequate without at least some mention of how we buy and acquire.

We have become used to the idea that satisfaction is to be found in shopping. We feel something missing in our lives and we may feel that this existential lack, this insufficiency, can be countered by filling the hole with material goods. There seems to be an impulse instinctive in us to search for things that will make us happy, a longing to devour; purchasing new things is this quest put into action. Consuming our way to happiness. I suppose all internet surfing and searching is a form of online shopping, looking for something to fill a gap. In the same way that we can fill our home with unnecessary 'stuff', we can also fill our mind with lots of useless internet stuff [38].

The desire for new things is widespread. An obsession with novelty. We want the biggest, best, tastiest, shiniest, cleanest, most comfortable, most pleasurable. When objects begin to show wear and tear, we discard them rather than mend them. Some of us buy new clothes and don't even wear them. We want the latest tech, the hottest app, the as-yet 'undiscovered' holiday destination, the top-ten gadget. There is always something greener, more sparkling, on the other side. And yet, we may have had the exciting experience of buying something appealing from a shop or online, getting it home, trying it on or turning it on, and then an hour later the buzz of getting something new just evaporates. Even to the extent of saying to ourselves, "Why on earth did I buy that?".

We are consumers of 'experience' in the present-day world; consumers of thrills, of novelty, of places we have been to, and things we have done. We may search to acquire something special or unique, so that we stand out from the crowd. At least, some of us do. Some of us apparently have the urge to possess what appear to be exceedingly mundane or bizarre items; a bidder was prepared to pay $48,875 for President Kennedy's tape measure at auction in 1996. I hope at that price that they got a lot of satisfaction out of it.

We may criticize others for over-consumption but frequently we gloss over it in our own behaviour. Rare is the home that is not filled with 'stuff', the by-product of accumulation, which is itself the by-product of coveting. The drive to acquire can have very serious financial implications as well, particularly given the ease of online shopping with a credit card.

Shopaholicism - the uncontrollable urge to acquire. Retail therapy – some of us look after our well-being through purchasing. Binge shopping - we may go on an alcohol binge, but we can binge-buy as well. We comfort-buy too; "Go on, treat yourself! You deserve it!" We may go on a shopping spree, splash out, get hooked on a good deal. Sometimes when we're stressed, our being is to binge (yes, anagrams).

We deserve our treats, as a sort of reward for the not-quite-right life we have to put up with which, as David Brazier explains, we consider to be unfair. 'We therefore seek compensation by looking for treats. To seek pleasure is to seek a change in the sensation. We want to be distracted. We look for a more compelling sensation that will pull our attention away from what ails us.'[39]

We shop in shops and shop online; shopping online is easier, we don't even have to move out of our comfy chairs. Shopping online is also a useful distraction if we're bored, at work or at home. An interesting term that I came across when the first lockdown of the COVID-19 pandemic started to ease in 2020 and people could start to go out and shop more freely was 'revenge purchasing' i.e., getting our own back (on what, on whom?) for not being able to shop for such a long time.

Compulsive consumption can result in enormous debts, often for those the least financially cushioned to deal with it. Anna Lembke, talking about the situation in the USA, but applicable elsewhere, writes, 'The poor and undereducated, especially those living in rich nations, are most susceptible to the problem of compulsive overconsumption. They have easy access to high-reward, high-potency, high-novelty drugs at the same time that they lack access to meaningful work, safe housing, quality education, affordable health care, and race and class equality before the law. This creates a dangerous nexus of addiction risk'[40]. Not only easy access to, and addiction to high-reward drugs, but also to cheap, unhealthy foods, high in carbs, sugar, salt and fats; obesity and consequent heart disease are widespread for those of us in low-income, poor housing situations.

All this of course is a reflection of the materialist societies in which we live, with the emphasis on the acquisition of 'objects' rather than on values such as generosity and simplicity[41]. And this is related very much to the craving for sensual pleasure that material goods appear to provide. Subhuti writes of 'the growth of materialism, with its glorification of the physical senses.'[42]

Taking a historical perspective, it seems rather ironic that the principles of greed and conspicuous over-consumption, which were seen as sins or undesirable personal qualities in more religious pre-industrial societies, are now placed on a pedestal and eulogized as not only desirable, but as the way that we as citizens should contribute to society's required economic growth.

Our modern patterns of consumption are induced, they are not natural. Our cravings are manipulated. Longing for avocado bacon ice cream (yes, it does exist) is not a natural urge; the craving is fabricated by the manufacturer. Encouraging, urging, provoking our desire to consume is of course the root of economic growth, the cornerstone of capitalist economics. The index of a successful economy is the amount of economic growth that can be demonstrated. If we do not consume enough, economic disaster would ensue we are told.

Our desires, indeed our whole psycho-physical being, are manipulated so that we buy. As good citizens we need to do our bit to serve the national interest and consume. In the modern world the primary test of how well a country is functioning is nothing to do with whether the population is content and fulfilled, but rather whether the national economy is growing. That is to say, is the population consuming and acquiring more and more? What a strange test! Acquire, acquire, buy, buy, consume, consume, waste, waste, you need it, you need it!......or else we won't survive.

We are bid to worship Mammon. Our consumer society constantly reinforces desires, and also creates desires for things we didn't know we wanted, ranging from the massive marketing and advertising budgets of multinational industries to little shopkeepers who put delicious things in their windows to provoke our appetite and entice us in. Advertising is designed to promote discontent, discontent which encourages us to exist in the acquisitive mode.

Mass marketing and advertising are not about catering to our needs, but rather about creating desires in us for products that companies wish to sell, and manipulating our inner feelings, forces, and drives, with the purpose of convincing us that we do need a certain product and that that product will make us happier. Spoken during the embryonic days of mass marketing in the 1920s, these words from a Wall Street banker still ring true today. 'We must shift America from a needs- to a desires-culture. People must be trained to desire, to want new things, even before the old have been entirely consumed. ... Man's desires must overshadow his needs.'[43]

In adverts we see people who do not appear to experience a lack, they patently seem happy by consuming whatever is being advertised. All adverts suggest that the satisfaction of craving will result in happiness. Perhaps I can cover over the deep anxieties and insufficiency in my predicament too if I just consume what they're consuming. In a sense, a whole host of new technological innovations has been thrust upon us in the 20th and 21st centuries, with no corresponding framework available for appropriate behaviour, leaving us in the dark, with uncertainty about how to relate to them in a way that makes sense, or indeed in a way that is in tune with our values, in an ethical way.

Desiring new things and new experiences can help us to be more open-minded, flexible and creative. But it can become a compulsive or impulsive habit and runs contrary to developing steady helpful habits. We may invest desire in things we don't have, instead of discovering contentment and interest in what we already have; we tend to value indulgence over frugality. "Do I really *need* a new pair of shoes? Or can I just manage with the ones I've got?" Most of us seem to care little about the drain on the world's resources caused by our voracious craving. If we wanted though, we could care for what is already in existence, for what we already have. And many of us increasingly do just that; the impetus to recycle in all sorts of ways has really taken off in recent decades.

Nothing is predetermined

We do have choices then. We can live in this world of *saṃsāra*, this world of unsatisfactory existence where we incessantly repeat our unhelpful actions [44], or we can refine our decisions about how and what we consume. Ultimately, we can turn our backs on *saṃsāra* altogether, and move towards a more liberated way of living, not bound by patterns of behaviour that are dominated by our cravings.

Maybe it's not really a question though of how our smartphones, for example, can intrude a bit less on our lives, but rather the emphasis is on being so engaged in doing something meaningful and fulfilling that we don't think about picking up our smartphone all the time, choosing a life that is so all-embracing that our smartphones can't match up. If the choice, when dealing with a habitual problem, is between 'stop doing that' (a negative) and 'do this instead' (a positive), then humans can feel more motivated and it will become more satisfying to choose the positive course of action.

As we saw above, we can say to ourselves that we are just relaxing, that we are just turning off our ethical sensibility switch for a little while and it will not matter. We can always turn it on again later, and the intervening turning-off phase is just a small aberration from the good, upright person we usually are (or think we are). "You know me, I never bad-mouth people, I'm not that sort of person, but that bloody idiot down the road is a complete and utter bastard and ought to be strung up". Unfortunately, life is not like that, simply a matter of turning on and off our moral compass. There is no such thing as an ethical rest break, a *karma* holiday.[45] This is because all of our intentional actions, great or small, always have an impact, whether we like it or not. The Buddhist law of *karma* is a law that deep down we already know - that actions, whether physical, vocal or mental, have consequences.

Psychologists talk about 'triggers' for a particular behaviour, for example, succumbing to our cravings when we're under the weather or tired; or walking past a cake shop, watching the news. Buddhists however talk not of triggers but rather of conditions, conditions which are supportive of behaviour that leads to positive outcomes, or the reverse, conditions conducive to negative outcomes. The power of situations, the effect of conditions on how we behave cannot be overestimated. The influence of our peers, the media, the weather, the location, are but a few factors that impact upon how we respond to whatever we are confronted with. Seeking out positive, helpful conditions then is central to the spiritual life. In the Buddhist view of the world, everything is interconnected, and everything shapes everything else. And it is the Buddhist view of craving that we shall be exploring in detail in the next chapter.

Reflecting Chapter 1

What are your 'favourite' sensual cravings? Can you think of an occasion when your craving for 'creature comfort' has meant that you have missed out on a possibly deeper experience? Do you recognise comfort eating in yourself? Is the pursuit of pleasure an important facet of your life? In what ways do you indulge in wishful thinking? To what extent do you feel that your sensual cravings are unhelpful? Are you in control of your 'screen craving'? To what degree does the purchase of material goods fulfil a need for you? How does the yearning for excitement manifest itself in you? Can you think of an example where a compulsive desire has led you to go against whatever ethical values you hold? Do you regularly indulge a craving secretly? Are there particular situations or factors which lead you to be more likely to indulge a craving?

Chapter 2:

THIRSTING

As we have begun to see, craving plays a central role in how Buddhism views the difficulties each of us faces in our lives. Its key message is that we can address those difficulties, transcend them, and come into a relationship with ourselves, other beings, and the world, which is clearer, calmer, kinder and more connected. This chapter looks at the place of craving in Buddhist teachings. Here is the background for an understanding of the rest of the chapters in this book.

The *dharma* is a term that covers many different interpretations of what the Buddha taught, interpretations across two and a half thousand years, in various parts of Asia and beyond, and in numerous Buddhist traditions. We have to be careful therefore in our use of terms and assume that all Buddhists will understand a word such as 'craving' in the same way. However, I hope that, irrespective of a particular school or tradition, Buddhists will generally agree with what I set out in the following paragraphs, about craving and its causes.

This simple definition from Subhuti will hopefully do for a start. Craving is a *longing*, for objects that we don't have, or for things to be other than they are; or a *clinging*, to an object we have, or think we have. 'Object' here is to be taken in a very broad sense - a material thing, a person, a mental state, a view.

Clinging then can be to material objects, but is particularly strong in the way we cling to views; views about our self, what sort of person we are - kind, weak, generous, pessimistic; and views about the world – for example, it's a hostile place, dog eats dog, it's unfair, together we can make the world a better place, it will all turn out right in the end. Another powerful characteristic of human beings is the way we cling to other humans, especially those close to us, our partner and our family members; we began to look at this in the last chapter in terms of intimate relationships.

The Three Thirsts

In the Pali Canon, the earliest Buddhist texts, there are several places where there is a three-fold categorisation of *taṇhā - thirst*. For example, in the Saccavibhanga Sutta, we find, 'And what, friends, is the noble truth[46] of the origin of suffering? It is craving, which brings renewal of being, is accompanied by delight and lust, and delights in this and that; that is *craving for sensual pleasures, craving for being, and craving for non-being* (my italics).'[47]

These three types of craving form the backbone of *Part One* of this book. In chapter 1 we broadly explored the 'craving for sensual pleasures', *kāma-taṇhā*. Desiring, and becoming attached to, anything via the five sense faculties is *kāma-taṇhā*. The 'craving for being' or 'craving for existence', *bhava-taṇhā,* will be the underlying theme for chapter 5, but we can say that essentially it is the craving to be something, to have some solid existence, to be a 'self'. The third type of craving is the 'craving for non-being' or 'craving for non-existence', *vibhava-taṇhā*. This will be the subject of chapter 4, but we can portray it here as the craving to avoid painful experience, to cut oneself off from life, to deny life's potential.

It is worth bearing in mind though that these three categories are just useful ways of looking at desire. They are not totally distinct types of craving but just different aspects of it. These three types of *taṇhā* are all bound up with each other. For instance, I may drink red wine because I want to experience the delicious taste of it in my mouth (*kāma-taṇhā*); or I feel it will bolster my confidence about myself in the company of others (*bhava-taṇhā)*; or I may drink it to drown my sorrows and not face up to the harsh realities of life (*vibhava-taṇhā)*. Or perhaps a combination of these. We can summarise the three *taṇhā*, for sensual pleasure, for existence, and for non-existence, as – elaborating Hamlet - to have, to be, and not to be.

The Buddha's teaching of the Four Noble Truths is useful to help us to understand craving and its importance for us. Put simply, the Four Noble Truths are (1) humans experience life as *dukkha* or 'suffering' (but see underneath for a clarification of this term); (2) the origin of *dukkha* is craving; (3) we can put an end to *dukkha;* and (4) there is a path that we can follow to bring about an end to *dukkha*.

In the same way as to understand Buddhism we need to understand craving, in order to understand craving we have firstly to understand the idea of *dukkha*. This word has traditionally been translated as 'suffering'.

In fact, *dukkha* covers a much broader range of emotions and feelings. If suffering seems too heavy a word to describe how we feel about life, and most of us don't feel that we are suffering all the time, then at least we can accept that life is difficult. It's a bumpy ride rather than a continually smooth one. It doesn't always go the way we hope it will, or expect it will. There is always uncertainty and the risk of our lives going pear-shaped should an unexpected event occur – losing our job, debilitating illness, or being involved in an accident.

We can put a range of different glosses though on the term *dukkha* – from not-quite-right-ness, through dissatisfaction, to difficult and painful experience. Our lives have peaks and troughs, it is far from being all negative, but, as Sagaramati has written in an insightful article, it is about 'seeing that the life one is leading, although it may have its pleasures and moments of happiness and fulfilment, leaves one's basic existential state untouched'.[48]

This last reference to our state of existence ties in with one of the three types of *dukkha* categorised in Buddhism. So we have the *dukkha* of physical and emotional pain; the *dukkha* of the psychological frustration at the changeable nature of things; and the *dukkha* of the unsatisfactoriness of existence - the nature of our existence is that we are born to die, that there is nothing in this life that can afford us lasting security, something that we may experience as a lack of meaning in our lives [49]. We can't avoid painful experience, *dukkha* is all around us, as well as within us, but Buddhism gives us a way of understanding *dukkha*, its cause and how we can address it.

I don't want to give the impression Buddhism is saying that life is painful all the time, that everything about the human condition is all doom and gloom - *dukkha, dukkha, dukkha*. Not at all. There are so many things in life in which we can find enjoyment – time spent with family or friends, a lovely holiday, a favourite bit of music. And we need to find enjoyment in our lives, to feel alive, to motivate us, to make life worth living.

What Buddhism is saying though is that at the end of, or despite, any enjoyable activity we engage in, there is still an underlying sense of incompleteness about the nature of our lives. We can enjoy temporary pleasure and respite, which is fine, but none of these activities will give us any lasting satisfaction, they can't quench a deeper longing that we experience. That is why we are always *Thirsting for More*, the title of this book.

It's as though we are cut off from something that we really need. There's a deficiency in our lives, a lack of completeness. And it's hard to put our finger on what that actually is. A character in Stefan Zweig's short story *Confusion* articulates this, '(I) was never able to say clearly what it was I really longed for, what I wanted, what I required and aspired to.'[50]

Because we don't feel whole in ourselves, we tend to turn with expectation to our outer environment, to look outside ourselves for the solution to this dilemma. We examined this in the previous chapter in terms our habits of consumption. If only we could possess something that would fill that dearth, that would give us what we want. 'The futility of this approach, however, should be obvious to us all. What person or thing could we possibly make our own so that this search for security might come to an end? Neither the most beautiful woman in the world, the most handsome man, the most fashionable clothes, the most precious jewel, nor the most ingenious new idea has the power to quench our desires as long as we remain incomplete inside,' writes Lama Thubten Yeshe.[51] And thirsting for things we cannot have causes frustration, that is to say, more *dukkha*.

The insecurity and possessiveness that dominates much of our behaviour, from this sense of not being whole, is at the root of all the problems in the world, whether it be the anxiety of one person, the conflict between individuals, or war between nations. Buddhism is clear that seeking completion through external objects will never satisfy us. It is to our inner resources and potential that we need to turn for a resolution of our difficulties.

The origin of *dukkha*

The very important insight that the Buddha gave us is concerning the source of *dukkha*. And, in the second of the Four Noble Truths, the Buddha said that the origin of our *dukkha* is *taṇhā*. And *taṇhā* means thirst, a rather imaginative word as we have seen for craving. It is our craving, in its many different manifestations, which brings about our unease. In Buddhism it is clear that craving is seen as a great 'fetter', something that shackles us, that inhibits our freedom and happiness. What happens is that because of a lack in our lives, which is *dukkha*, we search out things to fill this absence, to compensate for this something missing. In this sense, not only is craving the source of *dukkha,* but *dukkha* is also the source of craving - we can say that craving is a reaction to *dukkha*. Moreover, these longings that we all experience run deep. 'A human being' writes Sangharakshita, 'is a stream of consciousness deeply imbued with the dye of craving'.[52]

Buddhism is unique amongst spiritual traditions in declaring craving as the source of what is problematic in life. But, most importantly, it declares that *dukkha* is self-made. It is we who create our own difficulties. In my favourite Buddhist text, the *Bodhicaryāvatāra,* we read, 'We who are like senseless children shrink from suffering, but love its causes. We hurt ourselves; our pain is self-inflicted!'.[53] We looked at this at the beginning of this book. We bring upon ourselves these harmful emotions and often don't seem to want to do much about dealing with them. 'Lust and ill-will, these enemies of mine, have no hands or feet. They are not brave, nor wise. How then do they make me their slave? It is I who welcome them into my heart, allowing them to harm me at their pleasure. And yet I suffer all this without resentment. This servile forbearance is so ill-placed!'[54]

How are you creating *dukkha* for yourself at this very moment? I can feel a headache coming on right now, as I have been staring at my laptop screen for too long writing this chapter; I should stop and take a break, but I don't want to stop, I want to carry on writing before it gets too dark, despite this impending headache which will be a pain, literally.

It may be totally natural that we should long for things to block out what is difficult, seeking things 'out there' which are pleasurable. But the problem is that this behaviour cannot solve our problems, because it is the grasping at pleasurable experiences and the pushing away of unpleasant experiences that makes life ultimately unsatisfactory. Nothing in life will give us *enduring* satisfaction; we need to understand and accept this fact of life, said the Buddha. The nature of all phenomena is *dukkha*, incompleteness.

But craving is not only the cause of *dukkha,* it doesn't just lead to *dukkha,* it is *dukkha.* Wanting is in itself painful, it's uncomfortable when you're dying for something. Craving is characterised 'by a quality of ego-centred restlessness'.[55] To thirst is discomforting, *taṇhā* is *dukkha*. We suffer *by* what we do, not only *for* what we do.

We can easily test this out for ourselves. Sit and close your eyes. Bring to mind something that you habitually crave, whether it be a longing for a blackberry muffin, an urge for excitement, a sexual fantasy, or whatever. Don't imagine indulging the craving, just rest in the desiring stage. Now notice how that feels in your body, where and to what degree. Try it out with a different craving. When I have done this exercise with my students, we all tend to feel physical disquiet of different kinds.

We feel much more at ease with ourselves and calmer when we are in a state of equanimity, experiencing no strong desires. This is one of the benefits of meditation, that we able to notice the arising of unhelpful mental states and allow them to pass; more on this in Chapter 7.

It therefore follows that 'One insight is that grasping is the basis of all suffering. The other insight is that by the complete cooling and cessation of all this grasping there is no more arising of suffering'.[56] We create our own *dukkha* through our various cravings, and we need to recognize that the solution lies within each and every one of us to address those cravings. The transformation of our craving mental states therefore is the key to the ceasing of *dukkha,* the key to our happiness. Yes, it can be done, says the Buddha. Yes, we can stop being a servant to all these seemingly uncontrollable and compulsive urges, these emotional conflicts.

In English, as we saw in the Introduction, there are a lot of different words which express the idea of wanting something. We have the words craving, passion, desire, greed, urge, clinging, grasping, and many more. Each has a distinct meaning, but all cover roughly the same area of human experience. English is a very rich language in this respect. When we look in the Pali Canon, the early collection of the Buddha's teachings, we find many different words also in the Pali language for this area of our experience. Bruce Matthews mentions seventeen different words.[57]

With some exceptions though, it seems that in the Pali Canon the various terms associated with craving, although there are distinctions, are used fairly interchangeably. However, there is one particular area where a distinction does need to be made. If we look again at our definition of craving near the beginning of this chapter, we see that one aspect is *longing,* and the other *clinging.* Longing, as Rob Burbea describes, 'is the momentary impulse to have something or to get away from something. It can work both ways, as an aversion, aversive movement, to move away from something we don't like, what's unpleasant, or to move towards: I want that thing. I want to get it. I want to have it.'[58]

But when that movement of the mind - momentary *taṇhā* - persists, it becomes clinging, grasping, attachment; in Pali *upādāna*. The two concepts are closely related. As Rob Burbea clarifies, *upādāna* occurs when craving 'becomes more obsessive, if you like, or more entrenched, so we start circling around that thing, thinking about it a lot, scheming ways to get it, etc. There's a consolidation, a tightening, a reinforcing, a solidification that's happening.'[59] This fixation, this entanglement in our behaviour, particularly in relation to our attaching to views, is so fundamental to Buddhism that it warrants a whole section in these writings in Chapter 5.

The Wheel that is our existence

And this leads us, in our investigation of the place of craving in Buddhism, to the Wheel of Life. The Wheel of Life, also known as the Wheel of Becoming, or the Wheel of Cyclic Existence, in Sanskrit *bhava-cakra,* is a symbolic representation of the whole of our mundane existence, how we are trapped in an everchanging world of cause and effect, wandering round and round in the everyday world which Buddhists call *saṃsāra*.

According to the Buddhist principle of *paṭicca-samuppāda*,[60] everything that comes into being does so dependent upon certain conditions. Therefore, the sort of person we are, including what we crave and how much we crave, is dependent upon the conditions that have brought us to where we are now. This is consequent on factors that are genetic, social and cultural, how and where we were brought up, the impact of whatever experiences we have undergone in our lives, the decisions and choices that we have made, the people we have had connections with, events that arose before we were born, all of which have formed us. The principle of *paṭicca-samuppāda* describes the interconnected, interdependent flow of all phenomena and events; it is the essence of the universe, its guiding principle, its law. As all things come about according to particular conditions, this also includes *dukkha*, and *dukkha* arises in dependence upon *taṇhā*.

What the Wheel of Life illustrates is the realization which was the Buddha's Enlightenment when he sat under the Bodhi tree so many centuries ago. His realization, as Sangharakshita has put it, is this, 'He saw that everything was process…not only was there process on the material plane, there was process on the mental plane…that this change was not fortuitous – things do not arise and pass away by chance. Whatever arises, arises in dependence on conditions; whatever ceases, ceases because those conditions cease.'[61]

Much can be said about the Wheel of Life and its detailed representation of different realms that we inhabit, and stages that we pass in and out of throughout our lives.[62] Here though I mainly want to bring out certain aspects of the Wheel, those which explain and describe the arising of craving, and its ceasing; how exactly, according to Buddhism, this whole process of craving comes about.

However, before we explore that process, there are some other features of the Wheel of Life, which need to be mentioned. If we visualise the Wheel as a series of four concentric circles, the very inner circle is the hub, the force that drives *saṃsāra;* it consists of the three poisons of delusion, craving, and ill-will, portrayed in a circle as a pig, a cock and a snake respectively, biting at each other's tails. Craving then is represented by a cock, perhaps thought of as greedily scratching the earth, constantly searching for what it can find to satisfy its appetite. These poisons then drive our actions, our actions which determine whether, in the next circle outwards, we move in an upward or downward direction.

The following circle outwards consists of six different realms - we can think of the realms as psychological states - which humans pass in and out of during the course of their lives, some hellish, some less so, as we attempt to deal with the *dukkha*, the unsatisfying nature of our existence.

Here I only want to focus on one, the realm of 'the hungry ghosts', in Sanskrit the realm of the *preta*. Hungry ghosts are mythological creatures whom we can see as depicting symbolically the desperate craving which is endemic in human beings. 'They have enormous swollen bellies but thin necks and tiny mouths like the eyes of needles. All are ravenously hungry, but whatever food they touch turns to either fire or filth'[63]. This then is us, tormented by hunger and thirst but unable to satisfy either. Mark Epstein describes hungry ghosts as 'always searching for nourishment that they are ill-equipped to digest'.[64] This aspect of craving, the inability to fulfil our desires, we shall explore further in the following chapter.

However, it is the outermost circle of the Wheel of Life which I wish to concentrate on. This circle is usually described as a linked chain, a chain of cause and effect, the chain of *paṭicca-samuppāda,* the links that describe how all phenomena come about, and cease to be, in dependence upon certain conditions. We can say that this chain, known as the twelve *nidāna*, is a Buddhist model of how we go through life making the same old mistakes, how we go round and round fuelled by our delusion and craving. This twelve-link model is a detailed explanation of how we suffer due to our longing and clinging, an expanding of the first and second Four Noble Truths.

Let us start with the link 'ignorance', in Buddhism *avidya*. This is ignorance of the way that our *dukkha* comes about. We humans are born into a paucity of knowledge of how our *dukkha* arises, and how it can cease. The other links follow on from here, each one dependent upon the previous one.

A good way to illustrate this simply is through the example of smoking,[65] although we can easily apply this pattern to other compulsive behaviours. Smokers ignore, don't fully apprehend, or self-delude about, how bad smoking is for them (first link, 'ignorance'). Smoking becomes routine behaviour (next link, dependent upon the previous one, 'habitual tendency'). This impacts upon their thinking ('consciousness'), for example, a proliferation of fear or loathing may occur. This tension permeates them mentally and physically ('mind-body'). All of the senses in their body become primed to notice and imagine cigarettes ('sense spheres'). There is interaction between the senses and a cigarette ('contact'). In response to that contact, there is an automatic subjective sensation ('feeling tone', in Buddhism *vedanā*). The smoker reacts to that feeling with craving ('thirst', *taṇhā*[66]) - if a pleasant feeling, a desire to experience the pleasure of a cigarette; or if an unpleasant feeling, perhaps a desire to get away from the withdrawal symptoms since the last cigarette. That craving intensifies, reinforces itself and becomes more dominant in the smoker ('attachment', *upādāna*). The attachment or grasping for cigarettes is so tenacious that smokers become bonded to this craving way of living ('becoming', *bhava*). This way of living creates a particular identity with particular memories that keep us going in a certain direction ('birth').[67] And any birth has an inevitable conclusion ('old age and death'), which brings us back to being born into 'ignorance'.

So, as we can see in the *nidāna* chain, craving provokes attachment or clinging, and clinging then conditions becoming. What you crave is what you cling to is what you become. That is to say, your longings determine what sort of person you are. This process works both ways, your 'becoming' can be positive or negative, beneficial, or not, dependent upon the nature of your longings.

vedanā - always present, sometimes pleasant

Buddhism says that 'feeling tone', *vedanā*, is always present in our experience and we feel sensations as pleasant, unpleasant, or indifferent (that is, neither pleasant nor unpleasant). When our senses (sight, smell, touch etc) make contact with an object, a pleasant feeling, physical or mental, may automatically arise. In the Pai Canon we read, 'For some people, contact, the point where sense plus object meet, is enthralling'.[68] So is the thrill of the anticipation of fulfilling our craving, as Shakespeare wrote in *Troilus and Cressida*, when the ardent Troilus is conjuring up in his mind meeting his beloved, 'I am giddy; expectation whirls me round. Th' imaginary relish is so sweet that it enchants my sense'. So we can become giddy at the expectation of satisfying our craving. Or from the sensations may arise curiosity, nervousness or tightness.

The *vedanā* that we experience may be unpleasant, for example, if somebody threatens us or is rude to us, or if our back aches. Our desire is for the unpleasant to go away, or we desire for the discomfort of the unpleasant feeling to be numbed; we crave for the absence of the unpleasant. For example, we learn that something we wish for has not been fulfilled, an unsuccessful job application perhaps. We realize that we have lost a possession dear to us, a memento passed on by grandmother. And we experience unpleasant feelings of pain, unhappiness, sadness, or grief. From a painful experience we can choose whether to solidify it with ill-will or some outward expression of anger, bringing along with it whatever negative consequences that may ensue. Our lives are governed by these pleasant/unpleasant responses.

As we have seen, *vedanā* arises dependent upon a whole host of different pre-existing factors which will be different for each one of us, according to genes, culture, life experiences, etc. There will be differing degrees of pleasantness or unpleasantness as well, some very strong, some mild. Different types of *vedanā* will provoke different types of desire in different people; looking at a photo of one's deceased father may prompt a longing to visit his grave, an urge to share memories of him with others, a wish to tear up the photo, a need to visit a therapist, depending upon the type of relationship one had with him and the emotions that come with that relationship.

We saw earlier that *taṇhā*, translated as 'thirst', or even 'drought', is inherent in all human beings. Sagaramati widens its significance when he describes *taṇhā* as 'a notion that is best understood metaphorically, as a metaphor that evokes the general condition that all unenlightened beings find themselves in in the world: a state of being characterized by a 'thirst' that compels a pursuit for appeasement, the urge to seek out some form of gratification.[69] More than just an emotion therefore, *taṇhā* is what underlies the whole of our everyday lives, our human condition.

It is crucial though to understand what Sangharakshita points out here: 'While *vedanā* is something that happens to us, *tṛṣṇā* (or *taṇhā*) is something we do. We are presented with feelings, but what we do with those feelings - whether we manufacture positive emotions or negative ones out of them – is our own choice. Feeling is passive, but emotion (as the word itself suggests) is active.'[70] So, *taṇhā* is not produced automatically, it is something we create ourselves; it is our reaction to *vedanā*. Buddhism teaches that we are not responsible for the feelings or sensations that arise in our mind or body; what we are responsible for though is how we respond to them, how we relate to them. Feelings, which arise through our senses, are impersonal; they are not of our own making. We don't have to feel bad about them.

An instinctual feeling such as anger may arise in us and, if we just let it pass, then there will be no adverse consequences. However, if we choose to act on it, and get into an acrimonious argument, for example, then there are bound to be consequences, both for us and others. And the inevitable follows, we 'are washed by the tides of being, drifting along an empty, pointless road. Nowhere is there any sign of broken chains'[71]; we move inexorably along the links of the *nidāna* process. We cling to the *vedanā*, the feeling, we want to sustain it, and then we cling to the object itself which we think has generated the sensation. We crave it and we become attached to it.

Once we react to the *vedanā*, whether pleasant, unpleasant, or neutral, we become engaged, there appears to be no intellectualization at all involved. It seems as though it's instantaneous, a gut-reaction, a reflex. It can happen so fast that we are barely aware of what's happening. I see a chocolate biscuit on the table, as a result I grab it.

The digital world of course speeds up the process - from pleasant feeling, to craving, to the indulging action, to becoming hooked - to an extent that would have been unimaginable in previous generations. A hasty angry response to an email perhaps, without proper consideration of the consequences. This is quite unlike sitting down and writing a letter in reply, which requires reflection.

Managing our response

Fortunately, Buddhism teaches us that it doesn't have to be this way; we can interrupt this seemingly inevitable process of blind reaction. We can notice what's happening, interrupt the process, and even laugh at ourselves for being so silly. We don't need to be hopeless victims of desire. Desire only has sway over us and hoodwinks us for as long as we grasp at and react to it. Moreover, as Subhuti makes clear, 'By re-educating our desires we indirectly re-educate our feelings';[72] by training ourselves to respond differently to cravings which arise, our *vedanā* reaction will gradually change – the picture-postcard photo of a beautiful tropical beach hotel won't necessarily induce envy any longer – we can appreciate without wanting.

Craving then (and its corollary of aversion) is a response, a decision we make, subconsciously or not, to the stimulus of a feeling or sensation that comes about through sensory contact. Desire is not about guilt; we don't need to feel guilty if there arises a feeling of cheesecake-longing, irritating-neighbour-bashing, lust-in-awkward-situation, or alcohol-wipeout-urge. These sorts of feelings happen all the time. It's about how we respond to that feeling, with awareness or not, particularly with awareness of the consequences of indulging the feeling.

The idea of *vedanā*, and its connection with *taṇhā*, is crucial then in the Buddhist understanding of, not only how craving arises, but also most importantly how we do not always need to respond to a sensual trigger with craving. This is why Sangharakshita refers to the relationship between *vedanā* and *taṇhā*, 'the transition from sensation to craving, from passive feeling to active desire' as 'the battlefield of the spiritual life'[73]; this is where choices are made which determine what sort of person we become. Herein lie the fundamentals of Buddhist ethics, the principles that guide our behaviour of body, speech and mind, which we shall examine in more detail later.

Craving is reactivity to a stimulus and, in order to stop the cycle of craving becoming attachment becoming a harmful habit, we need to look at breaking the link between *vedanā* and *taṇhā*. The mind habitually reacts in an autopilot, we can say 'lazy' manner, but, with awareness, we can learn to short-circuit that reactive process and respond in a more open-minded, spacious, expansive way. There is a weak link in the chain between *vedanā* and *taṇhā*, which we can examine mindfully, and where we can insert a gap, a rupture, a breather.

'As the Buddha said, it is not the objects of desire that trap us', writes Traleg Kyabgon. 'It is not the beautiful object that we see. It is not the pleasurable sound that we hear, or the pleasant scent that keeps us entrapped. Rather, it is our response to these things.... we are not demonizing or denigrating the objects of our experiences or emotional responses. When we look at how we apprehend the world, we are trying to understand ourselves in terms of how we respond to the world—animate and inanimate—and how that engagement gives rise to disturbance in our mind.'[74] Chapter 7 explores this process more closely.

Don't kill off the passion

As I have hinted at, we need to be careful however not to misunderstand the Buddha's teaching about desire and attachment. 'The idea that Buddhism says that "all forms of desire are bad and that our ultimate goal is a state of complete desirelessness" is incorrect', writes Ringpu Tulku Rinpoche.[75] The solution to *dukkha* is not to lead a dry passionless desire-free existence, without any drive or longing. This is a misconception of the Buddhist path. When Western scholars first encountered and started to study Buddhism in the nineteenth century, particularly British, French, and German scholars, there was confusion about the Sanskrit term *nirvāṇa* (in Pali *nibbāna)*. This word, which we usually translate as the supreme 'Enlightenment' or 'Awakening' of the Buddha, has the literal meaning of 'extinction' or 'blowing out' - signifying the extinction of the three poisons of craving, ill-will and ignorance.

Partly perhaps because of the paucity of Buddhist texts which were available to scholars at the time, *taṇhā* in the Four Noble Truths and synonyms elsewhere were translated as simply 'desire' and the Buddhist path was seen as the extinction or negation of *all* desire.[76] Thus, *nirvāṇa* was perceived and represented as a state where desire was totally snuffed out, and the view became prevalent in the West that Buddhism advocated that all human desire was harmful, that it was a nihilistic spiritual tradition, a denial of natural life forces.

Buddhism is still today commonly portrayed in this manner, as a religion of passivity and non-action, even inertia. Where 'renunciation is the key to spiritual and psychological growth. Why search for pleasure if that search is the cause of suffering?'[77] However, "stop desiring and you will be happy and fulfilled" is not the Buddhist message; or, at least, not quite. Buddhism differentiates between desires which are 'unskilful', *akusala,* motivated by negative emotions such as craving, greed, anger, hatred, ill-will, confusion, selfishness; and 'skilful', *kusala,* desires motivated by positive virtues such as compassion, insight, wisdom, generosity, selflessness. The idea of something being 'skilful' implies a skill that we need to train ourselves in; this is indeed how Buddhists see ethical behaviour, a skill that requires self-training. We can call these 'unskilful' and 'skilful' mental states respectively 'unwholesome' and 'wholesome'. Unwholesome desires are those that lead to more *dukkha*. Wholesome desires lead to less *dukkha*, whether straight away or in the longer-term. As we saw in the Introduction, I use the word 'craving' for the first in these pairs of terms.

There is a near-synonym of *taṇhā,* the term *chanda*. It is often translated as 'interest', 'intention' or 'will'. In itself it seems to be a neutral term, neither expressing skilfulness or unskilfulness, and depends on accompanying mental states for its direction. A distinction is made though between *kāma-chanda,* the desire for sensuous experience, which we could also represent as 'craving' in the way that we have been using the word in this book, or even the desire which keeps the cycle of *saṃsāra* repeating itself; and *dharma-chanda (*in Pali *dhamma-chanda),* the desire for the truth, or the aspiration for progress in one's spiritual life. Hence, *kāma-chanda* is 'unskilful' desire, whereas *dharma-chanda* is 'skilful' desire, a desire motivated by the search for fulfilment and meaning, the search for wisdom and compassion in one's life. These are two radically different kinds of desires in their object and direction. We shall explore the idea of skilful desire in more detail in Chapter 9, but we can state here that *dharma-chanda* is the driving force on the Buddhist path, the aspiration which is 'the root of all skilful deeds'.[78]

What is *karma* really?

The term *karma* (not to be confused with *kāma*, sensual desire) has already been touched upon. Just a few words here though to clarify its meaning and look at how it relates to craving. Firstly, to clear up any confusion, in Buddhism *karma* 'is not some mysterious power standing over us, watching us unblinkingly, devising a punishment to fit each crime and an apt reward for every good deed', writes Subhuti,[79] 'it is the way we shape our future by shaping our mind'. He continues, 'In each moment, we experience the results of past actions, and also perform fresh actions that will produce results in future.'[80]

Although in Buddhism nothing is predestined, nor is anything random. There is a pattern to our life, a pattern to the mystery that is life. That pattern, that law, is *karma*. It is *karma* that determines the connection between an intentional action, such as craving, and the consequences of that action. The impulse behind a willed action (whether an action of body, speech or mind) - its motivation - determines whether the outcome is expansive or restrictive, uplifting or deflating, harmonious or troublesome, connective or alienating.

Other conditions also will have made us who we are – some physical, some biological, some instinctual.[81] We are made up of a bundle of habits constructed by these different types of conditions. It is difficult to unpick why we act in certain ways, but Buddhism invites us to examine our mental states, and to transform them so that we behave, speak, and think skilfully, for the benefit of ourselves and our relationships with others and the world.

This is the basis of Buddhist ethics. This is a natural ethics, neither created by society nor divine. This can be tested if we pause and reflect on how we are affected by a mean action that we have recently performed – how we are affected bodily, mentally, and our relationship with the world. And then we can do the same for a kind or generous action that we have recently performed. Our reaction to mean actions tend to be constricting, and to our kind actions spacious and outwards-looking. When I reflect on my habitual unskilful thoughts, I find that the upshot is a feeling of being in a tunnel, accompanied by a lack of awareness and lack of love; I feel like I have the instincts of a beast. I feel like an animal in a cage. This is *karma* at work.

An attractive person may appear in your eyeline; do you respond with a prolonged stare that may make you feel somewhat uncomfortable or guilty? Or do you just acknowledge their attractiveness and move on? The consequences for us of these two alternatives are either negative or positive. These consequences are called *karma-vipāka*, the fruit or ripening of our craving, the results of our actions when we crave.

Hangovers are the perfect example of the workings of *karma*. We can say that all of the consequences of our unskilful actions are hangovers – they carry over from the present into the future the costs of our behaviour. They 'hang over' us, reminding us of what we have done that has not been beneficial, to us and to those around us. Sometimes we learn from our hangovers – "Never again!" - and sometimes we carry on regardless, all of us human beings, making the same old gullible mistakes, even though we should know better by now.

To summarise

We can see that Buddhism, in pointing to the centrality of craving in explaining the causes of our dissatisfactions, our *dukkha*, has different ways of approaching, categorising, and analysing craving. We long for things that we don't have, or we want to be different; we cling to things we have, or think we have. Craving is not just the primary cause of our *dukkha*, but to crave is itself uncomfortable, if not downright painful. Craving, *taṇhā*, arises initially out of ignorance and delusion and is dependent upon the sensation, the *vedanā*, that arises out of sensory contact with an object; we react to the sensation most of the time without reflecting. In dependence upon *taṇhā* arises grasping or clinging to the object of our desire, and then we become a slave to the habits we build up as a result of the craving and grasping. 'Craving' writes Doug Smith, 'is the fulcrum around which *dukkha*, and its avoidance, turns our lives.'[82]

However, not all desires are a bad thing; there are both 'unskilful' and 'skilful' desires. We can have an investment in sensual experience but also an investment in searching for the truths of life. Craving takes many different forms and imbues many different emotions, one of which is aversion, the desire to push away or get rid of.

It is only actions then that are willed, consciously intended, that we have a responsibility for, and that will have consequences for the future; instinctual reactions such as the need to sleep, or fear in the face of danger create no *karma-vipāka*. Where we place our attention, for example, is a conscious action; for me right now, either on the distracting news on my smartphone, or on the calming spring blossom outside. What we dwell upon will affect our mental states. What we inflict upon ourselves may afflict us and constrict us. *Part Two* of this book is all about how we can respond in ways that are beneficial to us all.

Reflecting - Chapter 2

Do you have a worldview you cling to about how humans relate to each other? What *dukkha* are you experiencing today – and can you relate that to longing for, or clinging to, something? How are you creating *dukkha* for yourself at this very moment? What do you have a persistent attachment to? What can you think of, within you or around you, that arises and ceases dependent upon certain conditions? Can you think of an example in your life of 'what you crave is what you cling to is what you become'? Try to describe in your own words the link between *vedanā* and *taṇhā*. What are your thoughts on the Buddhist principle of *karma*?

Chapter 3:

DELUDING

Do you ever get the feeling that doing housework is a futile activity? Out comes the vacuum cleaner, whether out of a resigned acceptance of "Oh well, I can't leave it any longer" or alternatively out of a genuine desire for a clean and tidy home, and you whizz round, perhaps absorbed in the job fairly mindfully, or maybe begrudgingly, thinking of better uses of your time. But whichever way you approach it, eventually the housework gets done, and you stand back, satisfied with what you've accomplished. The futility comes in, at least for me, in thinking that the job is now done. I find it hard to accept that half an hour later there there's going to be something spilt on the floor or someone will come in with dirty shoes. And then the floor will need cleaning all over again. I desperately hold on to my clean floor and berate anyone who sullies it, for a few hours anyway, and then I give up the ghost and accept its fate, that nothing stays clean forever.

The same applies of course to washing clothes; no sooner out of the washing machine, sparkling white then ironed, when a rogue drop of soup escapes from the spoon, and it's back to square one, a dirty shirt. Why do I kid myself, even temporarily, that it would be any different? Why do I long for a home or clothes that stay spotless indefinitely, when I know really that will never happen? Maybe I just delude myself.

In the last chapter we explored how craving comes about using the symbolic model of our human existence known as the Wheel of Life, a series of linked events, each dependent one upon the other. At the beginning of this process lies ignorance, *avidya;* one of the three root poisons,[83] along with craving and aversion, which drive our unskilful unhelpful behaviour and which keep us locked into the repetitive cycle which we experience as *dukkha*, our incomplete, not quite satisfying existence. In this chapter we shall examine the connection between ignorance, delusion and craving and how we struggle to find satisfaction in craving. This chapter also explores the habitual persistent nature of craving.

The second of the Buddha's Four Noble Truths as we have seen states that the cause of our *dukkha* is *taṇhā*, our thirsting, our craving, in its many varied forms. However, in the Wheel of Life, the *nidāna* chain of connected steps shows us that we can go deeper and further back into how *dukkha* arises. And what we see is that *taṇhā* is not the first cause of *dukkha*. In fact, we could say that there is no possible first cause as, according to Buddhism, everything is related and inter-dependent. But we can also see that unawareness is at the root of all craving; we are born into the ignorance of how our *dukkha* arises, we have a lack of awareness of the processes that lead to craving and how it entraps us.

Ignorance though is not the same as stupidity. When Buddhism says that humans are ignorant, it is not saying that we are inane, thoughtless pudding heads. It is just saying that we are unaware. It is the fact that we are largely unconscious of the truths of *paṭicca-samuppāda*, *karma* and the impermanent nature of all phenomena that leads to our life being unfulfilled, troublesome, and painful. Ignorance is at the root of *dukkha*. At the same time, although craving may not be 'the first or the only cause of the arising of dukkha....it is the most palpable and immediate cause' says the Theravāda Buddhist writer Walpola Rahula.[84]

Blinkered desire

Craving and ignorance are inextricably linked. The emotional, affective side is *taṇhā*; the intellectual, cognitive side is *avidya*. It is unaware deluded craving that makes our world go round, a state of not knowing what we want. We can talk in a similar way about 'blind craving', not being able to properly take on board the impact of our actions. Or 'blinkered desire', where our perception is distorted. We ignore the effects of our behaviour. 'Ignorance of reality has consequences' says Sangharakshita, 'it automatically plunges one into confusion and bewilderment, which leads to a course of misguided thought and action. It's not just that one doesn't know something; one doesn't know that one doesn't know.'[85]

Obliviousness of our predicament is both innate - we are born with it; and acquired - the karmic consequences of our behaviour through our lives build up views of the world which we fix onto. We will explore the views that we hold in greater detail in chapter 5. Confusion, as Sangharakshita says, is an aspect of our unawareness – muddled thinking, misunderstanding and misinterpreting what others say and do, with consequent disconnection from them. We are confused: doughnuts –

fattening or fun? TV – sedating or soothing? Wine – toxic or thrilling? Social media – pernicious or practical.

Confusion can also result in denial – ignoring or blocking those things we don't want to face up to, distorting to our advantage, and numbing rather than confronting difficulties in our lives; more on this in the following chapter, in connection with 'craving for non-existence'. At times we appear to be so unaware as to be blind to what is happening to us, seemingly in a trance, our consciousness slanted or partial, with an inaccurate perspective of the world we live in. We make all sorts of misleading assumptions, about ourselves ("I'm a bad person, I get angry so often") and other people ("He's from Germany, so I bet he's organised and efficient"). We build expectations that may have scant chance of fulfilment ("My boss will really thank me one day for everything I've done for her"), and ascribe qualities to things and people that do not bear much resemblance to what they can offer ("People will think I'm really cool with my new haircut")

The Buddha's *dharma* is not about hating ourselves because we behave in this way; these are normal reactions because our minds are conditioned to be confused and unaware. What the Buddha's *dharma* teaches us however is that we can see through this confusion, recognising our customary thoughts and deeds as misperceptions brought about by the way we cling and grasp.

The word 'delusion' here in the 21st century may initially conjure up ideas such as 'fake news', how we can be misled, deceived and confused by 'information' that comes at us from the world external to us; from the media, and the worlds of advertising, marketing and promotion in their many forms. This is true, but there is also our 'internal world'; we fool ourselves. All *dukkha* has, at its root, delusion; misunderstanding, misinterpreting, misconceiving. Our understanding of the world and ourselves is frequently erroneous.

We may be unaware of our delusion, or the delusion may be conscious or at least semi-conscious; that is to say, we know that we are deluding ourselves. The truth can be very complicated and frightening, and deceiving ourselves might seem like a better option; the 1st century CE Roman satirist Petronius is attributed with the statement *mundus vult decipi,* the world wants to be deceived. We may turn a blind eye to our own and others' dishonesty and feel that being candid is an acquired taste that we don't want to sign up to.

If you're actually locked up in a prison for a period of time, at least there's one thing that you clearly know: that you're a prisoner and that you're not free. But when you're a prisoner to your desires, be they cyberworld surfing, looking 'cool', or the urge to be always in the right, then you may not be conscious of the fact that you're not free. How many of us who compulsively check our smartphones would actually admit to, or even be aware of, being chained to the object? If we are imprisoned in a web of our desires, this is however a web of our own making, like a spider that has got its threads tangled up. Are we crazy? 'The Parable of Quantum Insanity' of the great physicist Albert Einstein is usually quoted as 'Insanity is doing the same thing over and over and expecting different results'. Buddhism doesn't say we're insane though, just deluded.

Our minds have evolved to mislead us

I have made the point that humans are odd creatures in that we crave for things that are unfulfilling or are going to make us unhappy. And a lot of the time we know that this is the case but can't stop ourselves. How has this come about? One theory comes from evolutionary psychology, a discipline that studies how over time our minds have adapted, or not adapted, to solve problems in our evolution as human beings. Our biology is an important part of the puzzle that we as human beings are. Its connection to Buddhism and to the trait of ignorance lies in the hypothesis that our brains have evolved to mislead us, and that therefore we fail to see the world clearly.

At some levels our minds still seem to operate at the level of a primitive organism that has just emerged from the ocean with its instinctual urges driving it onwards, to feed, to procreate, to rest, to flee, to fight. It's just that over the millennia these primal urges have become overlaid with sophisticated coverings, ingrained patterns of behaviour, some of which have outlived their initial usefulness and raison d'être. What may have helped or enabled our ancient predecessors to survive is now, sometimes literally, killing us.

Craving is in essence instinctual, hard-wired into us, part of our inheritance. One of the types of Buddhist conditionality (that is, the processes which are the causal factors of all phenomena) is *mano-niyāma*, effectively our biological genetic instincts, including reflexes and stimulus-response reactions; this type of behaviour has no karmic consequences. But much of the craving instinct that comes from our genetic make-up is no longer really necessary, is in effect redundant, and in fact now unhelpful to our well-being. Surplus eating in times of plenty to prepare for times of dearth has now become over-eating at other times, leading us to obesity and premature death. Eating to survive and eating for pleasure have got their wires all crossed.

Emotions like greed, hatred and anxiety have not developed in order to give us a clear picture of reality, but rather to help our ancestors to get their genes into subsequent generations. Ultimately, they often serve little or no useful function now. The evolutionary psychologist Robert Wright states that 'the human brain was designed – by natural selection – to mislead us, even enslave us .... our brains are designed to delude us'.[86] He continues, 'pleasure is designed by natural selection to evaporate so that the ensuing dissatisfaction will get us to pursue more pleasure... the way to make us productive is to make the anticipation of pleasure very strong but the pleasure itself not very long-lasting'. The desire is more intense than the pleasure.

So, according to evolutionary psychology, our biology has developed to enjoy things which carry forward our genes, but not to give us long-lasting pleasure. If it did, we wouldn't carry on doing what is necessary, both in sexual and social terms, to procreate. The sexual act between a man and a woman, and the pleasure derived from it, hasn't developed (probably fortunately) to go on forever, just long enough for the possibility of conception to take place; and the desire for more sexual pleasure drives humans to go at it again, to give conception another chance.

In scientific terms, the 'reward' of getting what you want releases dopamine. Dopamine is triggered as we get closer to the reward. The dopamine buzz is just a temporary one, it merely gets us to the object of desire, the food or sexual partner which will help us, in respect of our evolution, to get our genes to carry on after we die. Pleasure is transitory and we are left unsatisfied, which is exactly what the Buddha said.

Sagaramati says something similar regarding craving in an evolutionary context - he uses the terms *rāga* (craving) and *dosa* (aversion). 'The most general and basic natural forces that were *necessary* for the evolution and survival of early man: *rāga* as the urge to acquire the necessities for survival; *dosa* as the aggressive drive needed when one is acquiring those necessities in a contest with others, as well as to defend one's possessions and family/tribe against aggressors'.[87] Biological, hormonal urges that developed to optimize our chances of survival have now effectively outgrown their usefulness.

It's like the appendage called the appendix that all humans have. Once upon a time it served a purpose for us in our digestive systems, but then it hung on in our bodies when it was no longer needed. And it's still there, frequently causing problems when it flares up for some reason. Fortunately, if this happens and we catch it in time, we can just get it cut out surgically. Unfortunately though, although sometimes we might fantasize about it, there is no surgical procedure available to remove our harmful cravings when they flare up. There is no one-off easy solution. As we'll explore in *Part Two*, we have to work at it.

Filling a hole

In the two previous chapters we saw how humans experience life as though there is something missing – this is what *dukkha* is about, incompleteness, something not quite right – and we crave to fill this void by grasping after various objects, both material and abstract. We always seem to be wanting for something to come along to satisfy us. Nature abhors vacuums it is said, and we humans can't stand the insufficiency that exists in our nature, the poverty that we need to alleviate, the cavity that requires a filling.

The poet Lord Byron described it thus: 'this "craving void" which drives us to gaming - to battle - to travel - to intemperate but keenly felt pursuits of every description whose principal attraction is the agitation inseparable from their accomplishment'.[88] We are drawn then to pursuits which bring stimulation to our ennui. We can dedicate much of our energy to looking for things to give our life meaning – football, fandom, fashion, Facebook. In the same way that sometimes we eat, not to fill a gap in our stomach because we are naturally hungry, but rather to fill an illusory gap brought on by an illusory hunger, equally we search to satisfy that which we experience as an authentic need but which in fact is an undefined existential longing.

One way of describing *taṇhā* is an urge for satisfaction. According to the Buddha's teachings, desire for ordinary mundane things can never be fully satisfied. The Buddha taught this from his own experience of life. In his youth and as a young man he lived in a home which was said to be like a palace, with all the sensual pleasures available to him that one can imagine, all of his worldly desires met. But this did not bring him genuine contentment and fulfilment, and he set off on a search for real purpose and meaning, his 'noble search',[89] the desire for transcendence and liberation from the *dukkha* caused by mundane desires.

The poet Bhartrihari, describing the way that we pursue unquenchable desires, wrote that we 'chase phantom rewards.'[90] The underlying things that we long for - security, permanence, identity – are ultimately unobtainable. They go against reality. Buddhism says that the three characteristics of existence (the *lakṣaṇa*) are the opposite of security, permanence and identity, that is to say, they are the characteristics of incompleteness (*dukkha*), impermanence (*aniccā*), and insubstantiality (*anattā*).

Like the hungry ghosts of the Wheel of Life, the *pretas* that appeared in Chapter 2, our hunger and thirst will never be satiated. That is, if we carry on in our same old habitual ways. We need to, and can, find different ways of responding to our longings. The Rolling Stones were only half-right when they sang about not being able to get any satisfaction. It depends on how and where we look. We tend to search for happiness in the wrong places or, to put it another way, we are all searching for fulfilment but just use rubbish strategies.

I remember, still with some pain, being madly in love as a teenager with a young woman who didn't feel the same way about me. Unrequited love, a lot of us will have had to suffer this aching at some point in our life. But in a sense our whole life is like this. It's as though we live with unrequited longings; we long, but our longings are never completely met. Mark Epstein calls this the "unbridgeable gap between desire and satisfaction"[91]. We desire things that we don't have; to want something is to be without it, to be deprived of it. We do not want things we have, we only want things we don't have. Longing therefore implies deprivation. And deprivation as we know is inherently unpleasant.

Our harmless cravings?

The behaviour of the mind that misleads itself plays out in many different ways. We may con ourselves into believing that gratifying our unhealthy urges hurts nobody but ourself, that our indulging is self-contained and a 'victimless crime'. But if we step back, reflect and look into the background story of how our objects of desire arrive in our lap, another pattern emerges.

As we saw in Chapter 1, in the production and use of pornography many people are exploited, abused and humiliated through this manipulative industry. In addition, we may compulsively buy cheap new clothes that don't damage our bank account too much but choose to ignore the often appalling sweatshops in which they are manufactured, mostly in Asia. Through our online purchasing we help to sustain processing centres where workers are often forced to work long hours for pitiful remuneration. For those who like to eat chicken, it's worth looking at how the demand for cheap chicken results in battery farms where the animals live in horrendous conditions, and their excrement is flushed into our rivers and lakes, to add to fertiliser run-off from farms, causing untold damage to the environment.[92] Do you know about the implications of the manufacture of everything that goes into your phone?

Not only do we dupe ourselves as individuals, but we are also susceptible to plunge ourselves into the abyss of mass, collective delusion. Particularly in unstable times, humans long so much for certainty, solidity, and belonging that, when a charismatic leader or movement comes along offering us these securities and much more, we can easily allow ourselves to be sucked into collective and mass hysteria. History, ancient and current, is peppered with demagogues and populist politicians who promise with simplistic answers to solve all society's ills, frequently by casting blame on a particular group, and invite us to close off our discerning minds and to sign up to their delusionary messages. We can dupe ourselves through hope and also through fear. Dupery through hope is wishful thinking.[93]

In Chapter 1 we looked at how consumerism pervades our societies, and how unsatisfying this turns out to be. We see this dissatisfaction playing out on a very broad scale, 'Transnational corporations that are never big or profitable enough, nation-states that are never secure enough, accelerating technological innovation that is never innovative enough to satisfy us for very long – our collective lack'.[94] In fact, our collective greed, collective ill-will, and collective delusion. This unsatisfied craving as it plays out in the affairs of the world, way beyond our own individual longing and clinging, has massive repercussions for the future of our planet and its population.

This is why I personally feel that a spiritual tradition such as Buddhism, which not only provides an analysis of the human condition and stresses our interconnection with each other, but also provides a path of practices that address delusion, as well as hate and craving, is so necessary to the continued existence of us all. If the human dream is to live in harmony, co-operation and peace with each other, rather than in warring inward-looking factions, then we need to cultivate the one and reject the other.

I don't want to be overly judgmental in describing the different ways in which we unsuccessfully try to satisfy the lack within us. After all, we *all* do it in one way or another. For all of us there is a kind of delusion underpinning our cravings, whatever they may be. I'm not trying to say that all our behaviour in seeking satisfaction wherever is unreasonable, superficial, or ignorant in a pejorative, belittling sense. Neither am I trying to say that we get no satisfaction at all from indulging our cravings. Clearly we do. We can assuage cravings temporarily and gain some peace of mind for a while. But let's not fool ourselves into believing that they will stay satisfied and those cravings will fade away. Unfortunately, they won't. Or they may morph and surface in a different form. We may think that we are in control but regrettably most of the time we are not; our thoughts and our emotions are disobedient. Our cravings set us up in order to let us down.

What I, as a Buddhist, am attempting to do is not to pour scorn on how and what we crave, but rather to give an analysis of something that we all experience, namely *dukkha*; what causes the undeniable *dukkha* that we live with; how we desire to bring about happiness yet our cravings go unfulfilled; and to examine solutions, to ask what we can do about it. What Buddhists say is not that we and the world that we live in are 'bad' in any sense, but just that our experience of the world is unfulfilling. And we are not fundamentally 'bad' people, we just fall into the trap of delusional craving.

The 19th century English poet John Clare, in his poem *The Vanities of Life*,[95] encapsulated I feel this futility of seeking for things which ultimately will give no satisfaction:

> *What are life's joys and gains?*
> *What pleasures crowd its ways,*
> *That man should take such pains*
> *To seek them all his days?*
> *Sift this untoward strife*
> *On which thy mind is bent:*
> *See if this chaff of life*
> *Is worth the trouble spent.*

Is pride thy heart's desire?
Is power thy climbing aim?
Is love thy folly's fire?
Is wealth thy restless game?
Pride, power, love, wealth, and all
Time's touchstone shall destroy,
And, like base coin, prove all
Vain substitutes for joy.

Topsy-turvy views

In Buddhism we call misinterpretations or erroneous understandings *viparyāsa,* translated as the four 'perversities' or the four 'topsy-turvy views'. These views are: taking impure things to be pure;[96] thinking that the unsatisfactory nature of things will bring happiness; taking impermanent phenomena as permanent; and taking illusory things to be real. We could broaden this out and say, for example, the misguided views that money will bring us joy, that making a list is the equivalent of getting the jobs done, or that jogging once a month will makes us fit.

We can summarise this teaching by proposing that there are two principal reasons why our ordinary cravings can never be satisfied: the impermanent nature of all phenomena (*aniccā*), and the fact that we ascribe qualities to our objects of desire which do not have any basis in reality.

The first reason then is impermanence. Nothing on earth remains the same. Just look at trees and how they change. Look at how we humans change over time - our bodies, our views, our cravings, our relationships with the world. Nothing is totally fixed and secure. And nothing endures enough to give us lasting satisfaction. The insecurity inherent in everything around us can be very unsettling, engendering anxieties. We fear to lose things that we do possess (or at least think we possess), so that owning things is in itself always tinged with unease, with the anxiety of possible loss and of being deprived of things we treasure. Our home could burn down, or our valued ring could disappear down the plughole; and we know for sure that our good memory *will* become less reliable, our good looks *will* fade.

Objects of desire enjoy the illusion of the static, the unchanging. We may impute longevity to things we purchase and seem surprised that they have built-in obsolescence, that the handle drops of the drawer after a couple of pulls, that the new hairdryer overheats and gives up the ghost far earlier than we think it should have. We attach to things because of the 'wrong view' that they can provide lasting happiness; well, if not lasting happiness, at least they should give us a bit more than just transient satisfaction. What we can rely on though is Śāntideva's dictum, 'All that may be wished for will by nature fade to nothing'.[97]

Of course, we don't really 'own' anything. We may be temporary custodians of a bike, a laptop, a jacket, but in the future we will have no connection with them; either they or we will disappear off the scene. Unlike Egyptian pharaohs and Viking chieftains, you can't take your belongings with you into the afterlife. In fact, we are only interim caretakers of what we think of as our arms, our legs, our eyes, even our heart. One day they will all wither away. We attach to things and people, and when they are no longer there, it can really hurt. We have to question the way we attach and grasp, and see what lessons we can learn. The message from Buddhism is not to cling to things which are by their nature impermanent. I have a favourite cup that my son bought me for my birthday with a Hokusai painting on it. I treasure the cup, but I know that one day I will wake up and it will have slipped from the draining board and crashed onto the floor into smithereens. I am ready for that moment and in the meantime I can appreciate it as it is.

Moreover, no object that we crave can be possessed in a form that is unvarying and stationary. By the time we managed to gratify our desire for it, 'possess' it, 'indulge' it, that is if we are able to so do, what we desired, what we acquired, and what we now possess will not be identical, due to the object's quality of impermanence. When we look for comfort in material objects, we are in denial of the principle of impermanence, one of the characteristics of all worldly things. We shall examine this principle further in Chapters 5 and 8.

The objects of our desire therefore and our relationship to them do not last forever and consequently they are unable to give us lasting satisfaction. Ordinary mundane worldly objects are called in Buddhism 'conditioned phenomena'; that is to say that they come into being dependent upon certain conditions. You need only to think of the book, e-reader or computer that you are reading right now and reflect on the incredible number of factors that have brought it about and brought it into your hands. These conditions are forever changing. We look for solutions, the fulfilling of our cravings, which are bound to be temporary for a problem which is always there, namely, our existential insufficiency, the something missing inside us. Long term longings cannot be slaked with temporary expedients.

Our phone, smart or not, will breathe its last one day, and so will we. However much we delude ourselves about the inevitability of death - and many of us do find it difficult to face up to our mortality - it is the one fact of life that we can be sure about; we will surely die one day. We are as impermanent as our phone, here for a limited length of time. Maybe if we can start to loosen our attachment to this 'me' going on and on indefinitely, we can perhaps loosen our attachment to what this 'me' grasps at for comfort; and vice versa. Living life with a certain lightness, not being weighed down by so many attachments, can be wonderfully freeing.

The word 'fix' says it all. Something that will 'fix' our longing, repair our unease, make everything right again. Fixing something also conveys the idea of making something stable or permanent. Of course, a 'fix' does none of these things. It is just a momentary manoeuvre at the very most. Fixes by their nature need fixing again and again. If they're not fixed, we find ourselves, well yes, in a fix.

Like the 9.08 train to Kings Cross, everything passes through and moves on, even though it may come back at you later from a different direction. Our difficult cravings come and go, disappear, accompanied by a sigh of relief, only to return escorted by a despairing groan. A painkiller may get rid of the symptoms of a headache, but it doesn't get rid of the causes. In a way, all of our objects of desire can be thought of as our painkillers, a limited fix. A health warning: this medicine will only give you temporary relief from discomfort.

Lama Thubten Yeshe talks about a change in our attitude, 'seeing the ultimate worthlessness of the transitory phenomena we are ordinarily attracted to. When we see clearly the unsatisfactory character of the things we have been chasing after, our compulsive striving for them will automatically diminish and the driving force of our grasping will subside.'[98] Positive thirsts can then take precedence – a thirst for life, a thirst for understanding, a thirst for clarity.

Idealisation and false projection

The second reason why our ordinary cravings cannot be satisfied is that we invest objects with qualities that they do not possess. Have you noticed that the more you actually long for something, the bigger it appears to you? At the moment, that millionaire's shortbread that I'm salivating for seems absolutely huge; to that extent it's taking up a lot of my mind space and attention. In our mind's eye we distort those things we crave.

As we saw at the beginning of this chapter, craving and unawareness are tightly intertwined; we are deluded about what we can get from the objects of our craving. The distance or separation between us and the object of our desire lends enchantment to it – the object of desire appears more attractive than it actually is, once it has been tasted. Hmm, that millionaire's shortbread was sort of OK, but it didn't really live up to its enormous billing. We can also gain more pleasure actually in the sometimes deluding-ourselves memories of how good an event really was than in the actual event itself; smiling, happy-go-lucky photos are often only a partial record of an event.

We can idealise those things to which we are drawn, attributing qualities to them that they hardly possess, the proverbial 'rose-tinted glasses' syndrome. Those of you who have ever fallen head-over-heels in love will know what I mean. When you become infatuated with someone, that person may indeed be attractive to others, but to you their attractiveness is colossal, exaggerated to a preposterous extent because of your desire for them. You may want to show all and sundry their photo to prove how beautiful they are, tell everyone about their great qualities.

Craving brings with it a false interpretation of the object of desire. We can easily reread too much into a word, a glance, a shrug, a text. For example, I might wrongly interpret the fact that a woman smiles at me as meaning that she must fancy me, because that is what I desire; we have a tendency to believe what suits us. We incorrectly construe therefore the target of our craving. We expect more pleasant *vedanā,* feeling tone, from an object than it is able to give us, we overestimate the positive benefits it can give us; "If only I get that job I've seen advertised, my problems will be solved." At the same time we edit out the unpleasant aspects of the object of our craving; "What do you mean, my new boyfriend has a drinking problem? I don't see it." We feel that indulging our objects of desire, because it initially brings us pleasure ("Oh, that joyful mouthful of chocolate truffle!"), is actually beneficial to us ("Something this delicious has got to be good or, at least, it can't be all bad"). We blind ourselves to the negative side of the indulgence ("I've overdone it on the wine…again…oh, my head!").

We don't really think that quaffing several glasses of Pinot Grigio is going to give us eternal joy. But what we do manage to do is to overestimate the amount of happiness it will bring us. We don't do this overestimating in a cool detached rational way. We know rationally that the wine won't give us long-lasting fulfilment. We may think more about the delicious taste, colour and bouquet of the wine than the hangover it might induce later; or we may simply do it because that's a blind habit we've got into.

So we don't see the object itself but rather a projection of the object, and the word object here applies to people as well. We project onto phenomena what we want to see. 'In making even horizontal and clear inspections' wrote Thomas Hardy, 'we colour and mould according to the wants within us whatever our eyes bring in.'[99] or, as Rob Burbea explains, 'perceptions, appearances, experiences are fabricated more or less dependent on the way of looking.' [100]

But sparkling tech goods inevitably and eventually lose their shine. And attractive aspects of things become irritants. Appealing download speeds aren't that fast anymore. We fall in and out of love with people, but with things too. We end up disappointed. Our ideas of what will satisfy us are warped, like images in a hall of crazy mirrors. We misinterpret, intentionally or not we don't see their true make-up.

Jnanaketu writes about how we attribute values to objects. 'An example would be gold. Gold is simply a material/mineral like any other material substance. But we impute something to it. We not only impute value to it, but some people seek to gather it, hoard it, and will even kill other human beings to get it and keep it. The value of gold is simply a human creation, yet 'it' creates in people all sorts of feelings, anxieties, attachments, views, and so which have no actual basis in reality. All these experiences are based on a mere metal that can be used to make wedding rings, and may be useful for capping teeth, but not much else.'[101]

The term 'clickbait' in our digital world describes the enticement held out to the user to try to tempt or manipulate us to click onto a hyperlink, an embellished or misrepresenting headline perhaps, leading to uninteresting, irrelevant or questionable content. We could use the word 'clickbait' as a metaphor for all sorts of deceptive *false friends* that promise but don't deliver, attractive packages disappointedly offering up precious little.

Craving disappoints, like John Clare's wildflower that when plucked lives only fleetingly;[102] being jilted by your lover in an affair you wanted to go on forever; or an unresolved conclusion to a film where you wanted a happy ending. A conflict is always present within us - the psychological conflict that underlies human dissatisfaction; the contrasting forces of craving, and the frustration that arises at the impossibility of satisfying it.

This is the anti-climax of gratifying desire – not long-lasting satisfaction but, in the end, frustration. Like sand that slips through our fingers, we cannot hold onto those objects of desire that we grasp at. It is a futile quest. Not getting what we want is wearisome. One day we will eventually tire of the seemingly endless routine of repeated unsatisfactory gratification. Eventually we will. Perhaps.

Seeking perfection

You may have had the experience, I often have, of being in a situation where just about everything is great, but you want it to be even a little bit greater. Sitting back relaxing in a comfy seat in a garden maybe, soaking up the trees and the sky. And all you need now to make this a perfect moment is for the sun to shine, a beautiful partner by your side, a glass of wine, some nibbles, a cigarette, for the background traffic buzz to disappear. Just like in some fantasy advert on TV really, where everything is just right. Because although this moment is great, it's not perfect. It's not quite complete. Half-good is regrettably not enough.

Thubten Yeshe elaborates, 'But what happens when we are successful, when we do get what we want? What we end up with and what we hoped to end up with turn out to be two very different things. For what we find ourselves in possession of is not the longed-for dream image — the permanent, complete, and ever-satisfying solution to our deepest problems — but something that is as imperfect, incomplete, and impermanent as we are ourselves.'[103]

The 'everything' in the phrase 'having everything' is of course a misconception. There is always something else. Just one more plant in the window box will make it perfect. Just one more shirt to add to my wardrobe. Just a slightly bigger home. Just a bit more intimacy in my relationship with my partner. There is 'this longing for an imagined wholeness'[104]. We seek after perfection, but it is unfortunately unattainable in our normal everyday lives. This is what *dukkha* means. In Chapter 7 we will see how we can start to look at life differently. We can be grateful for life as it is, not wanting it to be more than it is.

Enough is not enough

You may be familiar with vampires like Edward in the *Twilight Saga* series of books and films or, those of you a bit older, with *Buffy the Vampire Slayer*, or perhaps the most famous of the lot, Bram Stoker's *Dracula*. The characteristic of all vampires is that their bloodlust is never satisfied, they always want more. We may not continually prey on others as vampires do, but this vampire-like tendency is a feature of all human craving – our longings go unfulfilled and so we keep on wanting more. There may be the brief cessation of desire after sexual gratification, but the desire returns. As Robert Wright writes, 'One of the Buddha's main messages was that the pleasures we seek evaporate quickly and leave us thirsting for more.'[105] Whether it be a pinch of sensory input or a whole pile of it, the grasping does not satisfy and the grasping for more goes on, until we gasp our last, and we can grasp no more.

We may long for something to happen in our mundane existence, long to achieve something, long to acquire something new; only to discover that when a goal is accomplished there is still a deficit in our lives – we still carry on wanting. The more we crave, the more of a craver we become. Continually indulging my afternoon cake habit only refuels and strengthens my afternoon cake habit. For these types of cravings, you capitulate, they proliferate. According to Shakespeare, Cleopatra famously left her lovers always desiring more, 'Other women cloy / The appetites they feed, but she makes hungry / Where most she satisfies'.[106]

I used to chew a tab of menthol gum when walking to work every morning in a half-hearted attempt to wake myself up before I faced the onslaught of the day ahead. But one tab of gum soon wasn't enough to get me going, so I progressed to two. Alright for a while, but then that two too lost their clout. Before I knew it I was on three tabs every morning, mindless to the fact I reeked of menthol and eucalyptus by the time I presented myself to my work colleagues. Fortunately I stopped at three before I made myself sick of the stuff and changed my morning habit to caffeine instead. But then one cup wasn't enough...

Although generally speaking we want to keep having pleasant sensations and experiences, our body does have its limitations. It doesn't necessarily want to endlessly repeat eating whole boxes of Ferrero Rocher or keep on having multiple orgasms. In the end our body will tell us to stop, although sometimes we may have to keel over, pass out or throw up before we get to that stage.

The repetitive nature of craving is one of its most important characteristics. We indulge, we reinforce the habit; we indulge again, we reinforce the habit even more. Whether it be looking at ourselves in the mirror, smoking a cigarette, checking emails while eating breakfast, retail therapy, or gossiping about a work colleague, the pattern is the same.

The continual treading of feet through a field will eventually form a rutted pathway, which guides our feet. Along this pathway no grass will grow and flourish. Similarly, in the field of our mind, our unhealthy habits are like a series of ruts which guide our behaviour along well-trodden unhelpful routes, making it difficult for positive beneficial behaviour to flourish and grow.

There is an incremental aspect to craving, as we continue to grasp, the ruts get gradually deeper. We stupidly feed our desirings which, like other things we nourish, only makes them more powerful. Desire grows organically then. The more it is fed, the more we give it what it asks for, the stronger it becomes.

Our habitual behaviour, longing for the same things, means that we become very familiar with them. The more we become familiar with them, the more we grow attached to them. This is sometimes called the familiarity principle or what the social psychologist Robert Zajonc called the mere-exposure effect; the more often we are exposed to a stimulus, the more positively we will rate that stimulus.[107] Thoughts and ideas get lodged in our minds. An image that stays because it has provoked a strong emotion, perhaps a photo from a war zone or a region affected by famine, a sexual image, or a helpless puppy. The tune that stays in your head all day and that you can't stop yourself from humming. An unpleasant smell up your nose that won't go away, or a lingering metallic taste in your mouth.

Traleg Kyabgon writes, 'Strongly habitualized patterns of behavior set up tendencies whereby we begin to behave in a very predictable fashion. These habits, once established, do not stay the same but tend to become more intensely fixed and inflexible.'[108] The habitual tendencies that we develop are called in Buddhism *saṁskāra,* a concept we came across in the previous chapter as one of the links in the model of the Wheel of Life; *saṁskāra* arise out of ignorance, misunderstanding, and self-delusion, as we have seen in this chapter, and lead on to how our minds interpret the world and impact upon how we respond to it.

Our habitual tendencies condition then what we notice, what we pay attention to, seeing sometimes only half the picture. We may ignore beautiful things around us because we are focussing only on that upon which we are fixated. These *saṁskāra* then become our general disposition. There are tendencies which we inherit as human instincts from birth, those that are innate; and tendencies which we inherit through *karma* resulting from our behaviour, those that are acquired.[109] Acquired habits are learnt behaviour. For example, we learn from watching TV or films that when a character gets stressed or anxious they reach out for a cigarette or a whiskey.

In the Pali Canon we also find the idea of latent, dormant tendencies or inclinations, *anusayā*, the term always used in a negative sense; this can be compared to the unconscious in Freudian psychoanalysis, 'a deeper background, an undercurrent that sustains conscious craving.'[110] Our latent inclinations surface, given certain conditions, manifest as actions and become our habitual behaviour.

There is a disparity between understanding and practice. We find it easy to understand but difficult to practise. There is this gulf between knowing and doing, what is sometimes called 'cognitive dissonance', holding two conflicting beliefs, values, or attitudes, with the resulting mental discomfort. An example of this inconsistency between what we believe and how we behave could be wanting to build up our savings but tending to spend any extra cash as soon as we get it. We want to do wholesome things, but we end up doing the opposite. We know it's not great for us but we still do it. As the American author Mark Twain is said to have quipped, 'Giving up smoking is the easiest thing in the world. I know because I've done it thousands of times.'

It's so effortless to just slip back into old habits. We can get a temporary ending to our urges, but they always seem to return. They have the one-over on us. Compulsive behaviour is hard to get way from. Captain Ahab described thus his obsession with the whale in Herman Melville's *Moby Dick*, 'The path to my fixed purpose is laid with iron rails, whereon my soul is grooved to run.'

Ill-will - the flipside of craving - may pass in a flash, an outburst of anger, some shouting, and then it's all over; because it's obviously painful, ill-will can be easier to give up. Craving however, although its effects may be less harmful than hatred and anger, is associated with pleasure and is usually harder to abandon.

Reversing the magnet

However, one day we may just feel appalled enough with ourselves and have a 'lightbulb' moment. We come to a realization about what we are doing to ourselves and others, that continually putting people down to make us feel superior is not a great tactic for making friends, or that spending the hours when we should be sleeping playing online poker is seriously damaging our health. We may feel saddened that we have been carrying on damaging habitual behaviour for so long. This realization it itself may be sufficient to know that enough is enough, and it's time to address one's compulsive craving.

We can ignore the enormous potential that we have to address and transform our harmful urges. Our longings may seem like a magnet – a seemingly irresistible force. But magnets work in two contradictory ways; they either pull in or push away, either attract or repel. We too can attract or repel those things which cause us *dukkha*. Neuroscientists talk of neural pathways, imprinting and neuroplasticity[111], our actions ploughing furrows in our brains, both positive and negative, the ruts in our minds that mental channels that will lead us to lush abundance in our lives, lead us away from the unsatisfying repetitive world of *saṃsāra*. 'Whatever a *bhikkhu* frequently thinks and ponders upon, that will become the inclination of the mind.'[112] By setting our minds on positive longings, we can diminish the role in our lives of grasping after objects of desire, and eventually learn to go beyond those fixations altogether. In the next chapter, we shall investigate a particular type of desire that can entrench us in extremely deep ruts and is the very antithesis of fulfilling our potential.

Reflecting - Chapter 3

Can you accept that much of the time you walk around blinded by desire and see life in a distorted way? Do you sometimes feel confused about the pros and cons of your craving? Can you think of someone or something you have a misleading assumption about? Do you kid yourself about how much time you 'screen binge'? Do you feel you have primitive instincts that are no longer helpful to you? Does the Buddhist idea that mundane cravings cannot be satisfied make sense to you? Can you think of an example of where the anticipation or recollection of an event was more satisfying than the event itself? Are you someone who always looks to 'fix' a problem? In what ways do you invest objects with qualities that they do not possess? Can you think of an occasion when indulging a craving was a great anti-climax? Do you find it difficult to accept the karmic consequences of your actions? Do you feel that your cravings harm nobody but yourself? Do you recognize in yourself a longing for perfection? Reflect on what habits you have and note how they relate to craving. Do you experience a disparity between knowing what is beneficial to you and putting that knowledge into practice – why is that?

Chapter 4:

FLEEING

I want to tell you about Carlo, a good friend of mine. On the surface, he was in a very fortunate position in his life. He had a loving wife and children, work that was meaningful and reasonably successful, good friends, and relative financial comfort. He had undergone no apparent big trauma in his life, no major social upheaval, no obvious pressures then apart from the usual work-related ones. Indeed, nothing special about his life. And yet something wasn't right. Somewhere in his life there was something he was trying to escape from. He experienced a deep need to smother, to avoid.

Like many of his friends and colleagues Carlo drank alcohol, occasionally excessively, rarely to the point of being ill though. When he was younger, he was part of a drugs culture. Amphetamine to give him social confidence; LSD to rise into a world of heightened connection and transcendent, expansive experiences; regular cannabis to generally take the edge off of things. To avoid his day-to-day experience, his compulsive personality might have led him further and further into alcohol or drugs or work, or maybe he could have got sucked into a gambling habit to run away from his ordinary routine.

But then along came the Internet, and Carlo signed up for it hook, line and sinker. This was now the world he chose to bury himself in. Surfing from one topic to the next, one site to the next, anything and everything, it didn't really matter what it was, both the thrilling and the monotonous, the bizarre and the mundane; news, sport, porn, tittle-tattle. The Internet was a great drug for him; brilliant ease of access, although frustratingly slow in its infancy, simple to indulge in, private, cheap, and not immediately harmful. Or at least that's what he thought. With the sort of 'greed' personality that he had, it didn't take him long to become addicted to internet-surfing. It was easy to disappear into the digital world, the world that Prajnaketu calls *Cyberloka*.[113] Over time he cut back on sleeping, socialising, eating properly, exercise, paying attention to those dear to him, trying to be effective in his job.

He craved to shut himself off from the real world and live in a fantasy one. He wanted to hide away from that which he experienced as difficult in his life, and the Internet provided that escape. It was only when Carlo encountered Buddhism that he could begin to understand this compulsive trait in his personality, give a name to it, and start to address it.

The desire not to be

This chapter is about *vibhava-taṇhā*, usually translated as the craving for non-existence, one of the three types of *taṇhā* outlined in Chapter 2. Craving for non-existence is a desire for oblivion, for escape, a nihilistic urge, a pulling the quilt over one's head, ultimately a desire for 'death', not necessarily in the literal sense, but in a more metaphorical sense of closing the world off, or closing off to the world.

Traditionally, *vibhava-taṇhā* is equated with a belief in annihilation, the materialist view that when we die that is the end of matters, full stop, the lights go out and there is nothing more. In the Buddha's day, there was a whole range of views current as to what happens when one dies. At one extreme was the 'eternalistic' view, that our self or 'soul' carries on after death; at the other, the 'nihilistic' view that everything ends when our body expires.[114] The Buddha rejected both of these views, taking a 'Middle Way' between the two in supporting the view that a momentum or perfume goes on from our life after we physically die, formulated as the doctrine of rebirth.[115] To desire annihilation at death, to desire not to become anything after we die, was seen in Buddhism as a 'wrong view'.

However, it makes more sense to see *vibhava-taṇhā* in a much wider context than just what happens when we die. The more people I talk to about this rather overlooked or sometimes oversimplified aspect of craving, the more convinced I am that it plays an extremely important role, and often a very unhelpful one, in the lives of many of us. For me, *vibhava-taṇhā* means to give up caring - giving up caring about life, one's own life and that of other people; refusing to face up to life's challenges; the desire to be rid of what is inconvenient; and the consequent not adhering to one's values. This may not be the traditional definition of *vibhava-taṇhā,* but I feel that this is what it amounts to.

Like other terms such as desiring, clinging, and grasping, *vibhava-taṇhā* covers a wide range and depth of emotions. At one end of the spectrum is a craving to not experience the world, a longing for extinction; serious drug addiction and suicidal thoughts are typical illustrations of this. At the other end is the feeling of "I can't be bothered". Somewhere in between is the craving for an experience to go away or end; feeling humiliated perhaps by being in the presence of somebody who has superior knowledge or skills. In a mild form it may be not wanting to be noticed, wanting to fade into the background. Or wishing your life away on activities that don't amount to much.

In whatever form it takes for some of us, like my friend Carlo, *vibhava-taṇhā* is an extremely strong facet of our psychological make-up. For others, it is a recognizable tendency in our lives but does not overwhelm us. We saw in Chapter 2 that aversion, a strong feeling of dislike, repugnance, or antipathy toward something and a desire to avoid it, is in fact a form of craving; the wish to push things or people away. There is clearly a close connection between *vibhava-taṇhā* and aversion. Both are 'a wish to be separated from painful feelings', writes the Dalai Lama.[116] If aversion is a pushing away, *vibhava-taṇhā* is a running away from.

The not so great escape

We don't normally seek out hurt. We prefer pleasure to pain. To avoid hurt then seems on the face of it a perfectly reasonable desire. We probably all have a tendency to side-step experiences which we find difficult. There are those of us want to make their world beautiful and comfortable, where there is no challenge, no conflict. The problem is that there are things, people, events in our everyday lives, whoever we are and whatever we do, which we are always going to find challenging or troubling. This is the *dukkha* in life – nothing can be altogether right for very long. So what do you do? Do you just try to constantly dodge and duck those testing moments? Do you engage fight-mode or flight-mode? Do you stay around and try to deal with it, or take the first train to anywhere?

Have you ever feigned illness to get out of a difficult social event or other commitment, going to work, for example? Maybe you haven't but a lot of us have, even to the point of willing an illness to come on in order to relieve the burden of a social demand. Many of us choose to just flee difficult situations, whether it be physical, mental or emotional flight.

Psychologists use the term 'experiential avoidance' to describe this behaviour. It is an important aspect of *vibhava-taṇhā,* a longing for a predicament not to exist. If it's just a matter of retreating from boredom into Instagram now and again, then it's probably not going to be too problematic for our well-being. But this type of behaviour can easily become chronic, our default response to a complicated scenario, indeed any scenario that requires some effort. We may put off important jobs that need to be done, miss out on an opportunity for fear of failure, evade productive contact with others due to low self-esteem, shun deep relationships as a threat to our vulnerability, or suppress emotions that would be better aired. We may eschew physical exercise or even personal hygiene because of the imagined amount of energy they demand.

Avoidance strategies may provide short-term relief but, because they do, this increases the likelihood that this type of behaviour will be repeated. Avoidance strategies also reinforce the idea that anything perceived as discomforting is threatening. As we have seen, *dukkha* is an inevitable part of life; therefore, avoidance at its most can only be a temporary solution. Regrettably, trying to escape from emotional pain will never work; as we shall see in *Part Two*, sooner or later we will need to confront, see through, and release our troubling emotions.

Hankering for things to be different

So *vibhava-taṇhā* is a rejection of existence as we experience it. As Nagapriya has written, 'One way that we could define suffering is as a resistance to the limits of the present moment; we hanker for the moment to be different, we suffer because we say no to what we are presently experiencing, we want to flee from it'.[117] Our avoidance strategies are the different places that we can flee to – into hedonism, a dark warm cave, mind-numbing distractions, sometimes despair. In the American comic book series *Watchmen*, Alan Moore suggests that these strategies are a particular feature of our modern-day world, 'In an era of stress and anxiety, when the present seems unstable and the future unlikely, the natural response is to retreat and withdraw from reality, taking recourse either in fantasies of the future or in modified visions of a half-imagined past.'[118]

Particularly challenging times for many of us were the COVID-19 lockdowns in 2020 and 2021. Dr Andrew Doan, a neuroscientist and expert on digital addiction, argues that the lockdowns exacerbated the desire to flee from our everyday experience into our smartphones and computers, 'Stresses in life lead to cravings for behaviours and escape mechanisms. The pandemic has increased stress in people's lives, and a convenient way to escape is using entertainment digital media, such as gaming and social media. Excessive use to escape stress is a risk factor for the development of addictive behaviours.'[119] This is the risk; a helpful strategy becomes a harmful compulsion.

This type of craving is a diversion from our current reality. We are wanting to elude discomfort and confrontation. Often we want to avoid painful truths. We may be wanting to escape our fears, our inner emptiness, our helplessness, our inability to cope. We have already looked at how we can consume more food than we actually need. Over-eating is a typical manifestation of *vibhava-taṇhā*, blotting out troubles we don't want to face up to through indulging sense pleasure.

In 2022, the BBC aired a TV series *Avoidance*, a dark comedy about a character called Jonathan, played by Romesh Ranganathan. Jonathan was portrayed as a bit of a hopeless case, not able or willing to face up to anything that was happening in his life, especially the break-up of his marriage. He wouldn't turn up for work because he couldn't face telling his boss that he wasn't at work the day before. He'd lie to cover up his inability to accept his situation in life, constantly deceiving himself and unsuccessfully attempting to deceive others. No matter how many times his wife told him that their relationship was over, he continually denied to himself the truth of what she was saying. He went missing the evening when they were due to tell their son of the marriage break-up, effectively kidnapping his son, not answering his distraught wife's calls, taking the boy off to the seaside to avoid having to tell him about their split. His persisting delusion meant that he actually lived in a parallel universe where he told everyone that nothing was wrong.

Jonathan's inability to cope I found excruciating to watch. The programme cleverly demonstrates though that if you just try to run away from life's often harsh facts, your reality just becomes more and more complicated, one further avoidance to cover up a previous one. The programme also seems to be saying you can't really change your fundamental nature. However, this most certainly is not the message of Buddhism which teaches that we *can* change. The partner of the protagonist's sister does actually change during the course of the programme, from outright hostility to him towards a more understanding positive attitude.

Maladaptive coping

Buddhism recognizes that life can be very difficult; this is what the concept of *dukkha* is all about. So much can seem to weigh down on us. The phrase 'the oppression of existence' occurs in the text *The Sutra of Golden Light*, as an emotion which acknowledges this and which gives rise to unskilful acts of body, speech and mind to compensate.[120] This oppression is in Sanskrit *samkata,* 'those factors which by which we are surrounded, which crowd in upon us, which oppress us, which squeeze and limit us…as it were, under duress.'[121] Moreover, many of us will have experienced trauma of some kind in our life, and this will often lead to behaviour which tries to adapt to this trauma but can lead to loss of control.

The term 'adaptive behaviour' is usually used with reference to children learning the skills necessary to meet the demands of everyday living. But, in a wider context, we can talk about our adaptive behaviour as maladaptive, where we avoid situations to reduce anxiety, or because we fear that they will cause us discomfort. We may be trying to soothe our aching, wanting to be compassionate to ourselves. We may turn to a 'false refuge',[122] choosing a refuge that ultimately doesn't soothe, but can rather aggravate the pain. Maladaptive behaviour is not productive as it does not resolve our long-term problems.

Sometimes we are able to hide from our difficulties, burying ourselves in work, alcohol, TV, drugs and other cover-ups. At other times we cannot take cover from our pain, and that's tough. There's nowhere to run and hide. We are hurting. "Oh for an anaesthetic that could put me gently to sleep so that I do not experience more pain. Any blind comfort will do in a desperate effort to avoid this aching. Oh for the end to this mental chatter, this *prapañca,*[123] all this nonsense going around and around in my brain. Oh please, someone, get rid of it for me! Noise, noise, noise in my head. The noise is insane. I long to close it down for good. If not for good, at least for a few minutes, long enough for some precious moments of relief."

This is a desire for oblivion, 'a desire for dozing forgetfulness.'[124] There is a difference between the desire for sleep that comes from physical and mental weariness, and the desire for sleep which is a desire to close off one's suffering, the desire for shut-down, the desire to turn everything off – sleep as a narcotic hoodie. The widespread use of opiates throughout the world testifies to this craving.

I recall in my younger days, when travelling through Southeast Asia, finding myself in an opium den in Penang. There, with our heads on wooden blocks, I lay down with suited Chinese businessmen on their way home from work. I remember being handed a pipe and breathing in the acrid smoke. Of the next few hours I recall nothing. Total wipe-out, total oblivion. I could see the attraction. 'For the moment that interfering neurotic who, in waking hours, tries to run the show, was blessedly out of the way.'[125]

Seeking obliteration

Roll up, roll up, bury your pain here. Bury your anxieties and your turmoils. Your struggle to keep head above water. Bury your suffering - physical, emotional and existential. Your dissatisfaction and incompleteness. Your frictions and torments. Your stresses and strains. Bury your obsessive self. Roll up and be relieved. There is no need for the burying to be deep; a temporary fix will suffice. Deep enough for the pain to fade for a while. Leave tomorrow's woes for another day. This day we can be happy enough. Come, let us dive into today's nothingness.

Into the river Lethe, the river of forgetfulness; into the cave of Hypnos, the cave of sleep where poppies and other soporific plants grow. Each one into our own dark, murky hole in the earth. Warm and impervious to one another, alone but momentarily free. The desire for all-embracing, all effacing, total absorption, a craving for the void. A compulsion, a force that seeps in and obliterates. Here there is no space for rational thought. Our emotional and physical urges are the driving power of our behaviour. This is the gravitational pull of silent stupor.

Rob Burbea describes what lies beneath this wish for a kind of unconsciousness. 'For instance, someone wanting to just get completely plastered drunk. There's something seeking a kind of oblivion and a kind of dissolution of the self in that wish, that we seek obliteration, oblivion, a kind of extinction, *vibhava-taṇhā*. Sometimes what's happening is, in the object that we seem to be craving (maybe it's the chocolate cake or whatever), that there's actually a painful emotion underneath. Maybe we feel lonely. Maybe we feel unloved. And it's painful to be with that, and something in the chocolate cake, and in that whole putting it in the mouth and chewing it in this very primal way, there is pleasure involved in that, absolutely, but at another level of the craving, we're seeking to obliterate or cover over or numb out the painful emotion underlying it.'[126]

But although there may be real pain from which we want to flee, we are talking here about something which is different from physical pain. 'It is not really that the suffering is unbearable,' writes David Brazier, 'in the sense of being acutely painful, like a severe burn might be. In important respects, the psychological pain of being in flight from the present reality of one's life can be far more disabling than the effect of such a burn."[127] The running away from difficult experience can be as agonizing then as that from which we seek to flee. The flight takes more than it gives.

We can in the same experience be seeking both pleasure and forgetfulness. My own particular thirsts often seem to boil down to a combination of a craving for excitement and a craving for non-existence, and I find it difficult to work out whether either craving is primary, or whether it varies. There is a fascinating connection between sexual pleasure and oblivion in the French phrase *'la petite mort'* - the post-orgasmic state of a lessening or weakening of consciousness, likened to a 'small death'.

Perhaps it is no wonder we often seek easy solutions that do not require a great deal of thought or effort. A flick of the switch that would extinguish our troubles. Years ago I sometimes used to daydream of exploding things that were a problem for me. This included certain politicians whose views I found repugnant. This, I only realized later was a desire for my *dukkha* to just vanish in one fail swoop, to just negate my aversions with the simplistic press of a button. I did not care about the wider implications of what I was fantasizing about. I wanted to overlook the fact that life is much more complicated than this. It is simple to self-delude.

Can you be bothered?

I believe that the worse thing we can say to ourselves is "I don't care". Once we give up caring we give up the ghost entirely. That is to say, we give up our spirit, we give up what makes us conscious, discriminating human beings, a relinquishing of the life force within us even. We give up responsibility for our lives, we allow ourselves to be blown to and fro by the Buddhist 'worldly winds' - the four pairings of praise and blame; pleasure and pain; loss and gain; and infamy and fame. We give ourselves over to the push and pull of forces external and internal, and we allow our disparate energies to take us hither and thither. We become dis-integrated, directionless and disorientated.

Sometimes we explicitly say "I don't care" to ourselves; occasionally we say it to others. Temporarily we might push the 'oh-bugger-it-all' button. Most of the time however, it is an unconscious attitude, a hardly expressed state of mind. We can live our lives in a mentality of 'I-don't-care-ism'. It can be very subtle, we scarcely notice that this is our way of responding. We eat, drink, think, speak, behave whilst ignoring the consequences, the import, of what we are doing. If we did really care we would most likely act differently, in a more considered fashion. The French (again) have an actual term for this attitude towards life - *'je-m'en-foutisme'* - politely put, the mindset of 'I don't give a damn'.

One aspect might be not wanting to get out of bed today - "it's so warm and cozy here, the world out there is too much for me at the moment." Maybe we feel that everything we need is online - ordering food, social contact, sex, stimulation. The pernicious, delusional aspect of 'I-don't-care-ism' leads us to persuade ourselves that a little bit of this or that craving won't do us any harm.' Or "I'm only harming myself, so what?", as we saw in the previous chapter. "It's a waste of time caring about anything, a waste of effort, what's the point?"

This is a lessening of our ethical sensibility, a hardening of the shell around us, a barrier to connection with others. In this way *vibhava-taṇhā* can manifest itself as alienation. It can be a sense of not feeling good enough, comparing oneself negatively to others around us, not being able to relate to cultural expectations, and hence a sense of worthlessness. We can feel cynicism and blame.

Often it's not so much "I don't care" as "I can't be bothered". I'm just too tired to be bothered, what Stefan Zweig describes as 'the lukewarm mire of indifference.'[128] A sort of defeatism in which we can flounder, a morass we almost do not want to get out of. Feeling sorry for ourselves and helpless can be appealing, because we may feel then that we don't have to do anything about the difficult situation we find ourselves in. It absolves us of any responsibility.

'We fall ill and sink into self-pity', write Valerie Mason-John (Vimalasara) and Paramabandhu, authors and practitioners in mindful approaches to addiction. 'This lets us off the hook of taking action about our illness and working with our mental responses to it. Or we stay in a destructive relationship. It's unpleasant, we are full of self-pity, but we fail to do anything about it. We can even become addicted to self-pity and self-hatred. Every time something painful arises in our lives, we can flee to the place of self-pity because it's familiar, and we do not have to face up to what is happening in our lives.'[129] I don't care what happens to me, as long as I get my 'fix' (whatever that may be). At times we may be aware of a cloud beginning to envelop us, and we forget or ignore that we do have the choice as to whether we can be bothered to use the mind to disperse that cloud.

What about the consequences?

For example, does it matter if I say something callous to a work colleague? Does it matter if I don't say sorry? Does it matter if I throw a sweet wrapper out of the car window? Does it matter if nobody else finds out? Pema Chödrön, the American Tibetan Buddhist nun, asks in response to these questions, what would be the consequences of behaving like this, would I be causing harm to myself or others, what would be the larger impact on the world of my action or inaction: 'When we ask ourselves, "Does it matter?" we can first look at the outer, more obvious results of our actions. But then we can go deeper by examining how we are affecting our own mind: Am I making an old habit more habitual? Am I strengthening propensities I'd like to weaken?'[130] Here we are looking at the karmic seeds that we plant with our actions of body, speech and mind, and the effects that they will have in our future.

The attitude of 'I don't care' can lead to laziness and inertia on the one hand, and transgression and disregarding our moral values on the other. Let's look initially at laziness and inertia. In Buddhism there are traditionally three types of inertia.[131] Firstly, taking delight in lying down and not getting up; secondly, yielding passively to unskilful impulses which we should resist; and thirdly, the laziness of despondency and making excuses for ourself. Do you recognize these types of inertia in yourself?

So we have here an affliction that can be physical but also moral and emotional. It can manifest itself not just as a lack of energy but also as an actual preference for that which is unskilful. Somewhere in the middle it is the taking of the path of least resistance, the path of least effort. It is far easier to roll along on the plateau of indifference than it is to mount the hill of conscientiousness. Not caring in this context denies the one thing that can give deep meaning to our lives. It denies us a sense of purpose, it removes intentionality and replaces it with a drifting - a drifting on a lonely ocean where we are rudderless, where the currents randomly decide our fate.

Moreover, just because on the surface we may lead a busy active life does not mean that our spiritual energy is not in abeyance. Just as there is energy in pursuit of the good, which we shall look at in Chapter 9, there is an energy in pursuit of the spiritually unskilful, energetic cravings that lead us nowhere helpful, for instance, the pursuit of wealth, power and hedonistic pleasure. We can have a busy body yet a lazy mind.

We can excuse ourselves, seek to justify our resistance to bring about effective change to our harmful habits. Subhuti writes about a 'procrastinating inertia'. 'In this case, you accept that the spiritual life is possible and perhaps necessary. You even desire to live it. But say to yourself, 'Not just now. I've got too much on. Maybe next year, or when I retire.' '[132] Or even in the next life, an easy trap to fall into for Buddhists and others who believe in rebirth into a future life.

Stagnation, whether physical or mental, is not pretty; 'stagnation of both body and mind, a sort of dullness, a sort of deadness, a stiffness, a lack of resilience, a sort of - well, a force which is sort of pulling you down all the time and preventing you from making any further progress.'[133] It is not only in winter that creatures seek to hibernate. One of the greatest figures in Tibetan Buddhism, the well-loved hermit and teacher Milarepa, likened laziness to the robbing of an empty house, that is to say, there is no point to it.

I find that if I don't fill up the time and the mental space, I have a strong tendency to drift off. I drift off either into mental chatter, *prapañca*, or daydreaming, or a longing for something to fill the space. That may be a cup of tea, some cake, the latest news or, on bad days, a desire to escape into some fantasy life. I've got much better at noticing this habit since I've been a Buddhist, but it is potentially a dangerous area for me and probably for many of us. As we get older, we may develop the tendency to close down more, the desire to take things easier, to coast, to drift, to shy away from new or challenging experiences. We looked at this tendency also in Chapter 1 in terms of craving for comfort.

Straying into the forbidden

In Chapter 1 we also saw that our cravings can feel so powerful that it may lead us to turn a blind eye to our moral values. Let's explore that further here in the context of the desire to not face up to responsibility and not caring about the consequences. The gratification of one's craving can give an illusory, momentary sense of freedom; freedom from caring, freedom from inhibitions, freedom from holding oneself back, from restraining oneself. The 'I don't care' mentality can manifest as a mood of moral rebellion, of breaking 'rules'. There may even be a sneaking pride in breaking the rules. "Heh, I managed to get away without paying for that extra glass of wine at the end", or "I've found a way of getting Netflix without subscribing to it". *I don't care.*

There can be an excitement in straying into the taboo, of crossing over ethical, socially unacceptable frontiers. There may be a thrill in being drawn into a binge of transgression, gorging oneself on noxious substances or behaviours, overdoing for the sake of overdoing, a spree of indulgence, a bender of contravention. We may flaunt our lack of shame, boasting about how sick we were after Friday night's splurge. *I don't care.*

In a famous Buddhist metaphor, we lick 'honey on a razor's edge'[134] – the honey tastes so good that we don't want to stop even though our mouth may be torn to shreds; there is also the buzz of risky behaviour implied here. 'Again and again the tormented man strained to master a passion which diverged from the accustomed track by applying the lash of self-control, again and again his instincts impelled him towards the dark and dangerous.'[135] *I don't care.*

How many of us, I wonder, have a latent, or not so latent, tendency within us to be irrational and destructive? That kind of behaviour where you know that something is good for you (eating healthily, exercising regularly, taking time out to de-stress), but *intentionally* you don't do it, almost to spite yourself, because you know that it's supposed to be good for you? When we talk about indulging in self-harm, this may be in a literal physical sense, maybe inflicting wounds on our body; or, in a more indirect way, making ourselves ill by over-working, over-eating, over-drinking, over-exercising, or purposely, perversely, denying ourselves what promotes our well-being. *I don't care.*

This resistance to doing what is best for us is what Subhuti calls 'destructive inertia'[136], a case of knowing, but doing the opposite. At its worst this destructive urge can arise as malice, the desire to do harm to somebody; or its corollary *Schadenfreude*, taking pleasure in somebody else's misfortune. There is often a sense of spitefulness involved. I recall as a boy with my friends being fascinated watching lines of ants going back and forwards in semi-orderly lines, presumably from food source to nest. But, very sad to say so now, we used to revel in putting barriers up to stop them achieving their goal and, in the worst-case scenario, pouring hot water on them out of sheer vindictiveness.

There is a view that *vibhava-taṇhā*, because it can coincide with a materialist view of death, as we saw above – everything that is 'us' ceases to exist upon dying – gives us a licence to do whatever we please while we live, a "what does anything matter?" attitude towards life.[137] This can lead to a hedonist, living-for-pleasure, living-for-oneself, eat-drink-and-be-merry outlook, the view that we can indulge wholeheartedly in the sensual pleasures of life without any future comeback. Perhaps this view is widespread in the world in which most of us abide, with the hegemony of a materialist attitude to existence, and the falling away of spiritual traditions of ethics to guide us. Once again though it is crucial to stress that all actions of body, speech and mind do have consequences, and these consequences, the fruits of our action, carry on after we die, impacting on future lives. This of course is the principle of *karma*.

Our inbuilt tendency

As we saw in the previous chapter, humans are creatures of habit and our cravings have a repetitive compulsive nature; these habits then become very hard to break. Once we open the door enough, we find it difficult to close again, we are no longer in control. Mason-John and Paramabandhu begin their book on how Buddhist practice can help address obsessive behaviour with the sentence 'Human nature has an inbuilt tendency toward addiction'.[138] They go on to say that 'Even those of us who do not think of ourselves as having an addiction might be regarded as addicted to life: to physical wellness, to youthfulness'.[139]

So, we may not think of ourselves as addicts, but we all have compulsive tendencies which, if allowed to play out, can cause us a great deal of harm. Addiction is a powerful word with strong negative connotations and most of us would be loath to accept that we are addicts. But we will all probably recognize the habitual behaviour that we feel compelled to act out, despite the negative consequences.

In the Pali Canon[140] there is a list of activities that if performed obsessively can become addictive. These range from 'fairy shows' and 'rubbing the body with shampoos and cosmetics', through to 'talk of being and non-being', and not to forget 'fancy sticks' and 'combats of elephants'. In other words, one can become addicted to just about anything. There's nothing intrinsically wrong with 'cymbals and drums' or 'headbands' (some more), it is about our relationship to them, how we use them to flee our difficult experience.

Not all addictions are extreme, all-encompassing. Some are quite low-level, like drinking in company, regularly grabbing a donut, or watching the TV most nights; they are socially acceptable and may seem relatively harmless. Can we easily shake them off? Could we give them up tomorrow without missing them badly? Or are they an obsession, a compulsion that we can't live without?

Addictions can be seen as 'normal' cravings that have become magnified and in which we bury ourselves, longings out of control, desires gone wild. Addictions are often talked about in terms of substance misuse, the word 'substance' referring to a type of drug. However, if we think of 'substance' as any object of compulsive desire which gets in the way of us being more contented and at ease with ourselves, then substance misuse could apply to a whole host of objects, both concrete and abstract.

Technology misuse, online-retail misuse, or pizza-takeaway misuse. Use of which in small quantities may be fine, but when intensified and may lead to problems. It's not so much the longing that causes *dukkha*, as it's clinging nature. Typical characteristics of addictive behaviour are: wanting to cut down but can't seem to; spending too much time and energy on our 'substance'; experiencing withdrawal symptoms in attempts to limit use; usage getting in the way of other things you should be doing; adverse effects on work or relationships; affecting health adversely; needing more and more.[141]

Needs regularly need upgrading. There is an accumulative nature about compulsive craving. Because one can get inured, hardened, physically tolerant to the usual dose of the object of our craving, it's necessary to increase the dose to get the same thrill from it. We indulge as a habit but without any real high anymore. We need more and more, stronger and stronger, more explicit images, bigger wine glasses or more intense 'substances' to satisfy us. The eclectic writer and scholar Bradford Hatcher writes about this phenomenon 'also called "hedonic adaptation": we get used to the pleasant things and, until we can learn to control our subjective states, we are left with having to combat this by adding endless variations to our experiences'.[142]

Clearly our online activity is double-edged in the sense that it has benefits and downsides, including the potential to take over our lives. Dr Andrew Doan, formerly an addicted video gamer who at his peak invested over

20,000 hours of playing games over a period of nine years, has written that the internet should be seen as two separate parts. 'I break down digital media into two broad categories - digital sugar verses digital veggies. Digital veggies, such as online therapies, can be utilized to help people manage their stress and reduce their risk for addictive behaviours, [whereas] the excessive usage of digital sugars like gaming, pornography and non-work-related social media can increase the risk of addictive behaviours, in particular when these activities are used to escape daily stressors.'[143]

We can be so habituated to immediately reading messages received on our smartphone that, when we are driving, we put our life and the lives of others at risk through looking away from the road and fiddling with our phone in order to check a message. And even messaging back while at the wheel of our car. On the face of it, it seems like lunacy to endanger our very existence because we are too impatient to wait till later to check who has contacted us. So our irrational longings not only endanger ourselves but put others at risk also. 'When, under the power of the defilements in this way, they injure even their own dear selves, how could they have a care for the persons of other people?'[144]

Addictions of whatever nature are clearly harmful, but there is one especially insidious way in which they are dangerous. It is easy to say that one is addicted to a particular activity, in a sense treating it as an arbitrary illness, as a way of shedding responsibility for one's behaviour, as we saw above concerning self-pity - "Oh well, I'm just addicted to sugar, it's not my fault if I can't stop eating donuts". This can be compared to a helpless baby crying for its dummy. This view of course undermines the important role of agency in one's life, and the important ability that we have to change our habits.

Addiction is a murky abode, and we may notice ourselves sinking into the mire of negative thoughts and emotions. There can even be something quite beautifully attractive about what is usually seen as a negative state off mind, like melancholy for example. Strangely, because it goes against our idea that we all seek happiness in life, some of us often prefer to be sad. We may prefer sad music, sad films, sad images. They may reinforce or correspond to the darkness within us, our 'shadow' side, the comforting obliteration of oppressive reality. It may appear in this state of being as though we have a predisposition towards suffering, rather than a predilection for joy. Waves of *vibhava-taṇhā*, waves of night surge in.

Desire is a mixture of pleasure and pain. Pleasure can turn into pain and vice versa. We can continue pursuing a pleasure even though we no longer enjoy it; this is of course what happens in cases of a serious addiction. In his sonnet VIII, Shakespeare recognises this, 'why lov'st thou that which thou receiv'st not gladly.'

The power opposed to life

This rather nihilistic perspective on our lives may even be a rationalization for self-hatred. Leaning towards and into the dark may mean we see predominantly dark in ourselves and our capabilities; elements of ill-will towards ourself can be buried in *vibhava-taṇhā*. At its most intense we may feel ourselves 'writhing in the mud of the swamps' where we can 'only drift from one stone to the next'[145] or, in another metaphor, completely lost in 'the dark labyrinth of passion.'[146] However, as Traleg Kyabgon points out, 'When we get involved in negative thoughts, negative states of mind, we do not see the dynamism. We view everything in a very static and fixed way.'[147] That's to say, we are unable to see that we have the potential to change, to transform ourselves.

Ron Leifer, a psychiatrist who writes at the interface between Buddhism and psychotherapy, says, 'As the desire for life is based on the desire for pleasure and happiness, the desire for death is based on the desire to escape pain and suffering... the yearning for relief from pain, from anxiety, from disappointment, despair, and negativity.'[148] Or possibly shame and disgrace, seeing ourselves as a hopeless case, a compulsive indulger. Clearly this desire is most apparent in those who attempt to, or indeed, take their own life. But many argue that there is a death impulse latent within all of us. Sigmund Freud was renowned for introducing the ancient Greek personification of death, Thanatos, into his psychoanalytic theories, which he characterized as the drive towards death or the death instinct. At one point Freud claimed that the most basic drive for satisfaction is in fact a striving towards death.

Sangharakshita draws a parallel between Buddhism and psychoanalysis. 'It is rather significant, it is rather modern in a way that Buddhism traditionally has always recognised that there is in some people a sort of craving for death. It is what we may describe as something corresponding to Freud's death wish and its rather significant as I've said that Buddhism also does recognise this. We may also say I think that in the Buddhist conception of craving for conditioned or continued existence and also craving for annihilation these two I think we can see here also a correspondence with what Fromm calls biophilia, or love of life and necrophilia or love of death. It is also significant that the Buddha seems to have regarded many of the religious teachings of his time as not so much religious or spiritual teachings as rationalisations of craving, either for continued personal existence, or the craving for annihilation.'[149]

You may have encountered somebody who appears to have had a 'death wish', to numb experience, somebody maybe like the poet Dylan Thomas who drank himself to the point of death, as well as numerous rock stars. The Thanatos aspect of *vibhava-taṇhā* is extremely potent for some. Thomas Mann describes this force in the context of a character who is lost in a snow storm and is in on the point of giving in to annihilation, 'death, as an independent power, is a lustful power, whose vicious attraction is strong indeed; to feel drawn to it, to feel sympathy with it, is without any doubt at all the most ghastly aberration to which the spirit of man is prone[150]...a power in itself, the power opposed to life, the inimical principle, the great temptation....it is deliverance – yet not deliverance from evil, but deliverance by evil. It relaxes manners and morals, it frees man from discipline and restraint.'[151]

You may baulk at the term 'evil', which implies absolutist ideas of good and bad that are not terms generally used by Buddhists, but you can see that Mann is saying that there are times when we have to fight tooth and nail against the magnetic pull of a force which denies all our positive longings and values.

'Death' in its sense of closing off the world and everything that is uncomfortable or painful about it may seem like a simple, default cure for all our ills. But we can welcome death before its time is due. Death is part and parcel of life, certainly, but to prematurely 'gently sleep the sleep of death'[152] is a negation of our potential as human beings.

My apologies at this point if these writings seem to have become quite dark; you may relate to what I am writing here or not, or maybe partially even. However, to counter this, in Chapter 9 we shall look at the cultivation of spiritual energy in bringing about a transformation in our intransigent habits. We shall look at the idea of a creative impulse, a thirst for life, Eros or, in Buddhism, *vīrya*, the energy that is in pursuit of what is good and beautiful, as a force for driving us forward and bringing about change. If Thanatos is the death instinct, then Eros and *vīrya* are the opposite, the desire for life, the 'life energy'.

We are constantly presented with a choice between death and awakening. Taking on the confrontation with craving is more than just a matter of improved wellness. It can be seen as a confrontation with the very forces of life and death. And we are always gifted with the power of choice. We can choose between awakening or death when making decisions, between Eros and Thanatos, motivated on the one hand by all that is skilful – love, kindness, generosity, forgiveness, altruism, awareness and expansiveness; or on the other hand by all that is unskilful – hatred, ill-will, meanness, resentfulness, greed, self-delusion and egotism.

We can generate positive energy for the world, or contribute to the doom and gloom that seems to exist in many places. Our species and our planet are in grave danger of dissolution and degradation, and we humans appear to have our own death wish, a collective *vibhava-taṇhā*. If the positive skilful qualities listed above, which are the fundamental Buddhist virtues and which are inherent to all of us, are to prevail, then we need to say no to the craving of *vibhava-taṇhā*, no to Thanatos, no to inertia, no to not caring, no to running away, no to 'death'. We can settle for entropy if we like, or we can long for abundance.

Walking with our Shadow

Whether our cravings are great or small, habitual or occasional, intense or lightweight, we may experience them as a compelling force which feels as though it has taken control of us. In the quotes above, Thomas Mann seems to portray this force as a power which has a life of its own, a 'lustful power' which draws us in; it's almost as though Mann is representing this force as a person.

From the earliest times, humans have personified abstract experiences that they couldn't understand. And so we had, and in some cultures and religious traditions still have, gods, spirits and mythological figures manifesting aspects of nature, the weather, the sun, sea, trees and seasons, as well as emotions such as anger and love, good and evil. There are benevolent and vengeful, wrathful deities. There are God and the Devil. Dealing with an abstract concept in the form of a person can make it easier to relate to, talk to, rant at, pray to; to give power to an idea, or withdraw power from it.

To conclude this chapter, I want to look at the Buddhist figure of Māra, the personification of forces that are hostile to awakening. Māra is the insidious voice of doubt which is always latent in us, looking for a chink in the armour of our determination to be free. Can you hear his little whispering in your ear? "You don't really want to meditate right now, do you? Much better to just put your feet up and watch television". He is the Great Tempter, the Great Dissembler, the Great Seducer. He paces in the half-light, the penumbra of drifting unfocussed attention. This is where you are most vulnerable. Here are the shades where Māra conceals himself. He lurks in ambush, ready to pounce, to infiltrate when you are off guard. He is 'the friend of negligence.'[153] Much of the time Māra lays dormant, comfortable in knowing that you are sleeping away your life too. But he wakes up if he feels you are slipping away from him, if you are trying to break free of the bonds of *saṃsāra*; then he will beguile you with his wily insinuations. He is so easy to go along with because the urges that he represents are something instinctual within you, the personification of a primordial force within your mind, it is so difficult to say no to him. Māra is the snake in the grass, feigning friendship with the intent to deceive. He is the distracter, tempting you to think that there is something more interesting elsewhere. He is the incessant chattering of the mind. He is our inner voice telling us to do things that we know aren't good for us. He plays the beguiling tune of egocentricity and selfishness. He is both compulsion and obstruction. He is "You have no choice".

Māra is the equivalent of Jung's archetype of the Shadow, our dark side. We can easily wallow in our own Shadow and then drown in it. It is a part of us that that we will need to face up to and integrate, although much effort will be required if we wish to be spiritually whole. Our Māra-side can be locked away in us and blocked, and therefore not available to us as a source of energy. Or it may come out as guilt or unworthiness. It is a side of us that we tend to repress, deny, but also project onto other people; this projection of our dark side can result in scapegoating others, a phenomenon that we have seen played out in the world throughout history, but most horrifically in the 20th century in the German Nazi Party's treatment of Jews as subhuman, as well as in other acts of genocide.

The Buddhist teacher and writer Stephen Batchelor[154] suggests that Māra represents something like the personality of *saṃsāra*, what we are — grasping, clinging, deluded beings — and what we have to come to terms with. In the Sutta Nipāta we read. 'It makes no difference what it is you are grasping at; when a man grasps, Māra stands beside him.'[155] Although we might need to repress some of our dark emotions as a requirement of living in society, the danger of repressing Māra is that, unintegrated and blocked, he seems to grow stronger and more vigorous.

But why shouldn't you just go along with Māra? Why shouldn't you just give yourself up to the place where something inside you demands that you go? You know, although you may not admit this to yourself, that once you pass a certain point, cross that frontier, that the pull of the object of your desiring will be overwhelming, irresistible, that it will be impossible to turn round, to turn back. This time the fate of this particular event is decided. Māra has conquered once more.

In Buddhist mythology, Māra appears frequently as the Buddha's principal antagonist, putting all his efforts into trying to prevent the Buddha from attaining Enlightenment, employing various means including threats and temptations. As the Buddha sat meditating under the Bodhi tree, close to his realization of *nirvāṇa*, hosts of demons led by Māra hurled stones, arrows and flames at him, only for the Buddha to transform them into flowers that fell at his feet. The Buddha remained unmoved in the face of this horrendous attack. Next Māra sent in his three beautiful daughters, named Lust, Passion and Delight, all aspects of craving, to dance before the Buddha and try to tempt him with their worldly wiles. But still the Buddha remained unmoved. And the forces of Māra had no choice but to withdraw, defeated. The Buddha's Victory over Māra, whose name incidentally means 'bringer of death', can be seen as a symbolic victory of Light over Dark, the confronting and overcoming of our negative emotions.

Even after his Enlightenment the Buddha had to contend periodically with Māra, and undoubtedly us lesser mortals will have to face up to his traps from time to time during our lives. It is difficult to overestimate how powerful, how persistent are the forces of Māra. He is so strong and he just won't give up. It's as though he has his own agenda, the agenda of provoking our destructive urges.

The Buddha's life story however shows us that Māra can be countered. Māra may seem like our worst enemy, the devil even, but 'instead of seeing things as dreadful entities to get rid of, we can learn to embrace them,' writes Dzigar Kongtrul. 'When we stop rejecting our shadows and darkness, they lose their power over us. We become free of them'.[156]

One way of undermining Māra's hold, which I find particularly effective, is simply to smile at him or humour him each time he puts in an appearance, that cheeky little rascal who is trying to trip me up once again. "I can see what you're up to, but I've caught you at it this time. I'm on my guard to your silly tricks. Off you go."

Caring is freeing

We saw in Chapter 2 that we can choose whether to react in an automatic manner to a stimulus, or take a moment and respond in a more open creative fashion. 'I don't care' is a reactive response; 'I care' leads to a creative response. The former derives from the weight of our negative conditioning; the latter implies an emancipation from that conditioning. Caring is one of the most fundamental positive emotions that we can ever express, whether that be caring about ourselves, caring about others, or caring about the world about us.

You can try to run away from anything but you cannot run away from yourself. It is engagement however, not fleeing, which is what is so required in the world today; to engage in transforming oneself, and one's harmful habits, to engage with others in trying to transform the world, to cultivate an alternative way of living which is not founded on greed, ill-will and delusion. Buddhist teachings offer such a vision. We can develop our self-awareness and explore our mental states in order to see what our compulsive tendencies are, our thirsting manias, so that we can bring them to light, defuse them and rid them of their power over us.

Reflecting - Chapter 4

Do you recognize in yourself a desire for 'experiential avoidance'? In what situations does this occur for you? Is there anything you tend to escape *to*? Is this type of response a regular feature of your behaviour? Do you ever notice yourself retreating into a fantasy world when the going gets tough? Do you use digital technology as a place where you can bury yourself? Do you ever experience the feeling of 'I just don't care'? Does it matter to you if you are rude to someone? Do you recognize in yourself any of the three types of inertia mentioned in this chapter? Do you ever feel yourself straying into the taboo, of crossing over ethical, socially unacceptable frontiers? Do you ever experience self-destructive, self-defeating urges? What addictive tendencies do you have? Do you feel that you could easily give up tomorrow any compulsive behaviour you have? Reflect on how your compulsive behaviour may endanger yourself or others. Are you aware of having a 'dark side' to your character? Does the personification of negative emotions, such as the figure Māra, resonate with you?

Chapter 5:

CLINGING

I love early springtime where I live, when the dual-coloured blooms of the narcissus flower open up their beautiful hearts to the sky, timely heralds of renewal and fresh prospects. This flower is said to derive its name from the classical Greek youth of the same name. In his myth the handsome Narcissus becomes obsessed with his own beauty, turning down romantic advances from the adoring Echo and others as he falls increasingly in love with himself. So preoccupied does he become with his own appearance that he sits down by a pool of water where he can stare endlessly at his own reflection. This he does for the remainder of his life. Where he dies a flower grows which comes to bear his name.

We are familiar today with the personality disorder named after this ancient Greek youth - narcissism - a condition characterized by a grandiose sense of one's own self-importance, believing oneself to be unique or special. Narcissism is also an excessive seeking for the admiration and attention of others, accompanied by a sense of entitlement, and the inability to identify with others. A narcissist can only feel sorry for themself.

Now, although narcissism as a personality disorder is a serious condition, it seems to exist on a continuum between an 'abnormal' and 'normal' expression of one's personality.[157] The overlapping personal traits of egoism, of putting one's own interests and needs before those of others, and egotism, of having an exaggerated sense of one's self-importance, are traits which are not uncommon, although generally frowned upon.

It is fair to say though that we all have narcissistic tendencies to a greater or lesser degree - a fixation with ourselves, seeing ourselves as the centre of the world, an urge to perpetuate, promote and protect our precious self. Why do so many of us take selfies and post multiple pictures of ourselves on social media?

In Buddhism, this self-centeredness, this obsession with ourselves is an aspect of *bhava-taṇhā*, generally translated as the 'craving for existence'. It is the thirst to be or to become something. It is the clinging to the idea of 'me' as the central focal point of our lives, around which everything else revolves. It has narcissistic overtones in the sense that it turns us in on ourselves. Note that we have come across the word *bhava* before, as one of the links in the *nidāna* chain in Chapter 2, where it was translated as 'becoming'. Similarly, we could say that *bhava-taṇhā* is the 'craving to become', to become something or someone.

Both *bhava-taṇhā* and, as we saw in the preceding chapter, *vibhava-taṇhā* are rooted in the delusion that a fixed 'self' exists. The former is the desire for that 'self' to exist, to be defended and promoted, and the latter is the desire for that same 'self' to be annihilated or fled from. If *vibhava-taṇhā* is the longing for death, metaphorically speaking that is, then *bhava-taṇhā* is a fear of the death of 'self'. Mark Epstein describes the connection between the two in a similar way. 'What the Buddha called the craving for existence and non-existence, is what we today would call narcissistic craving: the thirst for a fixed image of self, as either something or as nothing. It is the craving for security wherever it can be found: in becoming or in death.'[158]

The fundamental craving

In fact, all the thousands of different cravings we experience can be reduced to one: *bhava-taṇhā,* this clinging to the idea of 'me'. This is the fundamental craving; the craving that is at the root of all craving. It is a general force that looks to express itself in a variety of different ways. This is the meta-desire; the desire to satisfy all our desires, the need to validate a belief about ourselves. And this is what Buddhism, a central teaching of which is that the concept of an 'I' is at the root cause of our *dukkha*, seeks to address.

In essence, this craving for existence is the *perpetuating, protecting, and promoting* of our ego. All types of thirst, longing, and grasping then have their origin in trying to satisfy, defend and boost our fixed sense of ourself, and in craving for our own continued individual existence. We could call it a 'lust for life' because this phrase can be understood in two different ways. Firstly, as a joyful healthy desire to make the most of one's life, to fulfil one's potential, to enjoy everything that life gives; and secondly, as *bhava-taṇhā*, a deep attachment to, and clinging on to, existence as we usually perceive it, hanging on for dear life to what we have or, at least, to what we think we have.

The philosopher and cultural theorist Byung-Chul Han talks about this focus on ourselves, as deserving individuals, as 'the mounting narcissification of the Self' with its accompanying 'narcissistic gratification'. He writes, 'Today, we live in an increasingly narcissistic society. Libido is primarily invested in one's own subjectivity.'[159] We primarily accept our own inner laws. In its most extreme form, it is as though anything that is outside of oneself is just an object there for one's own consumption and satisfaction.

In the same way that Narcissus was drawn to admiring his likeness in the pool of water, we too can become rather fond of looking at ourselves in a mirror, or at our reflection in a shop window, whether with admiration, disdain or just curiosity. I live near Cambridge in the UK, and when I'm in the city centre I usually see visitors taking photos of Cambridge's lovely historic architecture on their smartphones. I don't know why it still niggles at me, but I wonder why the visitors don't actually look at the buildings directly, rather than through the screen on their phone. And then play with the photo on the phone in order to post it on Facebook or Instagram. The experience of a beautiful city is mediated through the technology in their hands. The posting of the photos to friends and the world at large is about "Look at *me*, look at where *I* am". This is even more accentuated when the photo is a selfie.

I feel that a lot of the time this is automatic, habitual, unconscious behaviour. This is what one does when visiting a photogenic place or in the middle of a photogenic experience (or even not very photogenic – everything can be and is snapped on our phones). Underlying this it seems is a desire to propagandise ourselves, to form positive impressions of ourselves. Moreover, getting a 'like' back from a post is a buzz, based on the desire for validation.

Taking snaps just for their own sake, to look at and appreciate in themselves, perhaps as a memento of a nice visit or experience, is fine, but I don't believe that this is essentially what this is about, or at least not totally what this is about. This need to create a certain identity of ourselves for the consumption of others is I feel particularly strong amongst young people who are the main users of social media; the approbation, direct or indirect, of our peers. This is important stuff, not easily ignored when you are young.

Here we have though yet another example of how craving creates *dukkha*. There exists here a basic human need, the need for affirmation, the need for our ego-identity to be validated by others. The essence of this longing for self-validation is *bhava-taṇhā*, the desire to be someone. And the selfie-stick enables *bhava-taṇhā* to be made manifest through technology – to adapt the old Audi cars advertising slogan, '*bhava-taṇhā* durch Technik'.

I did consider calling this chapter *Selfing*, because that word seems to summarize the essence of this process, the process of endless self-referencing in which we are so firmly bound up. Selfing is our normal way of being – I 'self', therefore I am. It is, to use a psychological term, our 'default mode network', to which our mind reverts when we are not occupied with an activity and our mind wanders. We default to self-absorption.

I'm special

Our experience of the material external world is coloured by our self-centeredness. We perceive everything in terms of me and mine, or conversely not me or mine. We are of course the most important thing in the universe. We don't see anything more important than ourselves. And this can be very problematic when we clash with somebody else who is also the most important thing in the universe. Our unconscious urge to be the most significant will inevitably bring us into disharmony or conflict with others, and even ourselves. When self-importance is threatened we want to push back and put ourselves in the gold medal position once more.

The French, once more, have a term which is sometimes used in English - *amour propre*, love of oneself. When this *amour propre* becomes excessive it develops into conceit, being pumped up with self-admiration, seeing oneself as special, comparing oneself over-favourably with others, a desire to be superior to other people. Conceit can give one an inflated view of ourselves, and we can get carried away with our own self-regard; even though most of us though don't appreciate arrogance in others. Conceit is at base experiencing ourselves as separate and distinct from others, 'and therefore to be affirmed, if necessary, at their expense, or used as a basis for unskilful action with regard to them.'[160]

We sort of feel that other people will be fascinated by us and see our singularity. As the novelist Lionel Shriver writes quite bluntly about one of her characters, it's as if 'others will be mesmerized by your unplumbable depths, and we're sure to be fascinated by your amusing eccentricities, ironic inconsistencies, and arresting complexities. There's nothing special about you, as there's nothing special about any of us.... and you cling to the farcical fancy that your subtraction from humanity would leave a gaping hole.'[161]

There is of course a spectrum of the degree to which self-centeredness manifests itself in different individuals, from the stereotypes perhaps of the boastful, conceited, go-getting, narcissistic executive on the one hand, to the generous, selfless, altruistic, tireless caregiver on the other. But clinging to a sense of 'me' as something to be protected and promoted, is a trait, whether strong or weak, that is within us all.

This great self-centred 'me' has got a lot to live up to. Although there is such a thing as a healthy sense of self, this may harden into being engrossed with one's own thoughts and feelings. One outcome of becoming very obsessed with oneself is self-criticism developing into self-loathing. It may be about how we think we look, our habits, our relationships, becoming overly self-conscious. 'Preoccupied with thoughts of me,' writes Thubten Yeshe, 'our mind is filled with worry and anxiety — "Maybe I'm not good-looking enough," "Maybe others won't like me," "I wonder if I will succeed" — and so on. Everything related to this "I" becomes a problem, a worry, a threat to our well-being and security.'[162] And here we may be recycling old ingrained patterns.

What do we really want?

All surface craving is a manifestation of something much more profound. There is something deep-seated within us that seeks affirmation. When I have a yearning for salted caramel ice cream, what am I really after? What do I really want from indulging this craving? When I itch to impress those I meet with my knowledge of the *dharma*, what underlies this desire? What am I deeply hoping for?

As we have seen, it's as though there is something missing in our lives, there's a lack, a gap to be filled, a chasm that stops us being whole, an emptiness that goes to the very heart of our existence, even an ice-cream-scoop-shaped hole. Lacking means the same as wanting; wanting means lacking. We want to be complete, be self-sufficient, be whole. Previously we looked at this existential insufficiency in Chapter 1 with the examples of shopping, projecting fantasies onto the media, and romantic partners; in Chapter 2, as a characteristic of *dukkha*; and in Chapter 3, as something which is intrinsic to the nature of all humans. In this chapter I want to examine this dearth within us in terms of seeking completeness by trying to maintain and bolster our sense of selfhood.

The desire to be something is not something we acquire during our lifetime, like a pining for Prosecco. It is an innate quality of humans. Ron Leifer describes this craving for becoming or existence, this craving to be something. 'The desire for life is present in the body at birth, in its homeostatic, hormonal, and reflexive mechanisms... At the more subtle level of ego, the desire for life is the ego's striving to establish itself, to solidify itself, to gain a secure foothold, to prevail and dominate, and so to enjoy the sensuous delights of the phenomenal world. The desire for life manifests itself in all of ego's selfish, ambitious strivings.'[163]

So, this craving is a human reflex; a desire to be something solid; to have a place in the world, an entity with a past and a future; with a wish in the present to overcome and predominate; and a longing to be propped up and satisfied. This deep craving to be or become something can manifest itself in many surface ways – to be successful at work, a good parent, liked by all, the one who knows, a dedicated practitioner of the *dharma*. We can even want to be everything to all people. We can get snared up in creating an identity, something which we shall look at further below. We can really try our hardest to be 'something' that means something in the world. And this sort of trying can be very trying.

There is of course an overpowering will to just live. This is the opposite of 'metaphorical death', the desire for oblivion discussed in the previous chapter. There is generally in nature an impulse for continuation and we humans, as part of nature, are no different. An aunt of mine, in her nineties, spent her last years in a nursing home. With all the mental and physical pain and indignity she was experiencing, she came to feel that that there was no longing any reason to carry on living. She said to me, "I want the good Lord to take me now", she had had enough of suffering life. She even attempted to cut her wrists with the only thing she had to hand, a pair of blunt plastic scissors. But still something inside her would not give up, something that went against her conscious desire to die. It was her instinctual will to carry on living despite all her agony. But this 'life force', if there exists such a thing - and I think it does, judging by the story of my aunt in the nursing home - does not equate to the clinging onto the perpetuation of an erroneous sense of what we believe we are.

Our ego survival instinct

The physical survival instinct has always been there in humans, in order to enable our species to continue. It has been a crucial factor in our make-up, as we saw in Chapter 3, being able to ward off predators, protect against the elements, and distinguish poisonous plants from nutritious ones. Nowadays most of us are usually able to create safe environments for ourselves, although this is clearly not the case in every place in every country, in places where war, poverty, famine and hostile climatic conditions prevail.

However, what still exists from our earliest days as humans, is the instinct that we can call the *ego survival instinct*. Psychologically speaking, *bhava-taṇhā* is the ego survival instinct, the craving for continued existence of the concept we call 'me'. This is not dissimilar to Freud's concept of the *libido*, as the narcissistic self-regarding life instinct, a survival drive rather than just a sexual one. In the end our ego survival instinct is just doing its best to protect us – attachment, freeze responses, and 'fight or flight' reactions are all aspects of this. And we can acknowledge and be grateful for this, whilst at the same time being aware of the *dukkha* it entails.[164]

Fredrik Falkenström, an academic psychotherapist, writing about the input Buddhism has made to the study of the psychology of self, describes the huge outlay we make in perpetuating our 'me' sense. 'A great deal of the effort spent in a human life is an investment in the continuity and integrity of one's perception of a fundamental self. There are investments in finding it, in keeping it going, in keeping it the same, in keeping it protected from challenging information, in keeping it from not feeling wrong or ashamed, in maintaining its sense of sovereignty or independence.'[165]

Our ego survival instinct not only protects, it also promotes. We want to present the best of 'me' to the world; we don't necessarily want people to see our inner anguishes and struggles. We may want others to think that we are cruising along the road comfortably, rather than the reality, which is that often we feel stuck in an inescapable traffic jam, longing to be on the other side of the road in another car where everything appears to be moving along smoothly.

This is the desire to foster our sense of what we are, shore it up, propagandize it and elevate it. Bradford Hatcher[166] describes this desire well. He writes that *bhava-taṇhā* 'is the craving for more being, craving more than simply to continue our own existence. We want to be increasingly important, powerful, popular, or known, to be too big to fail, to be secure, to never slip back onto obscurity or nothingness.' This advancing of ourself solidifies into what we call our identity, the characteristics which seemingly make us different from others.

Our identity is our self-view, it is who we think we are, how we see ourselves, and how we think others see us. Our behaviour acts to affirm our sense of personal identity. What we do all the time can be likened to taking a selfie photo – trying to fix in time, to solidify something, which is fluid, constantly changing, ungraspable.

A lot of the narrative about lifestyles is about creating a particular identity, an identity based on what we consume and how we consume it. We wear certain types of clothes, eat certain foods, decorate our home with certain accessories, shop in certain stores, with a view to creating an identity for ourselves and for the eyes of others. We may believe that this will enhance our standing, and make others view us favourably. Group identity is also part of how we define ourselves; we may identify with a sports team, others who pursue the same interest, a religion, our country – and conversely, feel ill-will towards those who are not in our identity group. In the UK, shopping at either Waitrose or Asda seems to demarcate us; well-done the advertising industry in creating such identity myths.

This clinging on to our perceived identity presents itself in many ways – moral superiority, little digs at others, disguising what we really feel if we think it might be to our advantage or disadvantage, conceit about how clever we are, how more perceptive we are than others, competitiveness, the desire to retaliate so that we regain the upper hand, 'teaching a lesson' to someone, not giving way, dominating conversations, attention-seeking.

We can become so possessed by how we are perceived by others, that our thinking is governed by our views about our status, our reputation, our standing. We not only feed our own ego, but we look to - and use others - to feed it for us, a utilitarian way of relating to other people. Longing for status is a very good illustration of how much we value our self-importance. We may be prepared to lie and cheat for the sake of our reputation. And, as the *Bodhicaryāvatāra* playfully pointed out some thirteen centuries ago, 'When our reputation or status is attacked, our mind howls a wail of distress like a child whose sandcastle has been broken.'[167]

How we come to be

But how does this 'me' come to exist and sustain itself? In chapter 2 we looked at the Wheel of Life and the chain of linked conditions which lead from delusion, through sensual contact to craving, attachment and habit-forming; we saw that the 'becoming' of habitual behaviour gives rise to the creation ('birth') of a particular identity, supported by particular memories and a consciousness that keep us going in a certain direction.

The Buddhist academic and teacher Reginald Ray writes about 'the birth of the ego' in somatic terms, how it is created within the body, and how it develops and is fortified.[168] I summarize and paraphrase the process he describes: 1) disquieting phenomena, such as sense perceptions, feelings, thoughts, people, situations etc. burst into our lives, arriving unexpectedly; 2) we feel shock, and retreat into instant primal reactions of panic, dread, anxiety and fear; 3) we react with sudden anger, jealousy, irritation, neediness, pride, etc; 4) we tense and hunch up our body against these emotions; and 5) we shut out our body's feelings, and retreat into our conceptual thinking processes, strengthening the concept in our mind that there is an entity to be protected. We shall look at how we can work with this process in Chapter 8, but we can write here that discomfort in the body is frequently a message that we are holding on too tightly to our sense of self.

Another way of examining how the self comes to be solidified within us comes from the Buddhist philosophical and psychological school of the Yogācāra, which arose in India around the 4th century CE. The Yogācāra posits different types of consciousness; most importantly here, *store-consciousness* and *manas-consciousness*.

Store-consciousness is similar to the unconscious or subconscious in Western psychology; it is a processor which operates even in our sleeping hours, contains all our seeds, our potentials - joy, anger, sadness etc, - and consists of individual and collective consciousness, all connected. It is indeterminate, it is neither inherently good nor bad, it just processes. So it is open to cultivation in positive or negative ways.

Manas-consciousness is accessible to us in our everyday lives. It is 'infected' by *kleśa,* innate poisons that cloud the mind. These are: delusion; the view of a fixed self; the conceit of 'I'; and the clinging to this self. *Manas-consciousness* takes the *store-consciousness*, which is below the threshold of our normal awareness, 'to be a self, rather than what it is – an underlying process of ever-changing conditions, arising and passing away, which, as it flows on, gives a certain sense of coherence to a person's identity.'[169] It judges, mistakenly viewing *store-consciousness* as one's own ego, and thus creates attachment to this ego.

Manas-consciousness works day and night to protect our self. It decides which of the elements in our *store-consciousness* it chooses us to be, and then defends it, powerfully. It appropriates these elements of *store-consciousness* and says, "This is me, this is mine." Each time we act with craving, jealousy, hatred, anger, selfishness, we are watering those corresponding seeds in our *store-consciousness*. However, we can equally water seeds of compassion and joy through our actions of body, speech and mind.

A policy of safeguarding

Humans, like other animals, have a need to feel safe. When what we consider as part of us is threatened, we may go to great lengths to protect it - a possession, say a house, an organization we work for, our country. Even something we are sitting on, a chair or a cushion, can seem like 'me', because if somebody violates that thing, it's as though the boundary of 'me' is being violated. If somebody starts eating from your plate, for example, or elbows in on a point you're making in conversation, a sense of possessiveness can easily take over. All these things that we are attached to in different ways we want to protect. Noticing the boundaries of things we identify with, these are our identity, this is what we seek to protect.

Craving for ego survival is as we have seen a protective mechanism. We can say that *bhava-taṇhā* is the fear of death, the fear of 'me' no longer existing. Fear and craving are thus two sides of a fundamental instinctual emotion. Many of our fears are instinctual, descending to us from our predecessors' days in the jungle. Fears of hunger, thirst and attack are examples of instinctual emotions which developed in order to enable us to survive in harsh environments. There, the situations which we are afraid of can lead directly to our death. These are direct fears. Our fellow sentient beings in the animal kingdom have these instincts, if not their emotional counterpart of fear.

What we modern day humans possess though is another type of fear, which is an indirect fear. We are very unlikely to die if we mess up in a presentation we are making at work; if somebody who we think of as a friend tells us they don't like us; if the train is delayed and we get to our rendezvous ten minutes late; if our new bike gets a dent in the mudguard; and even if we are robbed. And yet these are common things that we are afraid of. Do they really warrant so much anxiety?

All our fears can be traced back to our fear of death. Our fear of the cold, of people laughing at us, not liking us, of being mugged, of being destitute, of our closest ones deserting us, all these and more derive ultimately from our fear of dying. And what is this but an expression of our craving for existence, our craving to exist. This is at its most intense when facing our own death. The Dali Lama writes, 'Craving for existence arises while dying because of terror that the continuity of the self will cease.'[170] We fear that we will no longer exist and cling onto any parts that we can of our 'self-make-up'.[171]

But, in reality, it is not exactly the fear of death which lies at the heart of all our anxieties, but rather fear of the annihilation of self. The two extinctions are not the same; one is essentially physical, the other essentially psychological, as Ron Leifer described above. We want to cherish and protect the thing we call our self, defend it from anything or anybody harming it, layer it with padding to soften any assaults, put our self in a suit of armour to establish a barrier between us and the outside hurtful world. We try to build a house of our self. Self-preservation at all costs.

We experience fear because we feel threatened. And when we feel threatened, our survival instinct gets triggered. Very often we feel threatened by others. We feel challenged, so we react. We feel derided, so we respond. We feel thwarted, so we hit back. We sense that somebody is trying to get one up on us, so we build ourselves up as big as we can so that we can ward off any attack. Something we think of as 'ours' is endangered in some way, say a project we are involved in which someone seems to be taking over; we feel a real ownership and anything that challenges that ownership can cause great upset because we cannot allow ourselves to share it or hand it over.

We cannot allow this to happen. We cannot allow someone else to have the last word, the winning shot, the deciding point. That would be a huge blow to our very being, to our essence, to our identity, to what we stand for, to what we see ourselves as. To our 'me'. And the bigger that 'me' is, the more I have to lose.

Our lives are often built around trying to avoid the threats posed by others. Sometimes it is easier to just run away, to not put ourselves in the position where threats can manifest themselves. Hermit-like, we may shun the company of difficult others. This of course is an aspect of 'craving for non-existence', as we saw in the previous chapter. Or we may cultivate secrecy about our unskilful habits in order to protect our ego from perceived shame.

Or we may retaliate, enjoin battle, slide into irresolvable conflict – "My ego is bigger and better than yours. How dare you challenge my centrality in the world, the importance of 'me'?" *You* launch an attack, and *I* fear that my fortifications may not withstand the assault. I continue to fire arrows of pomposity to try to defend my castle, pour the hot lead of clever words on the head of you, my enemy interlocutor, bring out my biggest shield to parry that which will wound my being. But all to no avail. We can never conclusively win a struggle to evade being threatened. As long as we think there are threats to be dealt with, then they will continue to exist.

Any attempt to protect our illusory self, of 'self-defence', is doomed to failure. It is a battle where we may see small Pyrrhic victories, but we delude ourselves in thinking that any victory can be final and complete. Instead we need to reassess our whole strategy and re-examine the dynamic of: I have a self > I need to protect it > I must put up defences > these defences are what I need > they will make me happy.

The inevitability of change

Our ego survival instinct also manifests itself as a denial of getting old, not wanting to grow sick or die. The poet Edmund Spenser expressed this force in a sonnet, 'Vain man, said she, that dost in vain assay a mortal thing so to immortalize; for I myself shall like to this decay, and eek my name be wiped out likewise'.[172] We are mortal but our vanity finds it difficult to accept this fact. We all know that dying is an inevitable fact of life, although we may choose to ignore it.

We saw above that we have an extremely deep-rooted urge to be somebody with a degree of permanence inherent in it. If we attach too strongly to wanting to be always healthy and to live forever, doing what we can to maintain our appearance of being youthful and vigorous, we are bound to make ourselves unhappy. 'We fear losing what we have,' write Mason-John and Paramabandhu, 'and we are therefore in denial of impermanence. It is as if, holding on tightly to what we have, we believe we can escape the inevitability of change.'[173] Ultimately, we shall have to give up everything that we prize, including our valued self.

Similarly, we seek security in an insecure world. We grasp after certainty, the need to know all is well, and thus be safe. If only the ups and downs of daily life could be flattened out. If only we could resolve the current upset, file it away as 'dealt with', and then slip back into our comfortable routine. Part of us jumps to conclusions because it wants certainty, but we have to be careful not to jump with it. Life is not like that – solid, guaranteed, secure. There is always uncertainty just around the corner. We cling to an idea of permanence which goes against the laws of nature. Wanting security is a manifestation of our ego survival instinct guarding itself against external threats. The desire for certainty hardens us and prevents us from being flexible and opening up to other ways of seeing.

Stability can seem so attractive. The craving for some sort of order in areas of one's life can become obsessional; a desire to control the flow, a desire to have an overriding influence on our chaotic existence. For me, this has sometimes expressed itself in silly obsessive behaviours, like digging deep into the peg bag to ensure that a piece of clothing on the washing line is secured with matching pegs of the same colour - not accepting the randomness of the peg bag. Or feeling uncomfortable that there are blank spaces on my weekly Buddhist group meet-up app, when everybody 'should' be marking their presence or absence with either Yes or No. Or wanting to take control in meetings if it's not progressing the way I think it should. It's as though I need reassurance all the time, to give my sense of self a big comforting hug. But, as we truly know, 'Life in any world is unstable, it is swept away. It has no shelter and no protector. It has nothing of its own, but must leave all and pass on. It is incomplete, insatiate, the slave of craving.'[174] Clearly, whenever we cling onto anything, we are making ourselves into hostages to fortune, since deep down we know that one day it will cease to be.

Conceding to what the ego demands

All craving is self-centred by nature. All craving is a reflection of, a concession to, the demands of the ego. Indulging in one's cravings is indulging one's ego, trying to satisfy the desires of this illusory thing we call 'me'. Craving, whether it be lust, greed, coveting or a wistful longing, is letting the self have its own way. The notion of selfness is always present in craving. It is always 'me' who desires. But, as Rob Burbea warns us, 'the stronger the sense of self, the more that tends to build craving', and the reverse, 'More craving, more self'.[175]

Along with conceding to one's ego comes the idea of entitlement, that we have the *right* to fulfil our desires. In our present-day societies which increasingly prioritize individual rights over collective responsibilities, this entitlement could be seen as a parallel sign of the times. There is a sense in which we *deserve* whatever it is we crave, it is our due to indulge our sexual fantasies, devour our calorie-packed donut, switch on our digital drug; we are justified in our desire for more clothes we don't need, somebody else's job, or in our entitlement to happiness. The individualism that is implied in 'my rights' can foster egotism and conflict between individuals and groups rather than lead to social harmony and selflessness.

Nevertheless, we have to accept that we have a pleasure-seeking mind. It is very hard to imagine what life would be like without the pleasurable feelings that we seek out. A life of trying to deny ourselves pleasure, a life of austerity and joy-renunciation (as we shall look at in Chapter 7), would be an extremely miserable one; it is just a question of how and where we seek pleasurable experience. Our entitled, self-focussed minds seem to be conditioned to continually seek pleasure, without moderation. There is an accelerator but no break.[176] Our minds can easily ignore moderation when we are pleasure seeking.

What we need to do is to recognize the different levels of enjoyment available to us on a daily basis, those factors which appeal to the pleasure-seeking function of our minds. There are of course chocolate, watching TV, and fine wine, but also the joys of nature, uplifting music, trusting friendship. We can get stuck in negative patterns of behaviour, pursuing pleasure to avoid suffering, running away from *dukkha*, ignoring the dangers of hedonism and over-indulgence, happiness seeming to depend on things always going to *my* liking. All self-gratification is a manifestation of ego-clinging, self-centeredness, selfishness – 'my' needs are more important than anything else, 'my' pleasure rules OK.

I'll keep holding on

Sometimes it seems to me as though the universe is a vast concert hall, with a multi-media, multi-sensory symphony playing. I desperately try to make sense of it all by snatching hold of small bits of output, clinging onto them, attempting to make them solid, trying to make them mine, in order to try to give an illusory sense of comfort in the midst of this mad cacophony. Similarly, Traleg Kyabgon likens this world we inhabit to a river. 'The turbulence within our minds is compared to the turbulence of the water. Our efforts to grasp onto various sensory objects, ideas, beliefs, abstract concepts, and experiences, are like clutching onto pieces of wood being carried down the river. We try in desperation to clutch onto the wood, in order to find some kind of secure ground.'[177]

Our latent tendency to cling onto what gives an impression of security and solidity becomes our fundamental craving to find substance, to secure and protect an identity. This predisposition leads us towards gripping on to this sense of our self like ivy clings to a tree, wrapping its adhesive tentacles around its host, literally holding on for dear life.

As we saw in the previous chapter, humans have an inbuilt tendency towards addiction. And what we are all addicted to is this sense of a static and enduring self. It's so difficult to shake off this feeling; it is extremely sticky. We are life-dependent, dependent upon the notion that there is a 'me'. This, as we have seen, is our inheritance; we *instinctively* cling to ourselves.

But although this ego clinging, and its correlate of ego survival, are innate and inherent in us, this does not mean that they are necessary and helpful attributes of being human. Subhuti writes about ego clinging, 'We solidify ourselves in our environments, patterning them to our own shape – although, oddly, our self-attachment may crystallise in worlds that give us a lot of pain and that we ourselves may rail against. We identify elements of our experience as 'mine' – and others as 'not mine' …. Our way of life coagulates, hardening into a carapace of self.'[178]

So, my craving for self-existence forms me, my habits, my personality. And the *dukkha* which has its origin in craving and aversion arises from the grasping of 'me' and 'mine', behind which lie delusion, ignorance and confusion. The false notion of self which we are Velcro-ed to is what causes our unhappiness, our dissatisfaction, our *dukkha*.

Unsticking the superglue

We can fixate on certain pleasurable sense experiences; we get fixated in our habits; and we can fixate on certain views about ourselves, others and our relationship to the world. We can get very hot under the collar if somebody questions our views, especially about ideas we are really committed to, like the crisis of human-made climate change, the availability of abortion, or the idea of fairness. We hold these views as set-in-stone, unshakable, non-negotiable pillars of our identity. If someone doesn't agree with our view of the world, doesn't affirm our view, and this annoys us, and we are set upon arguing our point of view till we are blue in the face, then we can see this as a sign of attachment, our attachment to the view. We want to feel that our view is the right one. A view in this sense can denote an opinion, a speculation, a theory, a belief, any type of philosophical and religious belief, as well as prejudices and assumptions.

This does not however mean that we should not entertain religious, political, and philosophical opinions and convictions. It does not mean there is something intrinsically wrong with those views. It just means that we should be wary of adhering to them blindly, rather than examining them, noticing how we cling, and being prepared to loosen the tightness around them.

We need to be open to whether our views are the last word about the world. Yes, accept if you will the teachings of the Buddha in this book, follow them and put them into practice. But if you hug them so tightly that you feel threatened if someone challenges your views and you react with hostility, then you are creating pain for yourself. This also is the teaching of the Buddha - hold on to views lightly. The most binding view that we hold onto, which is strengthened by clinging to the inflexible conviction that we are right, is our view that we have a fixed unchanging identity.

When we feel our views challenged or threatened, there is inherent in this a view or an idea. In reality, it is the view or idea that there exists a threat to ourself. We can however allow ourselves to move our awareness away from the object (what is threatening) towards the subject (what is being threatened). We need to be open with ourselves, examine what is really happening and investigate what it is that is being threatened. Maybe then we will discover that there is nothing that can threaten us, because there is nothing to be threatened. This idea will be developed more in Chapter 8.

Perpetuating, protecting, and promoting the ego takes up a lot of our resources. The ego is a hungry entity, and we waste much of our time trying to give it nourishment. In vain though, for the ego can never be satisfied, however much it is fed, boosted, praised and flattered. There is nothing to be fed, it is like feeding a phantom. It is the hungry ghost.

We cannot deny our innate ego survival instinct, but we have to be careful that we are not spending most of our energy in just trying to protect our sense of who we think we are - this energy, as we shall see in Chapter 9, which can be directed to recognizing what our potential is, developing more the joyful, wise, and compassionate side of our nature. Or, as the Theravāda Buddhist monk Ajahn Sucitto states: 'This thirst to be something keeps us reaching out for what isn't here. And so we lose the inner balance that allows us to discern a here-and-now fulfillment in ourselves'.[179]

As we examined in Chapter 3, the only constant in our normal lives is delusion – the delusion that we have a separate fixed self that controls our life, what Robert Wright calls our CEO, our chief executive officer.[180] This is the Buddhist teaching of *anattā*, sometimes called the doctrine of 'non-self', the teaching that we have no abiding essence, no imperishable 'soul'. What we think of as our identity is not stable and enduring. The 'I' exists because we designate it so. It is a fiction, a mental construct, albeit a very convincing one, a story which we concoct to help explain the multitude of events that happen in our lives. It is a convention, our prevailing narrative which we go along with. It is not unreal, but it is not what we want to think it is. We can think of ourselves as a case of 'mistaken identity', mistakenly identifying with, and grasping onto, this thing we call 'myself'. It's like clinging for all we are worth in a river to a raft made of cardboard, while forgetting that it will at some time dissolve and disintegrate.

Craving for existence, *bhava-taṇhā,* is a burden that we carry around with us, as are the other forms of *taṇhā*. However, Buddhism says that we can liberate ourselves of these burdens. With firm intent, we can set out on a path to do just that. Humans are much more than self-centred grasping - we also are endowed with great kindness and generosity, we have an in-built potential to develop these seeds of selflessness, to move away from self-orientated clutching, and expand those human qualities that make life fulfilling and purposeful. These immanent qualities within us we call Buddhahood, those qualities which we can uncover and cultivate, and which are our potential for Enlightenment. 'Since all living beings are bound by their craving for existence, you must begin by finding the determination to be free.' [181]

Reflecting - Chapter 5

Do you feel that you have narcissistic tendencies? In what ways do you feel 'a desire to be something'? How easy is it for you to accept that you will get old, deteriorate and die? What are your deepest fears, and how do they relate your sense of selfhood? Think of examples of when your ego has felt threatened. In what ways do you try to protect your ego? Which of your views would you find hard to 'hold lightly'? How do you seek self-validation? Do you ever feel an entitlement to anything? Do you feel that your happiness depends on things going to your liking? Do you agree that your *dukkha* arises from your self-centred actions? In what ways do you promote yourself? Do you feel you seek praise? How important to you is your standing in the eyes of others?

PART TWO:

THE SOLUTION

Chapter 6:

MEDICATING

I believe that there is an urge within us as human beings to be 'better' than we generally are in life. Ordinary happiness comes and goes. But whether consciously or not, I believe we long for something more fundamental. Something that brings about not only our own well-being but also touches upon a need for fulfilment and purpose in our lives, a search for a profound contentment. I believe we all long to be free, to transcend and be rid of our inner tensions and frustrations, to be at ease with who we are, not to be pulled this way and that by our urges and yearnings.

We limit ourselves by our likes and dislikes; we have the potential to be much more than these. In *Part One* we explored how our cravings - whether for sensual gratification, comfort, avoidance, or for protection and promotion of what we think of as 'me' - can never totally satisfy our deeper needs. Intuitively we know that this is the case, but this does not however prevent us persisting with our craving habits, slavishly indulging our unhealthy, unhelpful longings. In *Part Two* we shall look at how Buddhist practice addresses these obstructive habits. This chapter begins though by examining what it means to change our behaviour, and then goes on to give an outline of strategies and teachings which are developed in the remaining chapters.

This treasured opportunity we have

We are blessed with a treasure, this life that we have, this life which is too short and too dear for us to waste our hours pursuing unsatisfying cravings. The preciousness of our human birth is one of the Four Reminders[182] that Buddhists bring to mind as an antidote to a distracted life. Writer and broadcaster Vishvapani has developed a reflection on this reminder, of which this an excerpt: 'Here, now, I have a chance to make something of my life. I have health. I have energy. I have the ability to think and feel freely. I have enough food and enough money to meet my needs... All of these things can change, but while I have these advantages

I have a great opportunity... I have had the great good fortune to meet the Dharma... Am I making use of the opportunity this offers? How much time I waste! How much of my life passes in unawareness! How strongly my habits constrain me! I would be foolish to waste this chance. So let me commit myself to practising as fully as I can.'[183]

We have got to know when it is time to stop. We have just got to know when it's time to do something about our unfruitful, unfulfilling behaviour. There comes a time when we have to say, 'No, no more!' There comes a turning point or, better, a tipping point when we know that we need to change.

We become disillusioned with the way we are leading our life, with its petty delusional urges. We begin to see the shortcomings of a life based on sensual desire, compulsive behaviour and self-centeredness. We become weary and disillusioned at trying to satisfy our mundane longings and instead experience a desire to be more realized. We recognise that our object of desire is not our friend who helps us through the day or night, but rather the cause of our dissatisfaction and dis-ease.

We cannot just carry on consuming and grasping ad infinitum; we just make ourselves ill, whether physically, mentally, emotionally or spiritually. We cannot just carry on clinging to the idea that there is some kind of answer to our dissatisfaction about life in the things that we desire; Buddhism tells us that we can never find satisfaction in the attempted gratification of our mundane needs. We come to the realization that we are vulnerable to some of our emotions, easily led by them, and acknowledge that they are not always to our benefit. This is a start.

Then comes the awareness that we can be free of the emotions that do us harm. This is the essence of the third of the Buddha's Four Noble Truths – that we can put an end to our *dukkha*. We understand that there is another way. Throughout our life we may experience moments when we turn our back on old habitual unskilful ways of acting which bring about problems for us and adopt a new positive attitude towards our life which is liberating and progressive; we can think of these moments as mini-rebirths, opportunities to start afresh.

It's time for our cravings to not be such a big deal for us, to not dominate our lives. We delude ourselves if we think that we are in control of our habits when patently we are not. We have little control over our bodily functions and urges, and even less over our mind. Our mind has a mind of its own and just wanders off wherever it wants to, like a pet cat over which its owner has little influence. Impossible to tame, only possible to give love to. In Buddhism, love is at the heart of how we confront our cravings; in Chapter 10 we shall see how, with love - with *Mettā* - we move outwards, beyond the narrow confines of 'me' and my cravings.

It's time to get off the treadmill of repeated unhelpful habits for good, rather than stopping the treadmill now and again in those rare moments of clarity, and then getting back on it again when the clarity fades, continuing on our *un*merry-go-round that leads nowhere. The good news is that we can heal ourselves. We have everything we need to self-medicate our way to freedom; freedom from the urges that can plague our life and prevent us from realizing our true potential. Instead of self-medicating with intoxicants and other compulsive behaviour, we can find the medicine we need in the Buddha's *dharma*.

And this is not solely for ourselves, for our own well-being, but for the well-being of others as well. Everything we do has implications that reverberate all around us. Indeed, giving up something for the sake of others can be easier than doing it for oneself; we shall see more in Chapter 9 how having a greater purpose can propel our desire to change.

No more excuses

It's time to stop feeling powerless. It's time to stop making excuses. Why wait to take action? If you are not ready to stop your unhelpful cravings right now, ask yourself the question, "Why not?" Can you come up with a really good convincing reason?

As we have seen, each time we indulge a habit, we reinforce it. On and on and on, we indulge and make our habits stronger. The solution to weakening our habits now appears logical. Indulging our cravings reinforces them; freeing ourselves from indulging weakens them.

Meditation teacher and author Sharon Salzberg writes, 'It is never too late to turn on the light. Your ability to break an unhealthy habit or turn off an old tape doesn't depend on how long it has been running; a shift in perspective doesn't depend on how long you've held on to the old view. When you flip the switch in that attic, it doesn't matter whether it's been dark for ten minutes, ten years or ten decades. The light still illuminates the room and banishes the murkiness, letting you see the things you couldn't see before. It's never too late to take a moment to look.'[184]

If you're still not convinced that now is the time, reflect for a few minutes on what your main cravings are at the present moment and make a mental list of them. Try to experience what happens in your body when you think about them. Then reflect on whether these cravings are really helpful to your life, whether they lead to real satisfaction and happiness. Think about what life would be like without these cravings. What sort of person do I really want to be? Indulgent, self-obsessed, compulsive? Or generous, loving and free?

As my recovering-alcoholic friend Bill said to me, "Once I was drunk but now I choose to be sober. Once I was muddle-headed but now I choose to be clear." We always do have a choice. The medicine is here sitting patiently on the shelf. Are we going to reach out and take it (rather than the smartphone, the poison chalice, the remote control, the all-smothering quilt)? The more we indulge our cravings, the more out of reach the medicine may seem to be. But it is always here. We need just to choose to gather up our strength, to raise our arm, open our hand, take hold of the medicine and drink the first sip. Once we have made that decision, the medicine will start to work. It may start to take effect immediately, or we may need to bide our time. But have no doubt, the *dukkha* will begin to subside, and our cravings will begin to heal.

None but ourselves can free our minds

In reality, we have no choice but to make choices, every moment of the day. We have no choice but to try to make some sense of the world. These choices are based on our attitudes to what we are experiencing which we have developed throughout our lives. We make leaps of trust founded on our intuition; we then develop ideas which support and build our confidence.

Who do we think creates the *dukkha* in our lives? The ups and downs, the dramas, the itches, the unease, the dissatisfactions, the unhappiness. Is it somebody else's fault, is it always our circumstances? It's no use trying to find somebody else, something else, to blame. In the end, we should know that it all comes down to us.

Whatever our circumstances, however dire they may be – and for some of us they are really dire - we have the potential to relate differently to them, to change our attitude towards them. We can live to be pleased (to please ourselves) or lived to be fulfilled (to fulfil ourselves). In the end it is only *our own* actions that we can control and take responsibility for.

Nobody else can medicate us but ourselves. No one else can break us free from the *dukkha* which is craving; only us. Nobody else can free our minds. And if we decide to change our behaviour, it has to be because *we* want to change, not because it is expected of us, or to please somebody else.

Making choices about our actions is our ethical behaviour. Buddhist ethics is concerned with training ourselves to develop skilful states of body, speech and mind, and with the impact that this behaviour has upon us and the world around us. For Buddhists, behaving ethically is founded upon awareness and love. We train ourselves, we put into practice, and then we can see for ourselves whether the training works or not. We don't have to take anybody's word for it, not even the Buddha's. Chapter 8 looks at Buddhist ethics in more depth.

Guiding the change

Sometimes life sucks. Sometimes life is a bed of roses. But both types of experience will pass. Accept this and be prepared to move on. All things must pass, say a lot of Eastern spiritual teachers, as well as former Beatle George Harrison. And so too must craving pass, because it is an emotion that has no permanence; it arises and it ceases, like all phenomena in this universe we inhabit. We don't always have to end up feeling broke or bloated.

As I look out of my window this autumn I see the leaves yellowing and reddening; I see the neighbours' children growing up; I hear the rumbling of a train arising and passing; I smell cooking aromas waft into the room; I know that I am not a static Kuladipa but rather a fluid Kuladipa-ing, with new aches and wrinkles. Everything around us and within us is constantly changing. Once again we see that the truth of the principal of impermanence is vital: the fact that everything is constantly changing means that our cravings also can change and, given the right conditions, they are bound to change in a way that is beneficial to us and those around us. Since there is nothing that we *can* hold on to, there is nothing that we *need* to hold on to.

All we are is our actions right now. We are not what we were yesterday, let alone last year, and tomorrow we shall change again. That change is within our own hands. We are nothing but process. We are in a state of becoming. The person who wrote this book is not the same person as the one who originally thought about it. The person who reads it will not be the same person who picked it up. We begin the process of developing and growing from the moment we are born. We are just a changing process floating through this changing world. We have no choice about it, it's just nature at play. But what Buddhism teaches us is not only that we constantly change, physically, mentally and emotionally, but that we can influence that change, influence it in positive ways. We have the power to transform our lives so that the 'poisons' of craving, ill-will and delusion no longer plague us. We realise that we can have an impact on a situation, rather than it having an impact on us. We *can* take control, rather than being blown about by the worldly winds,[185] which we respond to with craving or aversion. We need not allow ourselves to be overwhelmed, rather we can stand back, stop what we're doing, pause and let go.

In order to change your habits, you really need to desire to change, you really need to be convinced that changing your habitual patterns of craving is what you *have to* do if you want to break the cycle of being controlled by them. Are you really deeply convinced?

Vessantara relates the desire for change to the Buddha's noble quest.[186] 'The noble quest will not be easy. The odds that it will turn out well may not seem very high. But what is the alternative? Wringing any real security or lasting happiness from the ignoble quest is simply impossible. We need to keep reflecting on this until we arrive at a definite conclusion, a decision that moves us to action.'[187]

My teacher and mentor Ratnaghosha amplifies this: 'The main obstacle to spiritual life is an unwillingness to change or an unwillingness to change completely. Sometimes we want to change, but only on our own terms; we only want to change what we find uncomfortable. But sometimes it's even more important to change what we find comfortable.... We need to be willing to change our behaviour, our ideas, views and opinions, our ways of thinking, our habits, our circumstances, our lifestyle, everything – everything is in the melting pot. We may not have to change everything, but the willingness is a key factor in making progress.'[188] Our desire for change will need to be stronger than our desire not to change.

But we may baulk against real change. Wanting to avoid discomfort can make it difficult to change. We know that craving is so powerful a force that it can be intimidating. We know that boredom, anger, exhaustion, low mood, distraction, loneliness can all lead us to abandon our good habits and indulge, give in to our craving. We know that shopping is easier than stopping. When we try to change we encounter our obdurate habits.

However, there is always a way to beat stubborn Māra, indeed many different ways. The forces of Māra may seem incredibly powerful, clever, beguiling, but his potency is in essence a blind one. We however have a quality that he lacks, a quality that is at the heart of our humanity, which distinguishes us from other sentient beings. We have the ability to look at ourselves, to observe the workings of our mind. We have within us the tools that enable us to break away from the 'mind-forg'd manacles'[189] of our cravings; the chains that we lock ourselves up with, we can also unlock.

I have heard so many times people say things like, "That's the sort of person I am (obstinate, aggressive, weak-willed, scatter-brained), I won't change" or "You can't teach an old dog like me new tricks". I often used to tell myself that I can't change my habits, I *must* have that glass of wine or two when I get home from work. When what I really meant is, I *don't want to* change my habits. Or I don't want to enough. Once we have managed to conquer an unhelpful habit and then look back at how we felt so trapped in it, we can wonder why we were so entangled. We need to change in order to accept change.

The teachings of the Buddha make it clear that it is within the capabilities of all of us to put an end to our *dukkha* by addressing our cravings, 'we all have the capacity' writes Lama Thubten Yeshe, 'to move from the confused, polluted state of ego-conflict to the natural clean and clear state of pure consciousness itself. We should never think that our mind has somehow become irreversibly contaminated.'[190] It is never beyond us to change, said the Buddha, 'Put aside what is unwholesome. It is possible to do so. If it were not possible...I would not ask you.'[191] Lama Thubten Yeshe once more emphasizes this. 'According to the Buddhist point of view, there is no human problem that cannot be solved by human beings. Each one of you should understand this personally and encourage yourself by thinking, "I can deal with all my problems; I can solve my problems." '[192]

If the Buddhist path to Enlightenment is the cessation of suffering through eliminating its cause - craving - then we can say that the Buddha, the fully enlightened one, did not suffer the dissatisfaction of craving. And by aiming to put ourselves in his position, by acting *as if* we were enlightened, we too can feel what is like to not suffer the dissatisfaction of craving. Buddhism in essence says that the way to overcome craving is to follow the Buddha's path, to become like the Buddha. Not for nothing was he referred to as 'the Thirst-breaker'.[193] If we follow in the Buddha's footsteps we can heal ourselves. We can heal ourselves from our compulsive self-centred thinking and behaving, from our cravings to have, to be and not to be.

Relinquishing our cravings is not about restricting our freedom to choose, but rather about liberating ourselves from the slavery of our unhelpful habits. And the change we are seeking in our habits is not just a short-term fix, not just a provisional relief from problems we are having at the present time. We are aiming at long-lasting fundamental change rather than just a temporary solution; or at least as enduring as anything can be in this transitory life of ours. Sangharakshita talks about 'the distinction between states of mind which are attained temporarily, and those whose attainment constitutes a permanent change. Spiritual states of mind are not necessarily permanent; as is all too clear, one can be feeling 'spiritual' at one moment, and far from spiritual the next. It is possible, however, to achieve continuously positive and refined states of mind.'[194]

What does this change in our behaviour feel like? Well, we may continue to crave, but the change in our behaviour is that we don't feel the need to always indulge that craving. It is not so much freedom from craving that Buddhists seek, but rather freedom from the enslavement to our craving.

Heirs to our actions

If we act in positive, skilful, helpful ways, the law of *karma* will take care of the rest. Indeed, the most obvious way that Buddhists look at the problem of craving is through the law of *karma* - seeing that our actions have consequences. Or as the Buddha made clear, 'Thus I say, beings are the heirs to their actions.'[195] The question is not "What does it matter if I do this or that?" but rather "What are the consequences if I do this or that? What happens to me if I carry on my habit of eating foods high in sugar, salt and fat? What's the result of my spending four hours a day peering into my smartphone? How do I honestly feel constantly putting down a friend to make myself seem superior?" If, upon consideration of the consequences of my habitual cravings, I feel better when I don't indulge in them, then I have learnt a lesson; maybe I can call this 'reward-based learning'.

Eventually my friend Carlo, about whom I wrote at the beginning of Chapter 4, as well as so many others who I have met and taught at my local Buddhist Centre, came to this realization, despite what they felt were intractable difficulties in their lives. They opened their minds and their hearts and, with guidance from the *dharma* and the help and support of those people they could share their experiences with, real change has taken place for them.

And it is important to mention at this point that the importance of help and support from sympathetic others cannot be over-emphasized. Although in the end the decision to address and persevere with intransigent craving habits is down to us individually, and we have to take responsibility for our decisions, in Buddhism the value of the community of fellow followers of the *dharma,* known as the *saṅgha*, is central to our practice - not feeling isolated with one's difficult cravings, being able to share and release, and to receive encouragement and affirmation.

You are not alone in your predicament. What in itself can be liberating is the realization that your cravings are a universal characteristic of humankind. It is not just you on your own struggling with your personal urges and longings, every one of us has cravings which we have to deal with, and which are problematic for us. This we can share.

We are not detached individuals, we have our passions in common with all other humans, and on this basis we can empathize not only with others but have compassion for ourselves. We all do foolish things sometimes. It's in our deluded nature. But we can also act wisely, with awareness, with kindness and with determination.

Stepping out

Making the decision to change, to change one's harmful habits with the wisdom of a spiritual tradition such as Buddhism, is to step out onto a path. If we feel that the path works for us, we will feel like committing to it. The Buddha was never one for giving out commandments – 'try it out and see' was more his motto. So we need to try out his methods for treating our dis-ease. There's nothing better than what our own experience teaches us, and Buddhism emphasizes our 'direct experience' as the best tool for making progress. The positive feedback we thus get from adhering to skilful habitual patterns of behaviour will keep us set on the right track. Addressing craving is not a one-shot deal. It is something that we will explore and investigate all our lives. Part of this path is allowing our mind to be more open to possibilities. Changing our behaviour means challenging our assumptions. The attitude of "I can't change" or "mindfulness is not for me" is the attitude of a closed mind. The mind is plastic and can be remoulded, which we shall explore more of in Chapter 9.

We may not be able to change things overnight, but what we can do is to make a beginning, and go to bed with a clearer conscience that now we have set off on a path. Ultimately, there is no magical one-off, instant solution to our cravings, but rather what is required is a graduated approach, working on our mental states, particularly when our cravings are deep-rooted and long-standing. We may have accumulated a lot of baggage over the years which needs unpacking, sorting and discarding, even though some of the items in our personal suitcase we seem to cherish and fear to abandon as they unconsciously make up our 'identity'.

Sangharakshita talks about the notion that it feels easier to be 'bad' (unskilful) than to be 'good' (skilful),[196] and yet there is no reason why we should not think the opposite, that it's easier to be positive and skilful in our behaviour. Freedom from the entanglement of unhealthy desires is our aspiration. Be brave. Dig deep and make the firm decision to change your unhelpful habits.

Immediate and ultimate goals

On our path to free ourselves of our seemingly intransigent cravings, we can think of immediate and long-term objectives. The ultimate goal of the Buddhist path is of course total liberation, Enlightenment. This will seem a distant aim that requires much practice. In the meantime our life can be amazingly enriched by seeking to transform our lives through addressing our longings. 'Our more immediate or relative goal' writes Traleg Kyabgon Rinpoche, 'is to put our effort into improving ourselves as human beings, to increase happiness, and reduce suffering. So we have two sets of goals, as Buddhist practitioners. As human beings we may not particularly expect to become enlightened any time soon but the desire to attain Enlightenment as our ultimate goal remains. The demarcation line between the states of Enlightenment and non-Enlightenment is not as clear-cut as many may think. In Buddhism, Enlightenment is not seen as a fixed state or place. That means that there are degrees of Enlightenment.'[197] And we may surprise ourselves how enlightened we can become.

On one level Buddhism is a therapy of the mind. It analyses causes of the human predicament and provides remedies to alleviate them. Vimalasara has called Buddhism 'the oldest therapeutic programme we know to date'[198] and, although Buddhism is much more than a therapy, for many it can be exactly that – a means to address the mental confusion or distress that we face daily. The Buddha may have been the world's first real psychologist, but he was not one whose aim was to help individuals to adjust or adapt to the norms of society at large. His message was not about restoring people to a certain degree of mental health and well-being. If we can talk about mental health at all, Buddhism is about becoming much, much, much more healthy, equanimous, at ease and in harmony with all around us than any sense of 'normal' mental health can imagine. 'Health is more than the absence of disease. And freedom is a lot more than freedom from unmanageable craving.'[199]

Following a spiritual path requires discipline, in the sense of respecting a training programme, comparable to that which an athlete follows. We require discipline in our life to prevent our ingrained reactivity, and to stop us back-sliding; we have a mind-blowing potential, but we are held back by our complaisance, our indulgence in time-wasting and energy-sapping inanities.

In my spare time, I am an amateur jazz saxophonist and I need the training of regularly and thoroughly practising chords and scales, the foundation of which will enable me to feel comfortable and grounded enough to let loose and improvise. The spiritual path is a path of regular and thorough training as well, leading to increasing ease and freedom. But this does not have to be an austere path of severity and self-denial. As we have seen, the Buddha called his path the Middle Way, the path that is neither self-mortification and asceticism, nor self-indulgence and sense pleasuring.

What we are renouncing is our attachment to *dukkha*. Whatever we do, we all need to find pleasure in life in order to motivate us, as a tonic to the system. If we don't find it in our spiritual life then we will search for it, most likely unskilfully, elsewhere. As well as being enjoyable, the principles that we follow on the path are of little use unless they have relevance and can be put into practice in this messy world that Buddhism calls *saṃsāra*. Words like compassion and kindness are fine, but unless they really mean something to us and we can apply them practically to resolve our dilemmas, then they are nothing but words. Going through the motions is not a viable solution to our *dukkha*. We can know, but not do. According to David Brazier, a Buddhist author particularly known for his writings on socially engaged Buddhism, 'Knowing a bit about how something works, however, does not stop it happening.'[200]

We can feel intensely the need to make good the unsatisfactory world we live in, to fix *saṃsāra*. Undoubtedly we can have an influence, great or small, on the manifold problems of this world, and engage in political, environmental, and community action to try to make the world a better place. I am very far from underestimating the necessity for social engagement, but we need to recognize that these actions, although crucial, will only result in limited success in bringing about the end of *dukkha* for humankind if our individual mindsets do not undergo a revolution as well. Indeed, scientists have now begun to talk about anthropogenic environmental destruction as 'a symptom of a deeper, more subversive modern crisis.... 'The Human Behavioural Crisis'. '[201]

What we most certainly can do is to begin to fix ourselves, transform ourselves. Buddhism is explicit in its teachings that our *dukkha* is embedded in the workings of the mind. The mind determines how we respond to the various urges that arise within us. The title of Danapriya's book sums it up – *It's Not Out There;*[202] searching for external solutions to our difficulties can only provide limited satisfaction. There are choices to be made. Craving happens in the mind, and the mind is liberated from craving by the mind.

I have heard it said that the Buddhist path, or indeed any spiritual path, is a path of escapism. That it's about not facing up to, or running away from, the crises that the world faces, whether it be climate change, or the many wars and conflicts, the social injustice and inequality that beleaguer so many people across the world. There are two ways of looking at escapism. Firstly, David Brazier once more: 'The Buddha did not teach escape. The Buddha taught noble living. Noble living is not pain-free but it is meaningful. Indeed, it is the very opposite of escape. The noble person is not a coward. The Buddha taught that a radical change is possible in the way a person lives their life and sees their world. This radical change is called Enlightenment. Enlightenment is a cathartic experience. One should not be deceived by the word into thinking this is a cerebral affair.'[203] So, not escaping but committing.

But secondly, as, Sangharakshita suggests, there is not only a negative escapism - the *vibhava-taṇhā* which we explored in Chapter 4 - but also a positive escaping. 'Well, why not run away from danger? If the house is on fire, why not get out?... It's not a question of running away blindly, but of definitely getting out of a situation which you see you ought never to have allowed yourself to get into.... Escapism can be a quite neutral word, the use of which is quite justified, and we could quite happily accept it. You could say, Yes, we are escaping... We want to get into a higher state of being, into a more satisfactory kind of consciousness. We want to escape from our present consciousness.'[204] So it's a question of whether we are fleeing blindly from our problems, or whether we are trying to free ourselves with our eyes wide open. Fleeing or freeing.

Not one but many

We have seen that mundane desires can never be fully satisfied. So, if we can't satisfy our desires, what on earth do we do with the darn things? As we saw in *Part One* of this book, there are many different ways in which people experience *dukkha*, and there are many different types of craving which are at the origin of that *dukkha*. Equally, there are numerous aspects of the Buddha's teachings which can address our cravings and the resultant *dukkha*, 'ways of dealing with desire that encompass a wide range of human experience.'[205]

It's not a case of one size fits all. Lama Thubten Yeshe points out that the Buddha's teachings 'contain thousands of different methods for overcoming the mental and physical obstacles to our happiness and well-being.'[206] We need to find which strategies work for ourselves and this will depend, for example, on the nature of our craving, the immediate need and the longer-term need, the strength of the urges, and what sort of person we are. And also where we are in our quest to address craving.

We can *suspend* our cravings; *reject* them; *weaken* them; *tolerate* them; *break* them *down*; *see through* them; *transcend* them; *transform* them.

Different approaches are appropriate for different people, at different times, in different situations, for different cravings; all though are steps on the path to greater freedom. For somebody experiencing an unhealthy sexual obsession with a friend's partner, the initial requirement may be to stay well clear of the person fixated upon, so that the stimulus of their presence does not evoke desire. It may then be a question of looking at what's happening here, what's going on in one's mind (and body) when the sexual longing arises. And then of seeing how the time and energy obsessing could be better employed.

It goes without saying that Buddhism doesn't have a monopoly on behaving ethically. All spiritual traditions have principles guiding their adherents' behaviour. Some of these principles are in the form of rules or commandments from God; others, like those of Buddhism, which has no place for an all-powerful God figure, are in the form of ethical training principles which we are encouraged to adopt. There are clearly humanists and others who follow no spiritual tradition but who nevertheless have an extremely strong moral compass. There is a Buddhist verse about the *dharma* which is frequently quoted, 'Just as the great ocean has one taste, the taste of salt, so also this teaching and discipline has one taste, the taste of liberation.'[207] Similarly, there are Christian, Islamic, Jewish, Hindu, and humanist teachings that also have the taste of liberation. Buddhism though is explicit in having freedom from suffering, from dissatisfaction, at the forefront of its teachings.

Over the course of its twenty-five-century history, unsurprisingly diverse traditions and schools of Buddhism have developed and flourished. They all represent aspects of the Buddha's teachings, but present them in different ways, with different practices. The three principal traditions of Buddhism have all sought to address the characteristics of craving. These three traditions are, in order of historical development, the Theravāda or Hīnayāna; the Mahāyāna; and the Vajrayāna or Tantra. The word *yāna* means vehicle – that is to say that the Buddhist traditions are vehicles or rafts to enable us to cross the stream of *saṃsāra*. All three are still very much alive and kicking. Other schools such as Zen, Pure Land and Nichiren Buddhism have developed out of these traditions.

We can see all of these traditions or schools as just models; models for practice, models of understanding how the mind works, models of how to change unhelpful habits, models for Awakening. It is important to realize that different traditions, models and strategies are interconnected and overlap; There is a lot more commonality between the seemingly different schools of Buddhism than may first meet the eye. 'Within the diversity, however,' writes Traleg Kyabgon Rinpoche, 'there is some kind of underlying current that is common and pervasive, which is to do with the grasping, clinging, and fixation.'[208]

In Mahāyāna Buddhism we find the idea of *upāya-kauśalya,* usually translated as 'skilful means' or 'skill in means'. This refers to the ability to teach the *dharma* according to the needs of people of different understanding, using whatever means were available. So there might be simpler teachings for those with less understanding, and more developed teachings for those who were capable of understanding them. This would be like a doctor prescribing different treatments depending upon the needs of the patient. The concept of 'skilful means' in our context of tackling craving is therefore about being creative, and choosing a strategy which is appropriate, practical and expedient; as long as it is motivated by and enacted with wisdom and compassion it will be skilful.

In the rest of this chapter I shall try to summarise how the models of Theravāda, Mahāyāna and Vajrayāna Buddhism tackle craving, and the approaches that they put forward. In the space available here this will inevitably be an overview or even a simplification of what can be quite complex teachings. This book is also just a model for understanding.

In the case of a sudden illness involving an infection of the blood which causes bleeding, we could stick on a band-aid for a temporary stemming of the blood flow; we could come to an understanding of its nature and apply this understanding to the malady; and we could get a transfusion, exchanging the poisonous blood for the pure. Three possible remedies or models – *halting* (model 1); *seeing into* (model 2); *transforming* (model 3).

Model 1

The primary emphasis in Theravāda Buddhism is on abstention, halting, renunciation, or a turning away from the object of desire. We might also use words and phrases such as quelling, subduing, silencing, suppressing, or stemming the flow of desire before it becomes unstoppable, like quickly staunching a bleeding wound or plugging a leaking pipe. This would be the approach, in the example above of sexual attraction to a friend's partner, where it might be best to keep away from the person you have a fascination with. Or if you're a smartphone news junkie, locking your phone in a time-controlled safe for a while. Relieving oneself of the distraction

The idea of abstention is inherent in the ethical precepts which derive from the Pali Canon. As Buddhists we have a basic set of five ethical precepts or training principles which we try to adhere to. The actual words in Pali (which we chant as well) are translated as 'I undertake to *abstain* from...harming living beings.. taking the not-given.. sexual misconduct.. false speech.. intoxicants'. Abstaining is being abstinent, refraining from indulging our desires. We can liken this to the abstinence of a state of sobriety, a state of non-drunkenness, non-intoxication, a state of moderation, where we feel cleansed and see more clearly.

There are strong arguments in support of abstention and renunciation as means to overcome craving. When an object of desire is no longer available within one's reach, logically there is less temptation present. For instance, the Prohibition of alcohol in the USA from 1920 to 1933 led to a 'sharp decrease in the number of Americans consuming and becoming addicted to alcohol. Rates of public drunkenness and alcohol-related liver disease decreased by half during this period'.[209]

A vow of abstinence may be exactly what we need, an approach which requires will-power and resolve. It can help as well to get some extra support, from friends for example, or from courses such as the Twelve-step Programme or Eight Step Recovery in the case of really obsessive craving. The Theravāda approach of turning away from or letting go of the object of desire is, I find, especially helpful in the here and now, in the immediate situation, when tempted for instance to raid the fridge. Avoiding the shopping mall when in town, switching off our phone, not keeping biscuits at home – suppressing temptation - these are all practical methods that can work for us.

Model 2

Perhaps the most important contribution of the Mahāyāna to addressing craving is to do with how we perceive all phenomena. As we have seen with the characteristic of existence known as *anattā,* Buddhism refutes the view that there is something fixed and enduring that we can call 'me', that this 'me' has any substance.

How does this relate though to our craving? 'From the Mahayana perspective, if we really want to let go of grasping, clinging, and fixation, we have to develop some understanding of emptiness or insubstantiality. The notion of emptiness keeps us from attaching too much significance to our response to what we encounter on a daily basis.'[210] We shall explore *śūnyatā* (emptiness) further in Chapter 8, but just to say here that when we begin to develop the insight that, not only the things we crave for, but also indeed the cravings themselves have no real substance, their spell over us will weaken. We begin to see what we call 'reality' quite differently.

Model 3

Unskilful mental states such as craving may disappear temporarily, through observing their arising and 'catching' them before they do too much damage. But ultimately we need to deal with them in a more thorough, more transformative way. This is the approach of Tantric or Vajrayāna Buddhism, the way of the thunderbolt. It is sometimes seen as an offshoot or an extension of the Mahāyāna. Rather than considering desire a purely negative quality, Tantric Buddhism embraces desire as a valuable resource, encourages us to be in touch with our longings, and to harness our inner drives, incorporating and using the energy inherent in craving to bring about liberation.

In Tantric Buddhism there is an explicit recognition that there are not only unhelpful harmful desires but also helpful beneficial desires, such as wanting to be free of an addiction, or wanting all beings to be content and fulfilled. So there is an emphasis on changing negative passion into positive passion, using desire rather than being used by it. Tantric teachings employ the means of our entrapment to free us, by tuning in to our vitality and a sense of purpose. 'Instead of advocating separation from worldly pleasures the way many other traditions do,' writes Lama Thubten Yeshe, 'tantra emphasizes that it is much more effective for human beings to enjoy themselves and channel the energy of their enjoyments into a quick and powerful path to fulfillment and Enlightenment.'[211]

Extricating, explaining and expanding

Part Two of these writings then looks at these three paths - a path of renunciation in which sense attractions are halted, released or avoided; a path of insight in which sense desires are seen through as having no substance; and a path of transformation in which sense desires are seen as energies that can be made positive use of. [212] They will help us to bring wisdom into our lives, to see through the foggy workings of our confused mind, and to let go of, purify and transmute the cravings that can plague and haunt us. Finally we shall see that we can move away entirely from a self-centred, self-obsessed way of living.

Reflecting - Chapter 6

Do you feel a need for purpose and fulfilment in your life? Reflect upon life as a precious opportunity, using Vishvapani's phrases. Can you think of turning points or tipping points in your life when you knew that something needed to change? Do you think to yourself that your cravings are not harmful to you? Have you reached a point in your life where you feel you need to address unhelpful cravings? Is there a reason why now is not a good time to take action? What sort of person would you like to be? Do you ever say to yourself that you can't change, when what you mean is you don't want to change? Do you feel that following a spiritual path is escapism?

Chapter 7:

RELEASING

What does the word 'renunciation' conjure up in your mind? Ideas associated with the life of a nun or a monk? Terms like austerity, self-denial, deprivation, or self-imposed hardship? As we saw at the end of the previous chapter, renunciation is the determination to be free of the mundane desires that we experience in our everyday lives. We need to be careful though not to tag on to the word 'renunciation' the suggestion of punishment or self-flagellation.

The Buddha tried out these ascetic practices and they didn't work for him; in fact, his lifestyle became so austere at one point that he almost died, depriving himself of adequate food. Although he came to live a very simple disciplined life, he most certainly rejected austerity as a worthwhile practice. But what the Buddha did do was to reject the way of life he was born into, a way of life predicated on wealth, status and sensual pleasure. He said goodbye to all that when he left his richly comfortable home and surroundings to seek the truth, to try to find real fulfilment. He knew that the life of indulgence he had been leading could provide no enduring satisfaction. Eventually he promoted a Middle Way, of neither asceticism nor self-indulgence.

Turning away

Like the Buddha, we too can turn our back on dissatisfaction in our lives. 'What the development of true renunciation implies' writes Lama Thubten Yeshe, 'is that we no longer rely on sensory pleasures for our ultimate happiness; we see the futility of expecting deep satisfaction from such limited, transitory phenomena. It is important to understand this point clearly. Renunciation is not the same as giving up pleasure or denying ourselves happiness. It means giving up our unreal expectations about ordinary pleasures.'[213]

We can give up then some of the unhelpful ways in which we relate to the world. Renunciation doesn't mean a denial of all our sensory input.

It is only superficially that we are renouncing 'pleasurable' habits. What we are really renouncing is dissatisfaction, mental turmoil, compulsion. We are turning away from the dis-ease of *saṃsāra*, the habitual ways of behaving that restrict us from experiencing our most profound potential.

The thought of giving up our habitual tendencies may involve an element of fear. Fulfilling our desires has a certain comfort associated with it. Casting off our comfort blanket may leave us feeling naked and defenceless in the face of the onslaught of reality. Putting aside our smartphone may leave us feeling bereft, experiencing a sense of lack or loss, as though someone close to us is no longer with us, no longer there to support us, nobody to turn to.

Although renunciation may seem to imply loss, we can focus instead on the joy gained from the freedom which comes with rejecting our unhelpful habitual cravings. We read in the *Dhammapada*, 'It is wisdom that enables letting go of a lesser happiness in pursuit of a happiness which is greater'[214]. We can experience far greater enjoyment when we come to the conclusion that 'our ordinary pleasures are second rate. They are inconsequential when compared with the extraordinary bliss to be had from awakening the energies latent within us.'[215]

We let go of our old habits in order to welcome in a freer, fresher, purer way of behaving, one where we can confront any cravings that arise with equanimity, since we are developing the insights that see through their persistent and harmful nature. What could be more pleasing than that? If we suffer any withdrawal symptoms as a result of renunciation, these are nothing compared to, on the one hand, the pain that our habitual afflictions bring about and, on the other, the happiness of emerging freedom. The only caveat is that we should be careful about trying to give up the 'lesser' pleasures of life until we have had some taste of the 'greater' ones.

Guarding the gates

This chapter is based on Model 1 that I set out in the previous chapter. Let's now start looking at what 'renunciation' practices actually look like. One of the most straightforward practices that we find in the Theravāda model is known as 'guarding the gates of the senses.'[216] The most basic form of craving as we have seen is *kāma-taṇhā*, the craving for sensual gratification, the craving that we explored in Chapter 1. Guarding the gates of the senses is therefore a stopping of, or a turning away from, the particular sense impressions that we normally react to with the response of craving, avoiding those things that cause us to crave.

For example, we can look the other way when passing a bakery window full of sweet carb delights if we know we might be tempted to pop in and buy one. If our attention is drawn to the physical attributes of someone we are sexually attracted to, we can learn to avoid staring or glancing a second time. We can decide not to read the TV schedule for tonight because we have something more productive planned. Out of sight, out of mind. This is a matter of self-control, being alert to the risk of falling under the spell of an object of desire. 'Because our eyes, ears, nose, and so forth are the very gateways of desire,' writes Thubten Yeshe, 'those wishing to break free and achieve liberation from this circle of suffering are encouraged to become especially distrustful of the five physical senses. These are to be recognized as exerting an unhealthy control over the mind and must be treated with the utmost caution'[217] Vigilance therefore is required so that sensory input does not overwhelm us.

Another strategy for developing abstention from craving is to focus on the negative aspects of an object of desire, those aspects of the object that will diminish our longing for it. There is a practice, *aśubha-bhāvana*, the contemplation of the unbeautiful, which typically was employed by monastics to curb sexual longing by concentrating on the impurity of the human body. You can see the idea, to put one off the allure of, and obsessing about, the glamour of the human body. We can however counter our longing for an attractive person by seeing them as a real human being like ourselves, in all their wholeness, with all their wishes and hopes, rather than just a vision of seductive body parts. We can also use the principle of *aśubha-bhāvana* to undermine the attraction of objects which have a hold on us; for example, eating meat (the dead flesh of a baby animal), a shot or two of vodka (alcohol that poisons us), donuts (heaps of white refined sugar), a nice new shirt (a load of dyed threads put together in a sweatshop by an exploited worker). Something very attractive and appealing suddenly becomes something not so nice.

It is shortish step from turning away from objects of desire to avoiding the places, people and situations which provoke craving and which thereby perturb the mind. There is a term *viveka* which refers to the physical detachment or seclusion from the distractions of the world. Since time immemorial hermits have withdrawn themselves from the temptations of peopled places, and of course monks and nuns in many spiritual traditions including Buddhism; although one can also see monasticism as not so much 'retiring from the world but rather, taking time out to a degree so that one can engage in self-reflection and have a better understanding of oneself and the world.'[218]

Clearly, *viveka* of this kind is one response to the many attractions of *saṃsāra*. Although most of us however choose not to follow this way of life, we can make the decision to avoid in our own way those places, people and situations which elicit our cravings, whether it be not going down the pub, hanging around shopping centres, or deciding who to socialise with. There is an interesting passage in the Pāli Canon in this context, the parable of a deer wandering in the forest wilds, out of the hunter's range and secluded from sensual pleasures. The deer is said to have blindfolded Māra, to have become invisible to him, depriving Māra of his opportunity to tempt it and lead it astray.[219]

As part of our practice, most Buddhists like myself spend some time on retreat, either a solitary retreat, or a study or meditation retreat with others. This is not fearfully running away from the world, but rather an opportunity to practise *viveka*, seclusion albeit temporary from *saṃsāra*, with the purpose of reducing distractions and deepening our practice.

A simpler way of living

We all have to make our own lifestyle choices but, if we are serious about addressing our cravings, then a simpler lifestyle based on gradually giving up those things which we are habitually attached to will make our path easier. Subhuti writes, 'it is at least possible to live in the midst of possessions and people and position with complete freedom from attachment....since the issue finally is within the mind. However, the less one renounces the more one will have to work to overcome one's attachments whilst immersed in their objects – which is not at all easy to do. Unless one has more or less decisively broken that self-attachment, anything but a life of progressive renunciation will simply tend to deepen it.'[220]

When I'm on a solitary retreat and left to my own devices (and not electronic ones), for the first day or two I usually experience the need for distraction, the desire to fill the mental space. After a while I can let that desire go. I have found a calmer more focussed state of mind which I have gradually relaxed into, and which is far more agreeable than a mind that constantly goes a-wandering. I have arrived at an attitude where I don't need, and actually don't want, to be searching for some sort of buzz, whether of a major or minor key.

We overfeed the mind by stuffing it full of input, especially electronic. What we need to do however is let the mind fast from time to time. The fasting of the mind can bring about great peace and mending, freeing it from constant longing for fake nourishment. Taking time out and doing nothing in particular. Doing less, realising more. There is a Buddhist meditation practice, Just Sitting, where we do just that, settle down, sit and watch. Watch sensations, emotions, thoughts come and go, not trying too hard. Spacious and still. No goal, no strain. In meditation generally we can also release what the mind fabricates, the stories which emanate from our fears and longings, the mental proliferation that just turns up uninvited.

Unfastening

There is nothing wrong with wanting pleasure in our lives, it's our clinging attitude to the pleasure that's the problem. And what we need to do is release that clinging to perceived but illusory comforters, and also our clinging to outcomes. We all need enjoyment, but enjoyment without clinging. We can enjoy things without wanting to hold onto them; for example, a rainbow is beautiful but we know it will pass. If we feel we are superglued to our habit of watching reality TV, if we feel tension when we longingly contemplate a Coke, we can start to feel less sticky or tight by learning to relate to these objects of desire in a different way. We can learn to step back and hold these tendencies more lightly, and not allow ourselves to chase after them, or seek them out. We can learn to let them go, 'When a *bhikkhu* has heard that nothing is worth adhering to, he directly knows everything….when he does not cling, he is not agitated.'[221]

In a new romantic relationship we feel a very strong passion for the other. But in a longer-term relationship, we don't necessarily feel shaken up by it, in the sense that we are now at ease with our love, it is a calm love, less needy, rather than a restless, dazzling, intense, unsettling emotion which seeks affirmation all the time, as it is perhaps in the early stages of a relationship. In Buddhist terminology we might say that the clinging has lessened; it is accepting, and it allows. It is not obsessed. It is not compulsive.

We cannot be strong and free if we are dependent on something outside of ourselves which, by its impermanent inconsistent nature, cannot be relied upon. Dependence and attachment mean fixation and inflexibility, and these are not helpful strategies to lead our lives by. But we can let the clinging that normally warps our experience fall away, 'like a drop of water on a lotus leaf, or a mustard seed on the point of an awl.'[222]

Imagine walking along a hot dusty road for what seems like forever, carrying a very heavy suitcase that you can barely keep off the dirty ground. In it is just stuff, stuff that you've accumulated over the years and that you just can't give up. It's a real weighty load that you're carting around, and it's clearly having an effect on your well-being. Really you're sick and tired of it but you still carry on carrying it along. And then a person appears by your side, travelling the road in the same direction, at ease and unencumbered. And they ask in a kind and gentle manner whether you really need to be carrying this load. And somehow you trust them, and you feel able to let go of the baggage and allow it to fall the ground. The relief, the release is immense. 'The suspension of pain, a letting go of clinging' says Subhuti, 'is the dawning of a state that is described as *paranaṃ sukhaṃ,* the highest happiness, the highest bliss.'[223]

Or remember that wonderful priceless feeling of letting go, perhaps on a warm sunny day in spring, closing your eyes, feeling the sun seep in, feeling whole, at one, uplifted. The relief that comes from a deep outbreath. The relief which alleviates. A catharsis that resembles but goes beyond any sexual release. A shedding. A shaking off of a prickly skin. The emerging of a chrysalis which is the true 'me', pure of taints. Take a moment to reflect, it's clear that totally at ease is the way to lead our life. At ease in any situation that arises, free of tensions.

Letting go is something you can do throughout the day. Feel those urges physically draining away from you. 'Breath by breath,' suggests Lama Surya Das, 'let go of fear, expectation, anger, regret, cravings, frustration, fatigue. Let go of the need for approval. Let go of old judgments and opinions. Die to all that, and fly free. Soar in the freedom of desirelessness. Let go. Let Be. See through everything and be free, complete, luminous, at home -- at ease.'[224] We can develop the ability to disengage from our unhelpful feelings and impulses. We have the ability to detach ourselves from the shackles that prevent us from meeting our real potential, from being the best that we possibly can be.

When we let go of one thing though, we can end up clinging on to something else. This may be fine, at least to start with, if the latter thing is less harmful than the former. So giving up a habit of drinking beer and then to take on the habit of drinking non-alcoholic beer may be a move in the right direction, as it will cloud the mind less. In the search for solutions though, we can get obsessed and fixated on an antidote to our unhealthy craving habit, developing a new unhelpful habitual pattern. For instance, countering the desire to smoke tobacco by sucking sweets; or avoiding acquaintances who regularly go boozing by avoiding socialising altogether. We need to hold any helpful strategy adeptly, not clinging to the idea that it will necessarily solve all our problems. Beware any type of compulsive thinking.

The Buddha told the parable of a raft,[225] the raft of the *dharma,* which we can hold onto on our spiritual journey while we navigate the rough sea of *saṃsāra,* the deep ocean of *dukkha,* ensuring that we don't drop off and drown; however upon reaching safe dry land we don't need to continue carrying the raft around with us. Any teaching can be useful, but we will need to avoid clinging to it forever. Crutches to support us are handy when we can't step out confidently, but to be totally dependent upon them as we go forward will handicap our progress.

Letting go of views

Some of us need to know how to fix everything, but the fact is that we can't. 'Letting there be room for not knowing' writes Pema Chödrön, 'is the most important thing of all. When there's a big disappointment, we don't know if that's the end of the story. It may just be the beginning of a great adventure. Life is like that. We don't know anything. We call something bad; we call it good. But really we just don't know.'[226]

We all have views about what is, and what is not, possible. Views and opinions come and go. We can easily see in our own lives how our views have changed over the years, even though they may have seemed at the time written in stone, unshakeable. I used to believe that violent revolution was what the world needed. I don't anymore. Maybe it's better to be an agnostic, in the general sense of 'I don't know' or 'I don't have an opinion on this', rather than be a sceptic or blinkered believer.

Amongst the unhelpful views that we hold onto are the labels that we apply to phenomena and, markedly, to ourselves. As we saw in Chapter 5, we attach to having an identity, something that we can call 'me', and we assign to that identity attributes which we feel define us and concretize us, but which often just restrict our potential and enslave us. These are labels which we give ourselves, and with which we label others similarly. Labels such as 'hopeless case', 'power-driven go-getter', or 'incorrigible cake-eater'

But these labels are only part of our story. We are much more than just a few words; nobody can just be summed up so straightforwardly. These are all identities that are at the most very partial, identities that we can do without, that we can cast off. Buddhists call the labels that we attach to ourselves 'wrong views'. They arise out of delusion about what we truly are. Don't limit yourself, you are worth much more.

It's not worth putting too much value on our views and opinions, it's not worth holding onto them tightly. They may change next month anyway, in the light of new experiences, new information, new connections. Can we really be sure what the truth is about anything in this world, 'truths' on which we base our views? We are capable of holding our views lightly therefore, being ready and open to modify them or discard them. We may even need to let go of everything we've ever believed in to be really free of our confusion, greed and ill-will. Some Zen advice from Shunryu Suzuki, 'The best way to find perfect composure is to forget everything.'[227]

One view we hold is around our expectations of security. We looked in Chapter 5 at how we grasp after security in an insecure world. But insecurity is the nature of the lives we lead all the time. We never know what's round the corner, whether we will fall ill soon, have a serious accident, the moment when we will die. Expecting permanent security in our lives is like hoping that that lovely long summer's day will never come to an end. We have to let go of this clinging onto certainty, in the same way that we have to let go of that summer's day.

Financial security may give us a sense of comfort in this unsure world, but it can only temper, it cannot put off, old age, sickness and death. Releasing can also mean relaxing into our own mortality, releasing our fear of death. There's no point railing against what occurs naturally. We cannot turn back the tide. So let's grow old gracefully, with dignity. Looking back on our lives we may feel haunted by what we have done in the past as a result of our uncontrolled urges. We can of course, and need to, learn from our past, but what is gone is gone, and it is pointless dwelling on our past mistakes if they only bring us pain and not wisdom. Instead focus on the positive, "May I see the good in myself, deep down

I am a good person, I am capable of acts of kindness and generosity, may I cherish and care for myself."

At some stage we will need to let go of even the things that we love. Parents will have to do this when their children leave home. You unattach but you do not stop loving, or stop caring. Parents need to provide space and let go of their children in order for them to flourish, however hard this may be. The same applies at the end of a relationship between two people.

Accepting life as it is

If we are determined to totally rid ourselves of our cravings, or are determined to avoid all things that cause us to crave, then we are likely to fail. A corollary of letting go is accepting this, acknowledging that life has its ups and downs, that we humans are flawed beings with all our urges and longings, that we are bound to experience discomfort in our lives. We are not sinners. Rather, as Buddhism points out, we are imperfect human beings who do not see clearly, and who sometimes act in unhelpful and harmful ways as a result of our conditioning, both external and self-induced.

Absolute perfection is very difficult to achieve. Better to change our relationship to our cravings; this we *can* accomplish. We can accept that we are not perfect, and then proceed to wanting to transform negatives into positives. Achieving little victories in our battle with craving will keep us going, keep us motivated to carry on, give us faith and confidence in what we are practising.

We may long to keep a brand-new car in pristine condition, only to get it scratched within the first week of getting it. This happened to me some time ago, but I managed to accept that stuff happens, and it was not too difficult to let go of attachment to an unscathed piece of metal; I did not sink into waves of guilt, resentment and disappointment. A cup of tea does not make you happy forever, as you realize the pleasure it gives you is only so much. So you are not devastated when you get to the bottom of the cup. 'And if we experience something pleasant we accept it comfortably, taking what enjoyment it has to give without demanding or expecting anything more from it.'[228]

We have to accept in life the clarity and the clouds, the soothing and the itching, the energy and the fatigue, the good days and the bad, the absorbing meditations and the distracted ones. We will have setbacks, what those recovering from substance abuse call relapses. We won't always be able to understand why it happens like this. But we can take the long view and try not to be shaken about too much by the daily changes in how we are, in how we experience life. We live, therefore we act, therefore we err. We pick ourselves up, brush ourselves off, and start all over again.

As Sangharakshita says, 'instinctual urges and old tendencies may emerge from time to time and result in a temporary setback in our overall spiritual progress and there is no point in getting caught up in self-recrimination.'[229] As we saw in Chapter 4, we have a 'dark side' to our character. This may include uncomfortable sexual or aggressive impulses. We need to understand these tendencies in ourselves and make the decision not to let them dominate our behaviour. Accepting and acknowledging is a better strategy than resisting or suppressing.

The vicissitudes of life are like ocean waves, some greater, some smaller. We can respond to the waves by building walls with the resources we have, to try to provide security from getting wet or being drowned; and we can hope that the waves won't come back again. Or we can try to ride the waves, to surf them, to accept that they are always there. The ACT (Acceptance and Commitment Therapy) practitioner Russ Harris writes about 'urge surfing'; 'we can treat our urges like waves and "surf" them until they dissipate.'[230] This sounds like a very Buddhist practice to me.

So life cannot always be how we want it to be. Uncomfortable feelings are endemic to what we are. In fact, we have to recognize that pain is part and parcel of living, since it goes hand in hand with the fact that we are cravers. These are the 'slings and arrows' of our fortune. Pain is inevitable in our lives. Suffering however is not; or, at the very least, it's optional. This is the teaching that Buddhists call 'the second arrow.' In the *Sallatha Sutta* we read, 'When touched with a feeling of pain, the uninstructed run-of-the-mill person sorrows, grieves, & laments, beats his breast, becomes distraught. So he feels two pains, physical & mental. Just as if they were to shoot a man with an arrow and, right afterward, were to shoot him with another one, so that he would feel the pains of two arrows; in the same way, when touched with a feeling of pain, the uninstructed run-of-the-mill person sorrows, grieves, & laments, beats his breast, becomes distraught. So he feels two pains, physical & mental.'[231]

Essentially then, we cannot avoid the pain that comes from 'the first arrow', but 'the second arrow' is our mental reaction to the first, which we do have control over. We may carry on replaying what has happened to us and by so doing add, and dwell in, the extra suffering of resentment, bitterness and anger.

For example, the bus you're on breaks down on the way to work. Your mind starts constructing a story: "I'm going to be late. I've already been late this week. My boss will be mad at me for missing the meeting. She probably thinks I don't care about the job. She's looking to make economies. I'll probably get the sack. I'll get a terrible reference. Oh, God!" This is the second arrow. You can't escape the initial pain of the bus breaking down, but you don't have to double it, as here. Mindfulness-based approaches to physical pain reduction and management are based on this idea, developing the ability to distinguish between objective sensory pain and the subjective judgement which we attach to it and which fashions how we experience the pain.

We have a choice about how to react to every situation, one of which is to just accept and sit with our discomfort, to allow whatever comes up to just come up. Rather than trying to bury our discomfort in action, we may need to give it the opportunity to arise, to be recognised, and to be embraced. We will look more below at the choices we have when we explore the alternative to a 'reactive mind'.

Accepting can also imply forgiving, not just forgiving other people for whatever perceived wrongs they have committed, against us or others. We have to learn to forgive ourselves for whatever errors we make. Forgiving is a releasing, and there is no action that we cannot pardon ourselves for. We can separate the 'me' of then, and the 'me' of now. The person who did those things is not me. That person is not the person I am now. This person might make new mistakes, but this person will not do what the old person did. Why carry around a burden of bitterness and pain when there is no need to? Blaming does not resolve anything, nor lead to ease and contentment. Perhaps the most important piece of forgiving that can take place is to forgive oneself. Forgiveness is a great healer. If we cannot forgive, we cannot be at ease.

A sense of lightness

You can take your own precious self and its longings far too seriously. We looked at this briefly at the end of Chapter 4. Alongside releasing and acceptance is the notion of 'play', in Buddhism *līlā*. You don't have to be so earnest about your compulsions, you can smile at them, and realize how inane they are. Is it really worth getting so hot under the collar about an unrealizable fantasy concerning an attractive Hollywood star? When you begin to let go and see through the stupidity of being tied to those disturbing emotions, the *kleśa*, you can't help but smile. Or maybe even feel a chuckle coming on. How can we be so daft as to be dictated to by a colourful object made of sugar and flour dressed up in a fancy way? This is reminiscent of Carl Jung's playful Trickster archetype who, by playing jokes and exposing our vulnerabilities, keeps our ego in check, stopping us from taking ourselves and our longings too seriously.

Hold your craving lightly and be prepared to laugh at yourself for your silly ways. Judson Brewer brings out this idea of letting go into playfulness, rather than battling with an object of desire; 'we can relax into an attitude that is more like a dance with the object, simply being with it as the situation unfolds, no striving or struggling necessary, as we get out of our own way and rest in an awareness of what is happening moment to moment.'[232]

As well as a sense of lightness, you can bring kindness to your longing and clinging. As Subhuti suggests, you can burst the bubble of grasping by regarding it 'with gentle irony and tender solicitude…. a *loving* approach to your own foolishness… A kind of gentleness and empathy.'[233] Why am I so obsessed in getting one up on an acquaintance who challenged my opinion, who put me on the defensive? What am I defending?[234] You can bring caring and loving kind attention, *mettā,* to these urges, give your painful craving an unconditional imaginary hug, for as long as and as many times as it takes to dissolve. Bringing *mettā* to our pain is such a wonderful and effective practice.

Cultivating contentment

With acceptance and releasing comes contentment and, eventually, equanimity – evenness of mind, and calmness in difficult situations. If letting go might seem a more passive act, then contentment is a quality that we can cultivate, an active, volitional, positive act. If the principal aspect of craving is wanting what you don't have, then contentment is being happy with what you do have. Happy, as well as grateful.

Contentment is thus the simple Buddhist antidote to unwholesome craving. This is easy to say, but harder to achieve, and so we can think of degrees of contentment, or relative contentment. Complete equanimity in the face of every adversity is the ultimate form of contentment. To my mind, the happiness which all humans seek is a combination of contentment and fulfilment. True happiness does not mean longing for excitement.

We probably all have experienced a degree of contentment at some time. For me, when I am content I can feel a real release - when I swim almost effortlessly outside, when I lay on my back and look up at the clouds drifting across the sky, or when I sit in harmony with a loved one. I do not experience any craving in these situations. When I think about contentment I feel warm and uplifted, sometimes even a serenity.

When you are no longer so full of yourself and your own preoccupations, you can at last chill out. You can be at ease with any cravings which may arise. The subject – you - is calmed when the object of craving ceases to exist as an object of craving. The object of craving ceases to exist as an object of craving when you, the subject, are calmed. It is through the relationship between the two that you have made peace with your craving.

With contentment there is no restlessness and boredom. One way of *experiencing* this contentment is to follow through the longing for something external which we think will make us happier – perhaps a big house, a change of job, a long holiday, a new phone – and then we can work our way through the shortcomings of that desire. Will these things really bring about a change in our state of mind? The perceived satisfaction and fulfilment that we thought they would bring is illusory. We can be happier where we are and with what we have right now. Realizing the shortcomings of longing and grasping for 'things' in our consumerist societies goes against the grain of how we are encouraged to behave. 'Learning to cultivate and acknowledge your own contentment' writes Diana Winston,' is a revolutionary act in these times.'[235]

We may not be able to do a lot about changing the weather, putting off old age, trying to enlighten unscrupulous politicians, transforming the fortunes of our favourite team, or being stuck in a traffic jam. But what we can do is to manage our responses to these phenomena. We can develop some equanimity and not get all worked up by them. This is the attitude of the loosening of preferences in our daily life. Having no preferences doesn't mean that we are passive in the face of whatever decisions we have to make. For instance, it's no good if you're planning a holiday with others and nobody has any preference about where to go. What it does mean however is not clinging doggedly to a particular point of view, but being tolerant and flexible, holding onto opinions lightly, letting go of unhelpful emotions, and deflecting the second arrow.

Flexibility, rather than a tight grasping onto the idea that there is only one way of doing something, links Buddhism once again with psychological therapies. 'Albert Ellis, founder of the first school of cognitive behaviour therapy and still the most widely cited CBT theorist', writes Josef Mattes, 'also seems to have seen inflexibility stemming from the belief that one must do certain things or that the world has to be a certain way – inner compulsion, or, in his somewhat colourful language "musturbation" – as the central impediment to a flourishing life. I happen to believe that this "musturbation" is the cause both of individual *dukkha* and of various problems at the societal and global levels, like religious and political fanaticism. It is what ties us, and what the *Dhamma* can liberate us from.' [236] The Buddha's *dharma* or *dhamma,* tell us that we need to see through and give up the inflexible attachment and compulsion of 'musturbation' in order to be free and to live in harmony with one another.

Ultimately, with much practice, we will be able to experience both sensual pleasure and sensual pain with equanimity, without excitement or disturbance. Free of clinging, we will be able to deal with difficulties that come along with a calm mind, without becoming overwhelmed. True equanimity cannot easily be rocked off course by the arising of a source of sensual attraction. Why would one want to compromise this wonderful calmness and sense of purity for a cheap thrill, a short-lived indulgence? Like the singer Carole King, we can ask ourselves, 'Is this a lasting treasure, or just a moment's pleasure?'[237] With equanimity comes a certain sense of dignity, of knowing that we are doing the right thing, of being comfortable with ourselves and the world around us.

With mindfulness, clear and radiant

What practice is it that allows Buddhists to step back, let go, acknowledge, accept and be conscious of their own reactions? In the Judson Brewer quote above, we 'get out of our own way and rest in an awareness of what is happening moment to moment'. This is *mindfulness*. The practice of mindfulness is a key element of Buddhist practice - cultivated through meditation - which permeates our actions of body, speech and mind throughout the day. None of the strategies outlined in these writings can be successful without the practice of some form of mindfulness.

This is how it is put in the Pāli Canon: 'In every direction, said Ajita, 'the rivers of desire are running. How can we dam them and what will hold them back? What can we use to close the flood-gates?' 'Any river can be stopped with the dam of mindfulness', said the Buddha, "I call it the flood-stopper. And with wisdom you can close the flood-gates."[238] The *Bodhicaryāvatāra* describes poetically how vital mindfulness is: 'Rutting elephants roaming wild do not cause as much devastation in this world as the roaming elephant, the mind let free... But if the roaming elephant, the mind, is tethered on every side by the cord of mindfulness, every danger subsides, complete prosperity ensues.'[239]

If indulging one's craving is like an action performed half-asleep, then mindfulness is being fully awake. What we decide to do with our attention is our choice – a mindful mind or a lazy, indulgent mind. Mindfulness is wise attention, 'just being with things as they are, accepting, paying attention to, opening to, without wanting to change, without being interested so much in that discrepancy between how I would like things to be and what is.'[240]

Mindfulness is not just about paying attention. It is very difficult to pay attention to something for long, for example, the breath as we do in meditation, unless we find it interesting. Bird song, say, might be more engaging and thus easier to pay attention to than the roar of traffic. A Tibetan word for meditation, *gom*, means to become familiar or intimate with. In order to develop interest, we first need to develop a curious mind. We allow ourselves to become curious, and interest arises. When interest arises we can find joy in the simplest things. With joy comes contentment. With contentment comes ease. With ease comes equanimity.

We need to be like intelligent fish – we may be attracted to the bait, whether it be digital 'clickbait' or other lures and enticements, but we have to remind ourselves what the consequences are of being hooked. Perhaps we can think of Māra as the Great Angler, intent on reeling us in. We however, clever creatures that we are, can just observe the bait on the hook, and swim blithely by. We will feed on what will nourish us without becoming hooked. We will develop into wiser beings. We get an inkling of wisdom by responding differently to our normal urges. Sometimes we may find ourselves in a conversation, dying to say something, barely able to hold back, itching to interrupt the other. What would it be like, what would be the difference, if we just remained silent instead? Could it be a wiser response?

We can ask questions of ourselves to examine our reactions. Better though to ask not *why* questions, but *how*. *How* do I experience this craving for excitement? *How* does it feel in my body? *How* can I respond creatively? 'How' questions are usually more helpful. Sometimes we have a tendency to want to know about the origins of things, but that doesn't necessarily improve matters. Paraphrasing the Buddha, spending time pondering *why* we are here on earth doesn't sort out *how* we are going to save this planet from extinction. Or, to put it more mundanely, puzzling why I am addicted to chocolate can be less helpful a question than how am I going to put an end to my compulsion.

We can however develop an awareness of how conditions trigger a particular craving. It may be tiredness, illness, boredom, fear of criticism of something we've done or not done, socializing with strangers, arguments with a loved one, or stress at work. What are the situations in which you are most at risk of indulging your cravings? Developing awareness of how our habitual mind works is key in tackling our unhelpful longings.

A foot on the brake

The most useful way in which we can use mindfulness to address craving is in the way we respond to a sensory stimulus; we began to look at this in the section on *vedanā* in Chapter 2. [241] As we have seen, Buddhism teaches us that it is not the fault of our objects of craving that we suffer; don't blame the bottle of booze, the internet, the beautiful person in front of you or in your dreams, the taste of chocolate, the poster of the tropical beach. Instead it is how we respond to these objects.

We can respond reactively, let's say automatically and blindly, which is how we are conditioned to act, conditioned by our genes and all the conditions in our life which have brought us to where we are now. Or we can respond in a more creative manner, in a freer, more flexible manner, giving ourselves the space to see more wisely, disengaging from the object, to understand what is happening in our mind if we indulge our desires.

It is blind reactivity then which is the real villain of the piece, giving in unthinkingly to immediate gratification. With mindfulness we can be in touch with what we are really feeling, so that our unhelpful habitual behaviour does not lead us astray. We can acknowledge what is going on in our mind (and, most certainly, in our body) when an urge arises to grab out for something, an urge to soothe, excite, or annihilate. Rather than being hooked on the object of desire, we can focus instead on the process of desiring and clinging.

This is all about creating a 'gap'. The mindful strategy that we are practising here, in Buddhist terms, is interrupting the link between *vedanā* and *taṇhā*, between the sensory sensation that arises from contact with an object, and our chosen response of craving for and clinging to that object.[242] And in order to do that we need to stop, put a brake on, and create a space for ourselves in this process. We need to bring about a hiatus, to separate the pleasant or unpleasant sensation from the grasping for it. What we can learn to do is to make room in order to see the craving arise, and then let it dissolve in the 'gap'. We can learn to watch the arising of a craving calmly, but not indulge it. The desire appears perhaps to eat that brownie; we make space for it, we are aware of the desire but we do not follow it, get dragged along by it. We observe, and it drops away.[243]

At first, trying to catch what we are feeling may be like trying to catch a mosquito that is zooming around all over the place. But with patience, stillness and attention we can catch the desire before it stings us. We can catch our cravings early before they have had time to bed in their toxin. Through the practice of catching a craving before it takes hold of us, we make room to ask questions such as "'What is my real desire here? What is it I really want? How much am I enjoying this? What will be the effect if I indulge?"

Some compulsive yearnings are extremely painful, and 'how we respond or react to the pain', write Valerie Mason-John and Paramabandhu, 'will exacerbate or diminish our suffering. Some of us have developed addictions because of pain and physical suffering. Others have become meditators and/or Buddhists because of physical pain.'[244] Relating differently to our longings and urges can change our lives. Mindfulness is bringing our attention to something and, wherever we bring our attention, there energy gathers and change can occur.

The more we are able to do this, like anything we practice, the easier it becomes next time the craving turns up. We can tolerate the desire and trust in its inevitable passing. From these choices, from these more creative, less autopilot, less lazy decisions, our unhelpful habits gradually will change into healthier ones.

I like what Ruben L.F. Habito calls replacing the 'acquisitive mode' with the 'contemplative mode.'[245] This is similar to what Sangharakshita calls replacing the 'reactive mind' with the 'creative mind.'[246] We observe the process of how the mind obsesses. Instead of instant pleasure, we delay gratification to the extent that we allow time and space for the desire for the gratification of instant pleasure to evaporate; we allow ourselves not to make snap decisions.

We can make room to introduce a word or phrase for support; perhaps "I acknowledge this…this is just craving…. this will pass". We can repeat the words for the object of craving, "jam doughnut, jam doughnut, jam doughnut…", until that word becomes nonsense and the object loses its power and its grip on us. It is as though the *vedanā* of the jam doughnut has changed from pleasant to neutral, or possibly even unpleasant. We can learn to disassociate from the pull of our cravings with affirmations, like this one from Mason-John and Paramabandhu, constantly reminding ourselves that nothing lasts forever:

This is a moment of craving
Craving is energy arising and ceasing
I don't have to identify with this energy
I trust the sensation of craving will pass.[247]

Mindfulness teaches us that we do not need to negate or suppress a craving. 'Letting go of a craving' writes Stephen Batchelor, 'is not rejecting it but allowing it to be itself: a contingent state of mind that once arisen will pass away. Instead of forcibly freeing ourselves from it, notice how its very nature is to free itself. To let it go is like releasing a snake that you have been clutching in your hand. By identifying with a craving ('I want this," don't want' that"), you tighten the clutch and intensify its resistance. Instead of being a state of mind that you have, it becomes a compulsion that has you.'[248] In the following chapter we will look more at how we tend to identify with cravings as 'me' and 'mine'.

The wisdom that comes from mindfulness practice, and mindful behaviour generally can be seen as a more effective method of addressing compulsive longing than will-power or self-restraint. If we look at the example of over-eating, the Buddha did not suggest cultivating an aversion to food or fighting against the compulsion. In the story of King Pasenadi of Kosala in the Pāli Canon we read that the King experiences a great discomfort due to over-eating.[249] The Buddha's advice to him is 'When a person is constantly mindful, and knows when enough food has been taken, all their afflictions become more slender'. Afflictions become slender and the body also it seems; as a result of this mindful eating King Pasenadi, undoubtedly savouring each mouthful, ceased his over-indulging. When we eat with mindfulness as to what is coming into our body, we don't usually want second helpings.

In summary then, mindful strategies for addressing craving are based upon: recognizing the arising of the urge; allowing a space around it; relaxing into and accepting the experience; observing the process of craving in the mind; realising that you don't need to react to it; and allowing it to dissolve. When we explore cravings within us in this way, really explore their nature, what they feel like, the tightness they engender, we can increasingly ease that tightness, relax that tension. The itching will fade, and our wounds will gradually heal.

One of the most well-known Buddhist texts is the *Satipaṭṭhāna Sutta*,[250] usually translated as the Discourse on the Foundations of Mindfulness or the Discourse on the Establishing of Mindfulness. In the *sutta*, four types of mindfulness are set out – of the body (*kāyā*), of feeling, sensations (*vedanā*), of mind, consciousness (*cittā*), and of elements of the Buddha's teachings (*dhamma*).[251]

I want to focus for a moment on mindfulness of the body. By observing the immediate physiological effects of craving as soon as it arises, we can avoid telling ourselves stories about our desirings, we can avoid *prapañca* - constructing conceptual justifications, or explanations like the story above about the bus braking down. Being aware of what is going on in the body brings us back to what is going on in the here and now, noticing our reactions and addressing them while they are taking place, before they spin off and work themselves through. Notice your heart beating faster, an adrenaline rush, a throbbing in your temples, what is happening in the pit of your stomach, the raw experience; really *feel* it and you will reach a point where it disintegrates. The body is purely somatic, it cannot grasp. Grasping and craving are *prapañca*.

The mind absorbed

If clinging is what causes discomfort, then logically letting go of clinging results in the letting go of discomfort. In a way it's as simple as that. And there is something very beautiful and appealing about that simplicity. We can experience this directly when we meditate. Often we begin a meditation with a 'body scan' in which we mindfully get in touch with the sensations of our body and our emotions, how we are feeling right now. We may take a few deep breaths, letting go of tightness, loosening muscles, softening internally, allowing our shoulders to drop, releasing pent-up feelings, dispersing discomfort by bringing attention to the place where the discomfort resides, freeing ourselves of the need to chase after things and ideas such as "There is something I have to do". By so doing we also train our attention, refine our awareness.

One category of Buddhist meditation is called *samatha* or 'calming' meditation. Thich Nhat Hanh[252] describes the several aspects to *samatha* meditation – stopping, calming, resting and healing. *Stopping* our thinking, our habit energies, the strong emotions that rule us; *calming* the emotions in our body and mind, becoming solid and stable as an oak tree; or, alternatively, *coming to rest* like a pebble sinking slowly onto a soft sandy riverbed, allowing the water around us to just pass us by; and then comes the *healing*, for which the other aspects are preconditions, the healing which we as individuals, communities and nations so desperately need.

Trying to 'catch' the urge to indulge our desire is difficult without a meditation practice. Meditation is the principal way in which we develop mindfulness. In meditation we practice mindfulness as above, and then we are able to take it out into our life away from the meditation cushion. 'In Buddhism the goal of meditation' writes Traleg Kyabgon, 'is to stabilize the mind.'[253] Stabilising the mind is a process of calming and releasing our 'monkey-mind.'[254] It is not so much the object of desire that we reach out for which is the issue, but rather the way we attach to it. It is this underlying attachment which we need to be mindful of all the time, by acknowledging how we grasp at those objects we desire. Meditation practice to develop mindfulness in our daily lives is crucial to this.

I do not propose to describe the different methods of meditation in these writings; these are amply explained elsewhere[255]. But the importance of meditation in quieting and purifying the mind is paramount in Buddhist practice. When we sit down to meditate we resolve, whether explicitly or not, to sit with whatever restlessness we may be experiencing. Whatever cravings may arise, through the senses, we try to observe and allow them to dissipate. Restlessness and sensual desire, together with aversion, apathy and laziness, and doubt and indecision, are known in Buddhism as the Five Hindrances – hindrances to meditation, but also hindrances to awareness in our daily lives. We become increasingly aware of these in our practice and learn how to relate to them.[256]

We may sit meditating for half an hour or longer. During this time, we practise not to indulge emotions like craving, which can plague our non-meditating moments during the course of the day. What this shows is that, despite the fact that we feel sometimes that we cannot do without, for example, our smartphone, our rant at our boss, a cigarette, a desire to dominate, self-referencing, we can actually do without all these urges for a significant amount of time when meditating.

Given the right conditions then, we can get used to being with difficult emotions for lengthy periods. We are able to 'renounce' anything which is not helpful to us. The more often we do this, the easier it gets. Next time you feel like a rant, a digital fix, burying your head in the sand, just sit with that desire for as long as you can, and observe it eventually subside.

In meditation we can learn to just 'be' and not 'do' anything. We can find this incredibly rich and calming. Less can be more. Seemingly doing nothing much, in reality transforming our habitual modes of responding. In the busy lives that we lead, the space that we can give to ourselves in meditation is so valuable. If we are really pushed, we can usually find time to allow ourselves a 'three-minute breathing space', where we become aware of our body, thoughts and feelings; gather our attention around the breath; and expand our awareness through all of our senses.[257]

We do really need to give space for our whole psycho-physical being to slow down. To pause and take a break. To allow our compulsions to emerge fully in that spaciousness and be seen and experienced. And to breathe out and let them drift away. Often. Regularly. This is what happens when we meditate, particularly in the mindfulness of breathing meditation. We can breathe out and let go and, when we focus on the breath, we are present in the here and now where compulsions have no space to exist.

Absorbed in the present, there is no craving, neither is there ill-well, nor self-referencing. There is only 'this'. The rest is just sensory experience which comes and goes. When we are absorbed in what we are doing right now, *dukkha* has no dominion.

This is the absorption that Ian McEwan's character Roland experiences, 'He was on his knees, scrubbing the sides of the bath when he paused at a sudden thought – he was oddly content, thinking of nothing but the next task, lost in the present, delivered from intro- and retrospection.'[258]

Whether we're scrubbing, meditating, ambulating, masticating, urinating, defecating or participating in anything, we can bring our energies mindfully to the present moment. Dwelling mindfully in the present moment, resting in pure awareness, we experience the wonder of no craving, no aversion. 'Let there be nothing behind you; leave the future to one side. Do not clutch at what is left in the middle.'[259]

Going further

In this chapter we have looked at how 'renunciation' does not mean leading a life of austerity and deprivation, although to address our cravings we may need to make changes towards a simpler lifestyle, with less busyness, less external input, turning away from clinging to things that cause us dissatisfaction. We have looked at how we can let go of our habitual urges, acknowledging and accepting them without suppression, smiling at our foolishness. We can also release views and labels which only limit us, limit what we can become.

Contentment and more equanimity in our lives are within our reach. Mindfulness is key to tackling our cravings, bringing space into our daily behaviour so that we can observe how we react and change how we respond. And a meditation practice is supportive to developing mindfulness.

So we have explored how we can release, let go of, unhelpful unhealthy desires. However, this needs some qualification. We must not get *too* simplistic about this. We obviously don't want to just let go of everything in our lives. We don't for example want to let go of all that is helpful and positively developing in our mind. We need to be discriminating, to understand those desires which are beneficial and those which are not. Moreover, there is more to Buddhist practice than just releasing unhelpful thoughts and emotions, such as craving. This practice is very helpful as far as it goes, it just has its limitations. There is a danger of complacency here as well, a certain passivity, which goes contrary to the Buddha's teachings. It needs to be coupled with other practices which are more active. If the message of the Buddha were simply that all suffering would cease through a passive non-attached quietism, then his teaching would have not inspired millions of people throughout the centuries to get out of their metaphorical comfy armchairs with a desire to change themselves and the world around them.

The same applies to accepting; acceptance does not mean the same as resignation. Accepting our current situation or limitations is not the same of believing that nothing can ever change. It is certainly not an excuse for letting ourselves off the hook, for saying to ourselves that it's not worth making the effort. As Traleg Kyabgon explains, 'It is not about saying "I'm just going to learn to accept who I am and where I am and leave it at that." '[260]

Similarly, we should not misunderstand what is meant by 'non-attachment'. It does not mean that we have to reject all enjoyment, reject relationships with others for fear of attachment. Concentrating on negation can blinker us to the immense gains that come from setting our minds on the liberation from our cravings. Negative emotions such as craving can be put into abeyance temporarily but not indefinitely; the energy of sexual desire rarely just disappears. It is not just about delaying gratification, fighting against our desires, holding them back provisionally in the hope they won't come back again, a limbo state when we're relatively desireless for the time being. Such tactics may be useful in the short term but what we are seeking is something much more transformational.

The idea of growing and expansion may seem much more appealing than the idea of cessation. The doctrine of impermanence isn't just about things ceasing to exist – this can lead to nihilistic thinking. Things arise as well. It is misleading just to think about the cessation of things. Things, events, feelings, phenomena arise and cease all of the time.

The idea of releasing, letting go of our cravings, accepting our ebbs and flows, is an approach to our practice that we may find useful but, as Rob Burbea makes clear, it is just one approach and we need many.[261] 'It's only the start… letting go, and the ease that comes from letting go of something that the mind is wanting, grasping, that is not liberation. Or rather, that would be a very limited view of what liberation is, if it's just a state of ease because the mind is not grasping onto the things of the world.' We may be searching for something much more profound than just temporary relief from *dukkha*, more than just stress reduction. 'Letting go' he continues, 'does not take us to where we deeply want to go… to varying degrees we want, human beings want *more* than ease and peace.' In the following chapters we shall explore what that *'more'* that we are thirsting for actually looks like, that which involves 'our deeper loves, our deep passions, our longings, the movements of our passion.'

If we want to free ourselves from unhealthy craving, then we need to go further and deeper. Letting go implies creating an absence. Now we need to develop, make present, more enlightened mental states; we can begin to open up to new ways of seeing, and explore new potentials within us.

Reflecting – Chapter 7

What do you feel you would be giving up if you give up your unhelpful cravings? Do you find it hard to just stop and 'do nothing'? Can you let there be room for not knowing? What labels do you give yourself? Is there a 'weight' that you carry around?

Reflect on how 'the second arrow' plays out in your life. Are you able to laugh at yourself for your silly cravings? How easy do you find forgiveness, both of others and yourself? If my examples of contentment resonate with you, what does it tell you? What does contentment feel like for you? When are you most at risk of indulging your cravings?

Chapter 8:

PURIFYING

Over-eating is one my favourite analogies, as you will have noticed. One of the highlights of my Sunday mornings when I was a child was to relish the thought that sometime in the early afternoon I would sit down with my family to a Sunday roast. It's still one of my favourite meals, and even now my mouth waters at the thought of it. Piles of crispy golden potatoes and parsnips, crunchy Brussels sprouts, fresh garden peas I'd podded myself, the hollow Yorkshire pudding drenched in lashings of gravy, with a dollop of creamy onion sauce on the side. In those days, there would be chicken, pork or lamb as well, but nowadays I have no appetite for meat, and these have disappeared from my plate.

The other thing that has changed since my younger days is my digestive system. If I allow myself to eat as much as I did then, as much as I would really like to eat now, I find myself pretty quickly with an uncomfortable stomach upset. And I know that. But, sad to say, even though I know that, I will still sometimes go ahead and over-indulge nevertheless. The appearance of the food, the smell, the taste, the expectation, these all overwhelm my better judgement.

Superficially something may appear very pleasant, like my Sunday roast, but I know I need to go beyond or beneath the surface and develop a deeper understanding of the surface aspects of the object I crave and what the craving really consists of. And I know that this deeper understanding will help me address my appetite.

We have seen that ignorance or delusion go hand-in-hand with craving. But what can we do to see through our delusions around craving and become more aware of what the consequences are of indulging our habitual desires? This chapter is based on Model 2 that we looked at in Chapter 6. The theme here is developing insight into our longings, by clarifying our vision, seeing their true nature, and refining them. We shall look firstly at purifying our motivations and our actions; and then at purifying our perception.

Honing our behaviour

A connoisseur of wine can work on and refine her sense of taste and smell to determine where and when a particular wine originated. A piano tuner can refine his sense of hearing to fine tune a complex mechanical instrument. All of us can refine our sense organs, but also we can refine the motivation for our actions. Our motives purify our activity, and our motives are purified by our activity. This is an ongoing constant process. We examine our motivations and work to refine them. It is through the purifying of our volitions that unhealthy craving is transformed into healthy desire, which is at the heart of the Buddhist path. So, not relinquishing our desires, but rather purifying them.

And what is the purifying of our behaviour? In the words of that little gem of a text, the *Dhammapada*, simply 'cease to do evil, cultivate the good, cleanse your heart.'[262] Unskilful deeds are ugly, skilful deeds are beautiful. You can give up 'lower' pleasures for 'higher' ones. Maybe you have already tried a digital detox or a sugar detox; now you can try to detoxify other aspects of your behaviour or, at the very least, become less intoxicated in your habits.

The Buddhist ethical precepts of training ourselves to act skilfully are usually formulated in a negative sense, 'I undertake the training principle of *abstaining*' from certain types of behaviour. Sangharakshita however has formulated positive ethical precepts, all framed in terms of purification; for example, 'With open-hearted generosity, I purify my body...With truthful communication, I purify my speech.... With mindfulness clear and radiant, I purify my mind.' We can think of this as a process of cleansing - cleansing in the sense of an ethical, moral cleansing, of our body, speech and mind; our *kleśa* gradually being flushed away through our skilful actions. Traleg Kyabgon describes how this feels, 'when there is less grasping and clinging, our sensory experiences become cleansed and purified... If one is not feeling so frantic and desperate, then what we experience will be experienced more fully and more completely.'"[263]

We purify our body, speech and mind then through ethical behaviour. Purifying ourselves of our unhealthy cravings is a question of behaving skilfully. Behaving skilfully is a question of being mindful of what motivates our actions, speech and thinking – not a motivation based upon craving, ill-will and confusion, but rather upon generosity, loving kindness and clarity of vision. In the words of Lama Thubten Yeshe,

'Pure motivation is a function of the wise and open mind, which is the total opposite of the narrow, psychologically defiled, obsessed mind that is overly concerned for one's own benefit and welfare.'[264]

We can refine our consumer choices, guided by the first ethical precept of avoiding harm to sentient beings - humans and other animals - as well as harm to the planet generally. We can cleanse ourselves of self-hatred and ill-will towards others by practising the *Mettā-bhāvanā* meditation, the cultivation of loving kindness. We can develop wholesomeness through seeking to give praise rather than to receive it, through listening attentively to others rather than speaking unthinkingly about oneself, through simply *being* with our space rather than searching for the buzz to fill it.

Cultivating inner purity

Imagine walking out one oppressively hot afternoon, and then discovering a cool crystal-clear lake. Imagine bathing slowly in the cool lake, and then emerging feeling refreshed and revitalised. Imagine enveloping yourself in a pristine white cloth, and then resting by the lakeside, beyond pleasure and pain, indescribably peaceful, totally at ease and profoundly cleansed. This is the image associated with a very deep, absorbed state of meditation known as the 'fourth *dhyāna*'.[265] This admittedly is a highly developed form of equanimity and tranquillity, but contemplating this image can help us to get a glimpse of what is possible.

In the same way that we wish, for the sake of our well-being, to live in an environment that is free from pollution, our mind has its own ecology which we need to keep purified. When the mind is pure and lucid, it is free from craving, from grasping, just as the Buddha's mind became in his Enlightenment experience. It is not only the body which is a temple which needs to be cared for and kept free from damage; the mind is also a temple which needs to be cleansed of harmful elements and kept unstained. With purification comes pacification, the pacification of those turbulent forces which trouble our mind.

There are many other images of purification in the Buddhist scriptures. We can imagine ourselves as an untainted shiny rock where the crow Māra has no purchase to be able to land; or we can make ourselves so pure that we are invisible to Māra. Both these images come from the Pāli Canon. In my Triratna tradition, at the start of a retreat we imagine the retreat centre as a sacred space surrounded by lotuses of purity, protecting us from the *kleśa* in the world outside. Moreover, there is the vision of Pure Land Buddhism, a widespread tradition in China and Japan, an imaginative realm, the ambit of the pure of mind. In the *Lotus Sutra* of the Māhayāna tradition we find the parable of the rain cloud that cleanses and refreshes the entire world. I love this image of being rejuvenated and restored by translucent water, being permeated through, outside and inside, by the most sparkling, clearest, freshest water - the purest rain or perhaps a gentle waterfall - our *taṇhā* slaked, all those nasty itches and sores neutralised, decontaminated, washed away.

When we start to feel ourselves being purified by our skilful actions, habits and practices, it is as though conduits within us are being cleansed and are becoming unobstructed, and we can act as a medium for *Mettā* to be channelled through our being, for the benefit of all beings. In addition, 'When we have developed our own inner purity, inner compassion, and inner love,' writes Lama Thubten Yeshe, 'we can then see the reflection of this purity and loving-kindness in others.'[266] When your mind is pure, what you perceive is pure. One of the things that happens when you begin to fine tune your perception is that you see the effects that your actions have on others, for example, your harsh speech, rudeness, bullying, belittling behaviour.

The road to reconciliation

Yes, sometimes the way we act does run contrary to our values. We are not perfect. We may be trying to purify, to deep cleanse our actions of body, speech and mind, but we are swimming in muddy, murky, messy waters. And we need to reconcile ourselves to the fact that we will act unskilfully sometimes. But what is important is that when we do, we don't just ignore it and carry on regardless. If we don't want to keep on having endless Groundhog Days, we need to come to terms with and address what we have done, so that it is less likely to happen again.

There is a Tibetan Vajrayāna teaching concerned with purifying ourselves when we have acted unskilfully, whether it be lustful longings, over-indulging, or wishing ill of another person. We can think of this teaching as purifying our negative *karma*. This is the teaching of the Four Opponent Powers or Four Opponent Forces.[267] These powers which address and act as an antidote to our unskilful actions are: *regret, resolve, reliance* (or *refuge*), and *remedy*.

I have developed and elaborated this teaching over the years to help with my own unhelpful behaviour and, in keeping with the initial letter of the English translation of the powers, I have called this process 'the path of R's', or 'the Path of Reconciliation'. The process is: *recognition* – seeing the unskilful action as such; *responsibility* – not blaming other people or situations; *regret* – real remorse or contrition for the action; *release* – sharing, confessing, admitting the action to someone I can trust; *reflecting* – reviewing what gave rise to the unskilful action, and what it reveals about myself; *resolve* – commitment not to repeat the action, perhaps making a vow; *reliance* – a plan of action built upon ethical, compassionate motivation based on the *dharma*; *revive* – reigniting what inspires me to act skilfully; and *remedy* – making amends, putting right, addressing where possible any harm that has been done.

The Path of Reconciliation: to reconcile is to confront. I feel that this process of facing up to our unhelpful actions with a view to changing our behaviour speaks for itself and needs little clarification. However, there are a few points which I would like to expand upon. When we speak of regret, this is not the same as guilt. We may experience guilt when we fear that somebody will not like us anymore because of what we have done – will not like us, will not approve of us, even will not love us. We can experience regret however as acknowledging what we have done, and the harm it has caused us and possibly others; just that, without the need to tell ourselves guilty stories which then linger on.

Confession, as a means of release, may seem like a daunting term. I remember it did for me initially, the opening up of one's private self to others. Sangharakshita talks though about the psychological, therapeutic value of acknowledging one's unskilful acts. 'So confession at least drags into the open something that we would prefer to ignore, but about which we have to do something if we are going to make any spiritual progress at all. Confession is good from that point of view in as much as it involves recognition of what is going on - involves seeing ourselves as we really are, on the empirical level.'[268]

I meet weekly with a group of fellow Buddhists where one of our practices is to confess any breach of our ethical code, the Buddhist ethical precepts, which we may have committed over the previous week. We take our ethical life seriously! But we also look upon it as an opportunity for forgiving ourselves. No guilt, but a sense of regret. I only wish that I had learnt to share my personal difficulties more when I was younger; it would have saved me a lot of grief later on, but it was not the 'done thing' for men when I grew up, and maybe still isn't for many men. One of the great things, for me and I know for many others, of being part of a Buddhist community is the emphasis on spiritual friendship and being able to talk openly in a safe trusting environment about one's 'difficult stuff', to release it, to get it off one's chest, and thus to feel 'purer'. As long as we realise though that releasing in this way is only part of the process of bringing about change.

We may experience an unpleasant feeling when we haven't lived up to our ideals. We may think of ourselves as a warm, compassionate person, but then realise that we just blithely looked the other way when we walked past a person begging on the street so that we didn't have to face up to ignoring them. We can feel a sense of shame about letting ourselves down, but this is not the same as irrational guilt. In Buddhism we have the connected concepts of *hri* and *apatrāpya*, which we can think of as rational or tolerant shame. Both can help us to refrain from acting unskilfully; *hri* is not wanting to let ourselves down, and *apatrāpya* is not wanting to let others down whom we respect and look up to, or who have put their trust in us. Together, *hri* and *apatrāpya* are the opposites of the 'I-don't-care-ism' that we looked at in Chapter 4. They are sometimes called 'the protectors of the universe.' Perhaps *apatrāpya* is more powerful and effective than *hri*, since we are social beings and may find it easier to be accountable to others rather than ourselves; this accountability is also at the heart of confession.

Refining our vision

If we choose to, we can take delight in objects for their own sake, rather than thinking how we can make use of them, or grasping at them, wanting to possess them; it may be a person who is attractive to us, an item of jewellery, somebody else's house or garden, a finely designed garment. 'But if you find it aesthetically beautiful', writes Sangharakshita, 'you will just want to stand back and contemplate it, surrender to it, absorb yourself in it. Aesthetic contemplation is therefore not only disinterested but, in a way, impersonal. You lose yourself in the object, forgetting your personal concerns.'[269]

Objects, people, landscapes are not necessarily inherently beautiful, it depends upon our attitude of mind how aesthetically pleasing they are; whether we look upon them with lust, greed, envy, or with a more open, non-attached, equanimous eye. This again is a refining of the way we relate to the world, detaching ourselves from our grosser emotions, cultivating less tainted, more wholesome, purer mental states. Instead of wallowing in the mire, our minds can rise to lofty heights.

We can appreciate the beauty of true friendship, a flower, a sunset, a work of art, without wanting to possess them, but we can equally find something, somebody attractive without desiring to have and to hold them. We can cultivate a sense of pleasant experience which is not based on our usual cravings. Aesthetic appreciation can thus act as an antidote to sexual longing and other yearnings; instead of focussing on an attractive outward form, we can become aware of a beautiful nature or essence.

We are now getting an inkling of what it is like to see the world and our lives differently. Along with an ethical structure in one's life comes lucidity, not just seeing the world through the eye of the flesh, but more readily with a clear conscience. Unskilful desires lead to clouded vision, skilful desires lead to clarity. And with more clarity comes the likelihood that we will continue to make more informed, wiser decisions.

Up to now in this chapter we have principally been exploring how we can purify our motivations and our actions, decontaminating them of the poison of craving. Now we shall be looking at how we can purify our perception, cleanse our vision, and gain a deeper insight into the nature of our longings and urges. As we have seen, particularly in Chapter 3, at the root of craving is ignorance or delusion, and we need to develop the wisdom to see through this delusion. In the words of the *Dhammapada*, 'seeing the creepers of craving, cut their roots with insight.'[270]

How we perceive our desires is crucial. Here I want to examine how we can gain insight, firstly into phenomena - what we crave – and our views of and reactions to those phenomena; and secondly, insight into our self-view – who is doing the craving and what that self-view consists of. These insights are at the heart of Buddhist wisdom.

Beyond appearance

In examining craving, Buddhism teaches us to move from a subjective view to an objective one. Rather than focusing on our needs in the moment, we can instead pause mindfully and focus on the object of our craving, and the process of craving, investigating it and thereby taking the wind out of its sails, as we saw in the previous chapter. When we begin to understand what our cravings are and how we can come to terms with them, a whole new world opens up, a world in which we see our relationship to all phenomena quite differently. We can see that our clinging has got much broader implications than we ever could have imagined.

Traleg Kyabgon explains. 'There is nothing wrong with how things appear to us. Our concern with appearance is that when our minds are myopic and confused, and they grasp onto an aspect of the appearance, we distort reality. When there is less tendency to grasp or be obsessed, we can perceive appearance in a more genuine and panoramic way. By seeing the interconnected and insubstantial nature of appearance we will see that appearance and reality are not separate.'[271]

One of the Buddha's greatest insights into the characteristics of everything in this world is a teaching that we have touched on before, the three characteristics of existence, the *lakṣaṇa*. All phenomena, all material objects, but also all sensations, feelings and thoughts - indeed all cravings and all things we crave - can be reflected upon, investigated and reimagined in the light of these three concepts: *aniccā* (impermanence), *dukkha* (unsatisfactoriness), and *anattā* (no enduring essence).

In other words, all those things which we ache for, pine after and binge on are ephemeral (*aniccā*), shallow (*dukkha*), and devoid of real substance (*anattā*). They are, in some sense, superficial thrills. We have already examined in these writings the relationship between craving and *dukkha*. Now we shall look more closely at how the other two *lakṣaṇa* relate to craving; then we can use what is sometimes called a *dynamic* approach to how we perceive things (seeing the object of our desire as impermanent, constantly changing, arising and passing in dependence upon a multiplicity of conditions); as opposed to an *analytic* approach (breaking down the object of our desire into its component parts, seeing it not as simple, but composite). Both are valid methods of examining the true nature of phenomena. With the 'right view' that *aniccā* and *anattā* afford us, we can undermine the power of *taṇhā*.

At several points in this book we have come across the notion of the changing, transient nature of all phenomena that is *aniccā*. Taking a *dynamic* approach, the more clearly we can see the impermanent nature of the world, including ourselves, the less attached we become to our objects of desire, their non-enduring fleeting nature. The more profoundly we can experience the evanescent nature of everything, the less enchanted we will become, for instance, with evanescent consumer goods; they neither endure materially, nor do they endure in the short-term pleasure which they are able to provide.

If we are experiencing restlessness, lust, anger, or an urge to indulge, we can consider the process we are going through. Most importantly, with practice, we can see the disturbing emotion as not the whole picture, but just as an impersonal phenomenon that has arisen because of certain conditions, and that will disintegrate given certain other conditions, that it is merely a passing cloud.

We may seek to escape difficult experiences by searching out pleasant ones. But the transience of all phenomena applies also to pleasurable experiences. 'The problem is that this syndrome of searching out pleasant experiences is no secure refuge. Pleasant experiences fade with time, and what seemed new and exciting yesterday seems dull and routine today.'[272] We may find it wretched to reflect that all that is dear to us will fade away one day, but all of what is painful to us will similarly evaporate. There is both a sadness and a loveliness in the concept of impermanence. 'In Japanese culture they have great appreciation for the chrysanthemum as it only blooms for a short time. Because of that it is considered very beautiful.'[273]

Not how we imagine it to be

And so to an *analytic* approach, using the concept of *anattā*. Not only are all phenomena transitory by their nature, but they also have no inherent core. When we break down the object of our desiring, for example a piece of furniture, into its constituent parts and investigate them, we find that we end up with something that has no real essence, and thereby something that has less of a hold on us. What happens is that we attribute, by custom and practice since the beginning of the consciousness of humankind, qualities to things, in particular the quality of 'having an essence'.

Geshe Kelsang Gyatso illustrates this: 'all phenomena exist as mere imputations. Things are imputed upon their basis of imputation by thought. What does 'basis of imputation' mean? For example, the parts of a car are the basis of imputation for the car. The parts of a car are not the car, but there is no car other than its parts. Car is imputed upon its parts by thought. How? Through perceiving any of the parts of the car we naturally develop the thought 'This is the car'.[274]

Mahāyāna Buddhism expands on the characteristic of *anattā* with an emphasis on the concept of *śūnyatā*, usually translated as emptiness, voidness, or even ungraspability. And *śūnyatā* applies to all things, not just 'me'. All phenomena are empty of any essential core, of any intrinsic nature, of any selfhood, they are only constructs which we ourselves have brought about. We can say that in this sense all things, without anything that we can hold onto, are 'like a face in a mirror; like the water of a mirage; like the sound of an echo'.[275] Saying that 'all things are empty' means that *they not there as such, not as we imagine them to be.*

It is as though there are two ways of experiencing the world - known in Buddhism as the Two Truths - our everyday *relative* reality, that is, our normal empirical experience, how things appear to us, a view grounded in distortion and delusion; and then an *ultimate* reality, grounded in insight, where we experience everything as how it truly is, insubstantial, empty of any inherent existence. The word 'experience' here is fundamental. 'Sunyata or voidness or emptiness - these are just the words,' said Sangharakshita, 'these are just the labels that we use - sunyata is essentially an experience, what we can only describe as a spiritual experience, even a transcendental experience.'[276]

Saying that all things are 'empty' is not the same as saying that nothing exists or matters. The term emptiness does imply an absence, the absence of our notion that things possess an essence. We don't need to be scared by the word. In a way, it is an optimistic term; we can think of everything being boundless, not tied down by the label of a car, chocolate, envy. These labels are just constructs.

The significance then of this teaching for us here, in looking at how we address our unhelpful cravings, is that, as we start to develop the wisdom that the targets of our craving having nothing of real essence in them, and neither do the cravings themselves, then their magic power over us dwindles. 'The great Madhyamika teacher Nagarjuna says in one of his writings that the teaching, or rather the experience, of sunyata is intended for the cure of all possible attachments.'[277]

Why do I allow this attractive person, this bottle of wine, this sugary delight, this smartphone, this idea about myself, have such a hold over me, when really it is nothing powerful and solid, but instead a flimsy, wispy, ephemeral hollowness? One could say it is laughable.

When Bāhiya persistently asked for a teaching, the Buddha said this: 'as regards things seen, heard, sensed or cognized, there will be in the seen only the seen, in the heard only the heard, in the sensed only the sensed, in the cognized only the cognized.'[278] In other words, here we have direct awareness of what we are perceiving, absent of any markers, pigeonholing or categorisation, and hence we are free not to react in our habitual ways.

The dissolution of the desirer

Next we ask the question - who is doing the craving? By virtue of the teaching of the *lakṣaṇa*, all phenomena then are both impermanent and insubstantial, and all phenomena includes the entity we call 'me'. We can again take a dynamic approach or an analytic one, as above, but this time what we are reflecting upon is our self, the one who does the craving.

Where is this thing I call my personality? We started to look at this Chapter 5. All I can find when I really look deeply are momentary sensations, thoughts, feelings, tendencies, desires – is any of this 'me' or 'my personality' or 'my soul'? However much I try to grab onto them, I am incapable. All is process, constantly on the move. From a dynamic point of view then, we can let go of our attachment to the fiction that we are fixed, enduring entities. In fact, all we are is flow, the ever-changing rhythm of life, the flow of nature that is the nature of all phenomena. In a paraphrase of Descartes, 'I change, therefore I am not.'

Several years ago, during a mindfulness meditation session, I came to a realisation which has remained with me ever since. My initial experience was the discovery that in the present moment, right now, in the awareness of 'now', there is no *dukkha*, no craving. This was followed by another discovery. Absorbed in that current moment, I realised that there is no such phenomenon as 'now'; it is constantly moving, changing, you cannot pin it down. But straightaway I came to a more miraculous discovery. As the moment 'now' constantly moves and changes, simultaneously so does the idea of 'me'; there was the realisation that 'I' was not fixed, 'I' was forever changing, moving. Along with this experience came a wonderful feeling of joy, of freedom. It was as though there was a releasing of a burden, the weight of being 'me'. At that moment I was no longer tied down by 'me', it had got in the way for far too long. I could breathe freely now that the burden had been temporarily lifted.

Traleg Kyabgon writes, 'We may think, "I'm getting emotional," but the teachings say that if we look into who is emotional, then there is not a single thing called "I" who gets emotional. That "I" is composed of our physical aspect: there is a body of a certain shape, weight, height, age, …background, cognitive capacities and feelings—and they all come together'[279]. From an analytic perspective therefore, we come to the same conclusion, that there is no such thing as a unitary fixed self with an inherent essence that is doing the craving. The 'I' only exists because 'I' style it so.

It is important to understand what is meant by this. In the same way that I wrote above about there being a relative reality and an ultimate reality, we can say that the self does exist, but only in a conventional sense, in a relative sense; it is useful therefore to use terms like I, you, she, we, mine, our, in referring to this relative self.

But, if we recognise that the self is an entity which is a construct, a practical one but not ultimately real, then we can begin to look at different, freer ways of perceiving ourselves which are less troublesome for us. The notion of I and me are a fabricated conceit; we can deflate our self-importance, our cockiness, by realising this. Identifying with a spurious autonomous entity is enchaining; liberating ourselves from this identification is enlightening.

Release from *bhava-taṇhā*

In the previous chapter we explored how we can let go of our cravings, but primarily in terms of release from *kāma-taṇhā*, the craving for sensual pleasure. Here we can think of release from *bhava-taṇhā*, the clinging to a sense of self which we looked at in Chapter 5; not just a physical letting-go but, ultimately, a letting-go of our fixed sense of being. Here too we can think of purification - purifying our wrong view, purifying our consciousness of the wrong conception of selfhood, purifying ourselves not only our normal cravings and aversions, but cleansed of the delusion that there is a fixed, absolute 'me.'

We can try out an exercise. Bring to mind and body, a particular craving, whether it be food or drink you'd like to consume, a sexual craving, a desire to purchase, or something else. Then try to experience this craving strongly. Now notice, if you can, your sense of yourself, as a human being who is craving. See how strong, solid and separate this sense of yourself is. You can see then that your sense of yourself is buffered and strengthened by the *dukkha* of your craving. Now do the opposite and let go of the craving. Feel the sense of calm and being at ease. This also works the other way round, noticing how our craving increases with the strengthening of our sense of separateness, our self-centeredness. This body/mind awareness can also develop into a practice to help us to dismantle our self-referencing. As Reginald Ray writes, 'By working with the body, by engaging the discomfort, the tension is present to our awareness, and we are able to engage the process of unraveling the layers of our self-concept.'[280]

No me, hence no mine

If, in the end, there is nothing unchanging or substantial that we can call 'me', then there is nothing unchanging or substantial for things – material objects, thoughts, bodily pain, emotions - to belong to. When you reflect upon this, you realise that the entity we call 'me' is not really in control of anything. Definitely not the body; it gets sick and ages however much we rail against it. Definitely not our mind, it roams all over the place like a 'rutting elephant'[281] and comes up with all sorts of difficult stuff that we have to make sense of and deal with that, basically, we'd rather not. If these longings and urges were mine, then surely I would be able to have some mastery over them.

Charles Dickens wrote in one of his novels of a suffering elderly lady, ' 'Are you in pain, dear mother?' 'I think there's a pain somewhere in the room,' said Mrs. Gradgrind, 'but I couldn't positively say that I have got it.' '[282] We need to remember this, that disturbing emotions are not 'me', and so 'not mine', they are not embedded within us somehow.

Cravings are impersonal, like other emotions and thoughts. They are not 'you' or 'yours' but they want to take over 'you'. Ownership of craving is an option. We don't need to think of this compulsive urge as '*my* craving'. Rather, in an objective sense, we can see it as just 'craving', something unowned and neutral; neither good nor bad. It is very helpful to look at our longings in this way, in trying to see their insubstantiality, to think of them as impersonal, not mine. It is just the mind throwing them out into the orbit which I think of as 'me'.

Buddhism teaches that there is nothing the matter with us. We are essentially pure, untainted. The *kleśa* are adventitious, they come about as a result of external conditions rather than being inherent in us. So we don't need to think badly of ourselves or beat ourselves up when we indulge a craving or long for something unskilful. We accept and we move on. There is no point in loitering in that place that says 'I am not good enough, I am hopeless'. Why cause unnecessary pain to ourselves? Buddhism can help us to see through those stories about our self-worth and let them go. We are not them. We don't need to always believe what we think, our minds deceive us all the time.

As described in the previous chapter, a choice can be made just to simply observe this impersonal craving. Observe it arising and then, giving it space, observe it passing. You don't need to identify with this aspect of your existence, you can watch it come and go like a passing storm. Do not identify with your desires, but just recognise them as neutral, not yours. In doing so you can naturally feel freer, more connected to what is around you, you can feel the joy of not feeling attached to what you have always erroneously called 'me.'

The dance of *māyā*

When the Buddha broadened out his vision and saw the immaterial, transient nature of all phenomena, including the subject, object and process of craving, his experience was the following: no craver, no craved, no craving. The subject, object and process of our longings (and the way that they are related to each other) are just a misconstruction of the mind.

In the *Abhidharma*, a part of the Buddha's teachings that deals with what we might call nowadays psychology, one of the unwholesome mental states listed is *māyā*, usually translated as deceit or pretence, or more often, illusion or magic. Without any basic essence, all phenomena are like an illusion – 'like the erection of a eunuch…like the track of a bird in the sky.'[283]

An illusion seems to be true but it is not. You perceive it, it looks authentic, and you take it for authentic, but finally it's not. Sangharakshita clarifies, 'The point of the comparison with a magical illusion is that they're experienced, but are not absolutely real. You're not denying the experience, but you're denying the ultimate validity of the experience…..Perhaps we can get closer to an understanding of the matter by recalling what happens when we've been in a really bad mood. Once the bad mood is over there's absolutely nothing left. It wasn't about anything at all. It was a storm in a teacup, and we think, Why did it affect me so strongly? Why did I get so upset? It was nothing really. Even the feeling I had was nothing.'[284]

In the *Bodhicaryāvatāra* we read, 'Where do the *kleśa* of craving and aversion abide? Not in the objects we perceive, not in the sense organs, nor in the relationship between them. There is nowhere for them to reside and yet they cause so much upheaval. They are but a mirage. So, free yourself from fear and devote yourself to striving for insight. Don't torment yourself any longer!'[285]

We don't have to speculate where the illusion came from, what we have to do is to see through it. Seeing through *māyā* at the same time as we are experiencing our cravings is seeing them for what they are, having no real solidity, empty of anything that we can call an essence. Sometimes we can only do this in retrospect, but the more aware we can become of this happening, the more likely it is that we will catch it in real time.

Goethe describes the illusion very creatively. 'When I consider the narrow limits within which our active and inquiring faculties are confined…whilst we amuse ourselves painting our prison-walls with bright figures and brilliant landscapes — when I consider all this, Wilhelm, I am silent. I examine my own being, and find there a world, but a world rather of imagination and dim desires, than of distinctness and living power. Then everything swims before my senses, and I smile and dream while pursuing my way through the world.'[286]

Our mind determines how we experience the world, how we interpret it; either as *saṃsāra or nirvāṇa*. One day we will see that we can dance happily and freely in the realm of *māyā*. The clumsy dance we perform in *saṃsāra*, tripping over and bumping into things will be no more.[287]

Once we see that the supposed 'I' inside ourselves that needs protecting is in fact illusory, we can begin to breathe more easily. This 'I' only exists if 'I' crave to satisfy and protect it. There is no lack, no chasm to fill. John Kabatt-Zinn writes, 'ironically, we are missing the fact that we are actually conspiring to make ourselves slaves to an illusion, to the compulsive longing to complete ourselves when, in fact, we are already complete, already whole.'[288]

Our Buddha-nature

I have written in this chapter that Buddhism teaches that there is nothing wrong with us, that fundamentally we are pure and untainted, that there is no lack within us, we are already whole. When we look inside ourselves we may see positives and negatives. When we look back upon our life, we may see skilful and unskilful things we have done. We may become guilt-ridden. I know that sometimes I have been prone to remember mainly the negative, the unskilful. But, unlike some spiritual traditions which emphasise that human nature is inherently sinful and needs taming, Buddhists believe that our natural underlying condition is essentially pure, but that it is overlaid with negative qualities such as craving, aversion and confusion.

All phenomena, including ourselves, are by their very nature intrinsically pure, free from the stains of the *kleśa* which are the origin of our *dukkha*. Beneath the coverings of our everyday reality lies another reality which is not subject to unhealthy urges and confusion. This is the essence of Buddhahood – pure, clear, unadulterated wisdom and compassion. We may experience fleeting glimpses of this selfless equanimous state, where there are no 'inner poison drives', in nature, while listening to music, in close human contact, or in other situations where we are totally absorbed in the absolute beauty of a timeless moment.

Buddhists frequently chant mantras. By chanting a mantra, either to oneself or out loud, our body reverberates to the sound, which can have a transformative and purifying effect on our mental states, refining the energy of the body. In this way, blockages of energy can be dissolved, and gross energies can become transformative. In the following chapter we shall look more at craving-as-energy. One of the many Buddhist mantras we chant is the *śuddhā* (purity) mantra - *oṃ svabhava śuddhā sarva dharma svabhava śuddhā hum* - which can be translated as 'all phenomena are by nature pure, I too by nature am pure', or alternatively as 'purity is the essential nature of all things, purity too is my essential nature.' Beneath the one who is craving is one who is not craving. The 'I' that craves is not the whole 'I'; the latter is able to really see what is going on and to do something about it. Beneath our craving is a calm and wisdom.

The term 'pure', which I have used a lot in this chapter, may be a difficult one, too abstract perhaps for us to conceive as our nature, as well as the nature of all phenomena. It may be easier to think of our being filled with light. We can imagine our mind as luminous - a term sometimes used in Buddhism - radiating light, shining, glowing, a clear blue sky within us. A luminous mind veiled only by our *kleśa*, like fog that masks that clear blue sky. Luminosity as transparent consciousness, unsullied, unpolluted, free of distorting and degrading energies, a domain of sheer happiness.

When we are able to create a chink in the armour of our selfing, then the bright sun of love and awareness will pour through. 'The more we can identify ourselves as having a body and mind of pure clear light,' writes Thubten Yeshe, 'the more we open ourselves up to the beneficial forces existing inside and outside ourselves.'[289] He continues, 'If we truly want to connect with this subtle essence, we need to quiet all distractions and loosen the hold our ordinary appearances and conceptions have on us. In other words we need to create space, space in which our essentially pure nature can function uninterruptedly.... bringing to the surface the inner, divine qualities that have always existed within the depths of our being.'[290]

And so finally, through refining our actions of body, speech and mind, through developing the wisdom that sees through our delusions about our self and the objects we crave, and through uncovering our inner purity, we can try to ensure that the impact we have upon the world around us is as positive, as untainted and as helpful as we possibly can make it.

Reflecting – Chapter 8

Do you ever 'let yourself off the hook' for your unhelpful habits by saying to yourself that that is the sort of person I am? To what extent do you try to insulate yourself from difficult experiences, and parts of yourself which are troublesome? Have you ever tried to detox yourself in any way? Do you have an ethical framework by which you try to live? Do you feel that the idea of reconciling yourself to your unskilful actions as described in the 'path of R's' is something that could work for you? How do you feel about 'confession', releasing your unskilful actions to others? Are *hri* and *apatrāpya* practices that might help you to behave more skilfully? How could you refine your lifestyle conditions and patterns of consumption? Take an everyday object, for example a table; reflect and investigate it taking first an analytic then a dynamic approach – what does this tell you about the object? Try out the exercise in the section 'Release from *bhava-taṇhā*'. Can you imagine yourself as filled with radiant light?

Chapter 9:

DRIVING

Some mushrooms are good to eat and some are poisonous. But we don't need to give up eating all mushrooms just become some are harmful. We need a certain amount of knowledge though in order to be able to distinguish between the two. Or we need somebody who is wiser than us to show us how to tell the difference; somebody who has studied the topic and who through their own experience has developed an expertise which they want to share with others. Eating the wrong mushrooms can destroy somebody's life. Eating the right ones can be very pleasurable. Being able to recognize the difference between the two is massive.

I don't know whether the Buddha ate mushrooms, but he could tell the difference between harmful desire and positive desire. As we have seen, and as the Buddha made clear throughout his teachings, craving is just one type of desire, a desire which is unskilful, unhelpful and unhealthy. In the previous two chapters, we explored how we can let go of unskilful desires, loosen the grasping that causes us unhappiness, developing acceptance and contentment; and also how we can see through the illusory nature our desires, refining and decontaminating our minds. This chapter takes another approach, based on Model 3 from Chapter 6. It is about skilful positive desires, and utilising energy to liberate us from our so limiting habits.

Thirst, wholesome and unwholesome

Up till now then, I have characterised *taṇhā* as the thirst, the craving, which is at the root of our ***dukkha***. It is now time to re-examine that proposition, so that *taṇhā* can be seen as skilful as well as unskilful. Both skilful and unskilful *taṇhā* are a search, a search for satisfaction, for fulfilment. Sagaramati describes *taṇhā* as 'the general existential condition we find ourselves in, it is the source from which spring the various means of seeking some form of gratification and purpose in life'.[291] Seeking then is also *taṇhā*, that is, searching for meaning, for purpose, for satisfaction. The 'skill' in the word 'skilful' means developing the ability and knowledge to search for the right things, those that will bring about happiness and freedom.

In a famous text from the Pali Canon, the *Ariyapariyesanā Sutta,* the Buddha, describing his own quest, talks about two kinds of search, usually translated as the ignoble search and the noble search; we might paraphrase them as, on the one hand, the search that demeans us and, on the other, the search that dignifies us. Vessantara compares this search to our own situation in life, 'The ignoble quest, according to the Buddha, is that – being yourself subject to impermanence, to old age, sickness, and death – you go in search of, or quest after, that which is also impermanent and liable to suffering. It is as if you are in danger of drowning, and in trying to save yourself you cling to someone else who is also sinking below the waves.'[292] In contrast, the Buddha compares this ignoble search with the noble search, the quest for the 'supreme security from bondage, Nibbāna'.[293] This is the spiritual path that Buddhism lays out.

We need then constantly to distinguish between these different desires, moving away from grasping after the one and moving towards cultivating the other. Humans possess the faculty of discriminating awareness, and the importance of this awareness on the path cannot be overstressed, differentiating between what is beneficial from that which is not beneficial.

This is not always as easy though as it might seem. Your wish to see a friend for example may have many different motivations – your concern for her well-being, to maintain contact for old times' sake, so that you can tap her for gossip, because you need her constant approval to make you feel worthwhile, or for simple human connection. Which of these seem skilful to you right now and which not? Which involve a clinging, a compulsion?

A stronger desire

We can compare our life to a long train journey, heading to some as yet unclear destination; we can stay on the train that stops at every station but doesn't seem to be getting anywhere, or alternatively we can get off and get on the train that takes us on and on to where we have, deep inside, always really wanted to go. The choice is ours; persist on the same habitual bumpy track, or decide that now is the time to take another tack. 'To overcome destructive or demeaning desires requires one to harness a stronger desire to motivate oneself towards a more positive direction and goal', says the Tibetan teacher, Ringpu Tulku Rinpoche.[294]

As we saw in Chapter 2, Buddhism has a term for this strong desire that motivates us and leads us to freedom from negative desires; this term is *dhamma-chanda,* the driving force on the Buddhist path, the aspiration for the *dharma,* the truth which is 'the root of all skilful deeds'. It is the antidote to kāma-*chanda*, literally the craving for sensual pleasure, but which represents all the kinds of unskilful craving that we explored in Part One.

In the Mahāyāna tradition of Buddhism there are frequently images of 'wish-fulfilling' trees and 'wish-fulfilling' jewels. This used to confuse me – how could a Buddhist 'paradise' be full of objects that granted your every wish, like a bunch of Aladdin's lamps? Wishes for fame and fortune, unlimited booze, sex and chocolate cake, a smartphone with infinite data that never needed recharging? It took me a while to realise that of course these were symbols of *dhamma-chanda*-fulfilling not *kāma-chanda*-fulfilling wishes; symbols of what your heart really desires, not your body or deluded mind.

We need *dhamma-chanda* to overcome *kāma-chanda*. Buddhism sees all desire as expressing our desire for Awakening and *dhamma-chanda* is a passion, a very strong desire for Liberation. Both *kāma-chanda* and *dhamma-chanda* are a desire for completion, for confronting a lack in our life. But only one of them is able to achieve its end. No longer is desire the cause of dissatisfaction, rather it is now what promotes the experience of feeling whole.

The drive that is *dhamma-chanda* is based on *karma*, the knowledge that positive actions have positive consequences. As the *Bodhicaryāvatāra* has it, 'Such misfortunes as befall me now are due to my lack of *dhamma-chanda*. The Buddha has sung that *dhamma-chanda* is the root of all virtue, and the root of *dhamma-chanda* is constant meditation on the consequences of our actions.'[295] There's some more good news; the developing of this aspiration to progress along the spiritual path to freedom is a process of 'eroding desire without harmful side-effects, with nothing else quite like it anywhere in the world"[296]. Not only will this path not do us any harm, but it is likely to do us a whole heap of good.

A drive that takes us forward

Hopefully by now we know that 'craving for stimulation, craving for affirmation, and craving to forget', which is how Prajnaketu succinctly describes the three types of *taṇhā*, [297] are not what we need. But what do we really want, what do we really need?

A new force, a different force from self-centred craving has to be our reason for being. We need a desire that is liberating, rather than desires which are imprisoning, which limit our human potential, which prevent us from being the best that we possibly can be. We need a drive that will take us forward, towards what we as Buddhists call Enlightenment; towards an increasingly awakened sense of what we are, and the deep interconnection between all phenomena in the universe.

Although this expansive state of enlightened being is impossible to describe, to conceive of even, with our current unawakened, undeveloped human minds, we can nevertheless point to a direction, a path to follow that leads us away from self-obsession and towards self-liberation. And this path requires a powerful force as its guide and motivation.

Desire needs to be recognised as an energy, then we can see how best to utilise it. 'We need two 'movements' in our life;' writes Vajragupta, 'withdrawal of energy from certain activities, and engagement in other activities.'[298] Desire is absolutely vital if we wish to aspire to, to commit to, and apply oneself to developing a way out of *dukkha*. Peace of mind does not come from just detaching from our desires. If we had no desire, there would be no desire to change for the better, no determination to move forward on our spiritual journey, no motivation to free ourselves. Everything would be flat and monotonous, and entropy would reign. Without desire, our lives decay into meaninglessness. There would be no civilisation, no culture, no quest for a better world, no drive to achieve success, no questioning of what life is all about, and thus no search for answers to our predicament. Life without desire is no life at all.

It takes skill to drive a car; it is something we have to learn. And from someone who failed his driving test three times, I know this learning process can take a long time. It takes skill also to learn how to drive forward on the spiritual path. We can accidentally turn left instead of right and end up in a one-way street, reversing frantically. The skill we learn is in being able to manage our desires. We can manage our desires to the extent that we can enjoy those things that we desire, without grasping and clinging to them.

When a positive thought or emotion arises, you can act on it, encourage it. What you do repeatedly then becomes your habit. In the same way that negative states of mind lead to more negative states of mind, positive states of mind lead to more positive states of mind. Compulsive behaviour such as craving is the fixing of the mind upon something. You can also fix the mind upon behaving skilfully, so that it is your skilful behaviour which drives you. If your mindset changes so that you begin to act more generously and kindly towards yourself, as well as others, and you realise how much better it makes you feel, then you naturally want to carry on making generosity and kindness central to your life. You then become addicted to being a force for good. Kindness and generosity generate more kindness and generosity. In this manner, you are attracted to, drawn towards Awakening.

By strengthening your positive longings, you empower yourself, you develop forces within you which take you away from unhelpful habits. You learn that positive desires can be fulfilled, the desire for example to be open-hearted in your relationships with yourself and others, unlike negative cravings which, as we saw in Chapter 3, can never be satisfied.

The energy of Eros

This vital purposeful energy that I have been attempting to describe, the energy that is required to take us beyond our mundane existence of petty longings, resentments and confusions, has a counterpart in philosophy and psychology, the concept of 'eros'. Eros covers a wide range of connected meanings – the Classical Greek god of love; erotic love or desire; the life instinct; the impulse to satisfy our basic needs; the creative urge; the sexual drive; a desire for transcendence.

Fundamentally though it is a creative impulse, a thirst for life, as conceived originally in Ancient Greece by Plato, but goes beyond a purely sensual or sexual element. It is an energy that can be easily dissipated in solely sensuality and sexuality, but that can also be diverted to be a vehicle for the transformation of consciousness. In Plato's Symposium, eros is described as a universal force that moves all things towards peace, beauty, harmony and union.[299] Much later, Carl Jung took up the use of the term eros from Sigmund Freud in the field of psychology and saw it as, not unlike Plato, a desire for wholeness, for relatedness and for connection with other humans.[300] This is clearly the force that is the direct opposite of, and corrective to, the craving for non-existence that we examined in Chapter 4.

It is in the sense of a desire for transcendence that the Buddhist teacher Rob Burbea uses this term, 'A desire, a movement of the psyche, of the being, that opens out, deepens, enriches, complicates also, our sense of sacredness. A desire, a movement of the psyche that *opens* the being, unlike craving.'[301] As put neatly by Mark Epstein, 'erotic experience can be transcendent and spiritual experiences erotic.'[302] Perhaps what is needed then is the taking of the erotic - eros - out of sex, out of the sensual, and bringing it into all aspects of our life, to try to find the intensity and intimacy of sexual and sensual experience in everything that we do.

Facing up

The Buddha's own life story illustrates how long and hard he struggled to attain Enlightenment.[303] His dying words to his disciples are said to be, "With vigilance, strive on". There is I feel determination and fervour in these words and in the example of his life, a passionate search for the truth. Like the Buddha we need aspirations - to attain certain goals, to improve ourselves, to move forward – in order that we can feel motivated, vigorous and energized. But there is a difference between determination and willpower. There is a plethora of apps and books out there, based upon bending our will, which promise to curb our desires, for food, alcohol, or our reluctance to get up off the sofa. Some of us switch from app to app for help in 'improving' our behaviour. If they work for us, all well and good. But often it's back to square one, and the craving remains.

There has to be a different way, a way not just based upon willpower. Willpower suggests constantly fighting *against* something difficult, rather than working *with* it. When we fight against somebody or something, rarely does it end happily, rarely does any enmity just fade away. Similarly, when we fight against our cravings, the fight does not end in a harmonious way, as if all is now be resolved. The cravings are still there, bugging us and stopping us being at ease. If all we can do in relating to objects that we desire is to avoid them or push them away, then there are bound to be grave limitations as to how far this will take us in our practice of addressing our ingrained habits. As with certain diets, you can't eradicate a habit just by battling against it; that can simply magnify its importance and power over you. And we can make ourselves very miserable by inflicting a regime on ourselves and then feel that this state of misery is somehow worthwhile. Misery has no value in it.

Part of our aspiration has to be *not* to run away from our demons. We have a tendency to bypass parts of us we don't like, a kind of internal censorship, refusing to accept those elements that are troublesome. We opt for this but not that part of us. In doing so, we are not treating ourselves as a whole. We may feel that facing up to our *dukkha* will mean that we will get overwhelmed by it. We may have grown up to believe that we need to shield ourselves and others from challenging experiences as they may lead to psychological disturbance and harm. But sometimes we need to challenge ourselves. Insulating ourselves from difficult experiences will not help us to develop the resilience we need to face life's struggles. We need to challenge our unhelpful habits, our unhelpful cravings.

Returning to that old demon Māra once more, we can envisage him as a noisy neighbour, there a lot of the time, and who just won't go away. Often at his most invasive when we are at our most vulnerable, for example, in the middle of the night, or when we are feeling low or under the weather. And we have to find some way of coming to terms with our neighbour. I am not suggesting we slay him, as metaphorically we might do with Māra. In fact, we can't slay our demons. Demons are inside us, not external to us, so they can't be killed. We need to be honest and observe them. If we try to kill our demons, or give them too much or too little attention, we only make them stronger. If we can't destroy our demons, what we can do is neutralise them, take the power out of them.

We need to face up to the discomfort Māra is causing us. To confront the deep psychological forces that he represents. Sangharakshita has said, 'we have to drag them all out into the light of day, into the light of the Buddha, and dissolve them. And at least to recognise that they're there and see them clearly, and face up to them, before they can be purified. Purification is possible, but the condition is that at least we recognise the need for purification.'[304] We cannot deny Māra, we have to open a dialogue with him, cultivate intimacy with him. Before you can change any emotion, you need firstly to get to know it. You can then let it be your guide to freeing yourself from *dukkha*. That which weighs heavily when concealed, weighs more lightly when brought out into the open

This requires honesty and courage. Confronting our painful experience may be the very last thing we want to do. Experiential avoidance, particularly when that experience is very demanding, may run deep in us. Facing up means bringing to the surface, but with kindness to ourselves, emotions which we have done everything we can during our lives, by distracting ourselves, to keep buried. The *Bodhicaryāvatāra* recommends that we start off by dealing with our small urges, and then build up to the bigger compulsions. In this manner, we can begin by confronting our lesser, material cravings, perhaps cake in the afternoon, which will then give us the strength to address our deeper ones, maybe wanting to dominate and have the last word in any conversation, always to be right.

Trying to renounce strong emotions can just lead to their conscious suppressing or their unconscious repressing. What we suppress, repress or deny lies buried, or even not so buried, as a shadow, a shadow that can easily re-emerge at any time, ready to catch us unawares and overpower us once more; we looked at this shadow side of us in Chapter 4. What is suppressed just has the nasty habit of turning up again, like a plastic bag of dog poo which someone has mindlessly chucked into a pond.

Some religions have often been perceived as killjoy, exhorting its adherents to keep strong desires under wraps. 'No wonder, then, that organized religion has such a bad name,' writes Lama Thubten Yeshe. 'Instead of being a method for transcending our limitations, religion itself is viewed as one of the heaviest forms of suppression. It is just another form of superstition to be overcome if we really want to be free.'[305] Similarly, Traleg Kyabgon writes, 'Within much of theological discourse, this belief was endemic, the belief that it is paramount to keep the beast that is within us contained. If we allow the beast to come out, it will go on a rampage and we will become sinful and be condemned.'[306] Early Buddhism has been described in this way, with its emphasis upon renunciation and abstention; later Buddhism, as we shall see below, sees things otherwise.

Not allowing oneself to experience a certain part of oneself does not mean that that part has ceased to exist. It will often make its presence felt in terms of mood. Have you ever felt that restless unease in the presence of an acquaintance for whom you still bear resentment for something they said or didn't say, but you have not aired it with them or tried to resolve it or come to terms with it? Holding on to buried resentment is I feel very widespread and an extremely unhelpful emotion; Bradford Hatcher quotes the Buddha as saying that 'holding a grudge is like drinking poison and waiting for the other person to die.'[307]

It took me a long time to realise that suppressing, concealing strong desires, only leads to unhealthy, unbalanced, unintegrated states of mind. To be truly free we have to integrate all aspects of ourselves; really get to know them and bring their energy together so this energy drives us towards liberation.

Not indulged, not suppressed, but transformed

Craving, and its reverse manifestations of ill-will and resentment, cannot just be eliminated by waving a magic wand. They cannot be simply crushed or willed away. Looking at the different Buddhist approaches to craving once more, there developed in the Vajrayāna or Tantric tradition a different emphasis. Instead of extinguishing desires, we find the idea of their transformation. Not cutting off the electricity, but rerouting it. Not snuffing out the candle, but passing the small flame on to a much larger lantern whose light will guide us on our path to freedom.

The Tantric Buddhist path of transformation is in a way the opposite of suppression, the suppression that is of our negative side, our shadow, our afflictions, our *kleśa*, our delusions, our unhealthy cravings. Instead it brings them out into the light of day, and integrates them into our being, our becoming, and transmutes them into positive drives of our body, speech and mind

These transformed drives are what lead us towards Awakening. Through integrating our energies we also are learning to experience ourselves more fully. As we saw in Chapters 7 and 8, we do not need to suppress our desires, nor identify with them, we can observe them as they arise and see through them. Our desires are not us, they are impersonal, they are energies that we can harness and utilize skilfully.

Craving is like some mollusc whose purpose it is to attach itself to a rock. It is energy that searches for *something* to cling to. Usually for humans, that is something pleasurable; but not always, we can cling to grief as a way of holding onto a dear one who has died. Our task as humans who wish to be free is to detach that craving mollusc, and to direct that longing energy into moving forwards, away from clinging and towards an awakened mind-heart.

'There is no question' writes the Buddhist scholar Dhivan 'of somehow getting rid of this kind of passion, hard-wired, as it were, into humanity. The path consists rather of gradually seeing desire for what it is, and letting go through insight. Since this task involves a kind of passion for truth and for liberation, it is a matter of desire transformed through spiritual practice; or, in Buddhist terms, of *kāma-chanda*, desire for sensual pleasure, transmuted by and into *dhamma-chanda,* desire for the truth.'[308] So, seeing desire for what it is; and transmuting it.

There is then another way. We do not have to give in to craving, we do not have to try to destroy it completely, or suppress it. This other way is using the energy inherent in desire to take us beyond unhelpful craving.

I am no physicist. In fact, I didn't get on with science at all when I was at school, and I gave up physics as soon as I could. Nor do I think that everything in this universe which we inhabit can be explained by science. But I have been interested for a long time in one particular law of physics, the Law of Conservation of Energy. From what I understand, this law is one of the principal laws of physics and states that energy cannot be created or destroyed but may be changed from one form to another, that is to say that it can be transferred or converted. Everything that occurs in the universe, everything around us and within us, does so through energy transformation, whereby a particular form of energy moves from its original form to another form.

Our lives depend upon this transformation. We can see this when we cook our dinner: our cooker uses the energy of fuel to transform raw food products into something which our body, using chemical energy, transforms into calorific energy, which gives us the energy necessary to operate as a breathing, moving human being. And then wherever we apply our energy, that itself has an impact; for example, applying our energy to cleaning the bath.

So again, if we consider craving as an energy, we see that *craving-as-energy cannot be extinguished.* We can't just turn it off, as though with a flick of a switch. The law of physics has its parallel in this truth of Vajrayāna Buddhism. Craving-as-energy though may be transformed; in this case, from one form of desire into another. Energy is what we are, it is what makes up the universe. Instead of fighting it, denying it, we need to get in touch with it. Energy is always there, it's just a question of locating it, putting our hands on it, and applying it. Harness, convert and channel.

At the heart of Tantra is an alchemy that delivers a universal elixir; base energies can be transmuted into the wisdom and compassion of Enlightenment. For followers of Tantric Buddhism, desire is the actual path, transforming our burning desires, our flames of greed, into blazing flames of joy. We can dedicate our energies, dedicating ourselves to the pursuit of freedom, freedom from craving. The blind passion of neurotic craving becomes the bright compassion that comes with insight. And the energy that comes from clarity galvanises us. We feel coordinated rather than controlled, at ease rather than on edge.

Perhaps it has always been thus, but it feels as though here in the 21st century humans are more desirous than ever, in an infinite number of ways; so many things to wish for, consume, covet. And 'while the great explosion of desirous energy in this century is considered to be a serious obstacle to most spiritual paths,'[309] it has been suggested[310] that, out of the three main traditions in Buddhism,[311] Vajrayāna or Tantric Buddhism may be the most well-suited of paths to the Western mentality. Lama Thubten Yeshe writes, 'the principle of transformation of energy — on a material level at least — is well understood in the West, like those ingenious scientists who know how to extract energy from everything — from sunlight, the tides, wind, and so forth…..the West has discovered how to tap so many powerful sources of energy in nature but still remains largely unaware of the tremendous force, even more powerful than nuclear energy, contained within each one of us.'[312]

Tapping into transformative energy

Try this. Sit down and think about what you have done over the past week. Find a few obvious examples of how you expended your energy in ways that weren't helpful to you – perhaps how you wasted it in activities that on reflection weren't very productive; how your energy may have seemed all over the place, dissipated and unfocussed; how you felt frustrated, maybe resulting in anger, resentment, ill-will, blaming, nihilistic avoidance; how you ruminated in fearful, anxious ways; how your energy was engaged in physical cravings, greediness, lust. Yes?

Now look again at each of these examples individually. Try and relive the energy that was experienced in each incident. How does that feel, particularly in your body? Can you feel it as tight and restricting? Dark? Uncomfortable? Is that really what you want to carry on experiencing in your life? Examine the experience closely, look at the consequences of the experience, and find its source of energy.

Now try to open that energy up; feel your chest and heart unlocking; feel the energy as warm and bright; let the warmth and brightness become friendliness, kindness, generosity, caring, and gratitude; let this permeate your being, let it embrace your entire mind-body; expand it outwards, to those near, and to those far. Just rest with these feelings for a while. Then ponder how you can use your energies in ways that will benefit you rather then hinder you; and how this will benefit others.

Whenever any of your senses makes contact with an object which gives pleasure, instead of grasping and attaching to that pleasure, you can try to channel the energy of the desire in more creative, expansive ways. When you feel yourself craving, notice the energy within your body, where it is in the body, what actually feels like, its strength, its range, its qualities. See it as energy, just energy. Let it permeate you. See it as a positive force. Let it expand outwards. Feel it as connection with all around you.

When I feel my positive energy waning or difficult to contact, and I sense in me a drift towards indolence, I can invariably get in touch with *mettā*, that universal undiscriminating kindness and love for all beings, which takes me out of my narrow sphere of concern for myself and energises my whole being. In Chapter 10 we shall explore more of this outward expansive movement that is the greatest medicine for our *dukkha*.

Energy is generated by the mind as much as lying dormant in the body. So you need to be careful what you say to yourself about having low or no energy – thoughts are actions, and therefore have consequences. You can think yourself into all sorts of physical states. Try, when you wake up in the morning, to think to yourself that you have bucketfuls of energy for the day ahead. You may not necessarily leap out of bed, bound downstairs and do 40 minutes of yoga, but you never know.

The drive that needs direction

Our energies are not always integrated, they are dispersed, they are not all working in the same direction. Even when we have some intellectual mastery of its operations our body may refuse to be disciplined. And so we indulge our unhelpful cravings. You know that a couple of hours spent Instagramming, Facebooking, youTubing are not the most fruitful use of your time, and yet does that stop you from doing it?

We know things with the conscious mind, intellectually, rationally. But we are not just conscious minds. There is another greater part of us, there are other energies - instinct, intuition, volition, emotion - which are not accessible to the intellect. We have to get this part of us on board if we are committed to freeing ourselves of those pollutants of the mind which plague us. This emotional side of us is more powerful than reason in bringing about change. We need mindfulness, but we also need heartfulness. We need to engage our emotions, to put our heart fully into the path to being free. We need both a wise mind and a wise heart. In Buddhism, there is no difference between the two. In fact, there is a Buddhist term *citta* which means both mind-heart and heart-mind.

Many of us have been brought up to believe, implicitly or explicitly, that the rational mind can solve all the problems of the world. This after all has been the central plank of scientific and much philosophical thought for several centuries in the West. Interestingly, although religions and philosophy in the West have talked a lot about the importance of desire in our lives, it is rarely in any positive sense. As Traleg Kyabgon points out, 'Rather, you will see everything that is distasteful about human beings traced back to the fact that we have desire. Having desire is somehow related to our bodily, carnal nature, according to much of western philosophy, and there is nothing redemptive—in Buddhist terms, nothing "liberating"—that will come out of it. Therefore it is often concluded within the many western traditions that reason and rationality is what human beings should aim towards and excel in, to overcome our desires.'[313]

Rationality though can be a handicap to being in touch with the real nature of things. By contrast, look 'how the creatures of the air,' writes James Joyce, 'have their knowledge and know their times and seasons because they, unlike man, are in the order of their life and have not perverted that order by reason.'[314] The constantly thinking, cogitating, cognitive faculty of the mind can get in the way of us directly experiencing what is right, true and beautiful.

Buddhism does not belittle the importance of reason on the spiritual path, far from it. Reason and conceptual thought are crucial, for example, in observing how our craving mind works, and so in developing awareness and wisdom. But reason has its limits. Can reason rule desire? Buddhism says no. We have to harness the unconscious emotional side of ourselves if we wish to make progress in the direction of liberation.

In Sangharakshita's phrase, we have to 'find emotional equivalents for our intellectual understanding'[315]. Intellectually we often know what the right thing is to do, the right thing to bring about a positive outcome, but we need to engage our emotional energy to inspire us and bring about a change in our habits. I like this sentence from the human rights lawyer Philippe Sands, 'An abstract principle is not enough to be heroic; it has to be something which is emotional and deeply motivated.'[316]

Wherever energy is applied, there is change. The application of energy is what is required of us in order to address those unhelpful urges, longings, clingings. We have the choice about what we set our mind upon and, whenever we attend to something, we apply energy to it. We need to integrate and incorporate our scattered dispersed energies, all our diffuse energies, and direct them so that they become determination.

And so, an amalgamation and a harmonisation of our energies. As many holistic therapeutic approaches put forward - ancient and modern, across the world - whether we are in good health or poor health depends on whether our mental, emotional and physical energies are in balance and harmonious, or not.

But how do we harness our emotions? Emotions are our inner drives and they prepare us to take action. They are energy, and without emotions there is no energy; at least not the type of energy that gives us the power to change our habits. It is worth reflecting on what really engages you emotionally. I did this on retreat several years ago and came up with a tentative list: family, teaching the *dharma*, music, kindness, nature, interconnectedness, and generosity. If I did this list again now it might be different, or maybe not. I might include swimming and writing. These are things I can easily put *my* energies into.

Most Buddhists engage in imaginative devotional practices which awaken positive emotions; these may involve bowing or kneeling in front of a shrine, and thus paying reverence to a statue or other representation of the Buddha, the Buddha who reminds us of our own potential to become enlightened; offering gifts of flowers, lighted candles and incense to show our gratitude for the teachings; chanting a *mantra,* a sacred phrase, invoking the qualities of the Buddha or other Buddhist figure; and performing a *pūjā* - a ceremony in various parts which includes all of the above. A *pūjā* is a very rich and heart-opening practice. Some newcomers to Buddhism take to it straightaway, whereas for others, including myself initially, raised in a culture of materialist scepticism that disparages the elaborate trappings of ritual observance, it may take time and the opening of the mind and heart before one can actively engage in a *pūjā*.

Something bigger than ourselves

Buddhist devotional practices work on the basis that there is some force vaster than ourself with which we can align. Sometimes it may feel as though we are a hapless salmon swimming upstream against the natural flow of the river. But the salmon has a purpose, to lay its eggs in a safe place, and it is the determination that comes about from this purpose that drives it on, drives it on against strong oppositional forces.

Living beings are purposive. Whether plant or animal, we all pursue goals, although we may not necessarily be conscious of it. Ultimately our goal may be just survival and reproduction. Acting with a purpose can in many different ways influence the evolution of us all, of humankind.

In order to gather together all our diverse energies so that we can direct our whole being towards transformation and liberation, we need to find some purpose or meaning which is greater than our normal everyday concerns. When you give yourself over whole-heartedly to a project, something magic happens. In hospitals all over the world nurses, doctors and carers work long gruelling shifts, often at the expense of their own health and well-being, frequently go without proper sleep, food and exercise, yet find resources of energy which can seem superhuman. All because they are focussed on the welfare of the people they dedicate themselves to.

We can all too easily sink into the morass of self-obsession. We need an anchor which we can hold on to and which pulls us up out of our self-referential murk, freeing us to get in touch with those energies which take us beyond our limiting views about ourselves. I find it fascinating that in the Twelve Step Programme devised by Alcoholics Anonymous for recovering alcoholics, the eleventh step is about getting into contact with a higher power, a higher plan or one's higher self.

We can all contact a powerful urge within ourselves, an urge to relate to something that we are meant to be doing; it's as though we all have our own individual private story, our myth, which represents our profoundest nature wanting to articulate itself. We need to uncover this deep nature which consists of our loftiest values. We shall look at this again in the following chapter.

Perhaps the problem is that our desires are too petty, they need to be a lot grander. And the urge to be free of our neurotic cravings, the energy that we wish to align ourselves with, has to be more appealing, more engaging, more satisfying than our common everyday longings. What is more fulfilling, an hour spent kicking around, clicking around on Instagram, or an hour passed in harmonious conversation with a good friend who is open to you, and to whom you are open?

To challenge the powerful urges and attractions we all experience, we need always to feel motivated so that our efforts are enjoyable, not a drudge. We will need inspiration, which we will have to keep on renewing. I wrote earlier that my inspiration usually comes from getting in touch with *mettā*, the loving kindness for all living beings. I also turn to verses from the *Bodhicaryāvatāra* where I offer up symbolically all that is beautiful in the world to the Buddha, my inspiration.[317]

There are many ways in which we can be become inspired and motivate ourselves. Some depend upon having the right conditions in place, for example, being in the company of positive others. We can be inspired by what we hear, listen to, see and read; a stimulating talk, moving music, an awe-inspiring sunrise, a sacred shrine, a commanding presence, an uplifting book. There is a pleasure also that comes from skilful action; an act of generosity, a deed of kindness, words of appreciation and encouragement. When we see the fruits of our skilful action, say in managing to successfully address the cravings that have haunted us, then we will feel inspired to continue acting in the same way.

Effort in pursuit of the good

I wrote above that we need to find something bigger than ourselves in our lives to find the determination to change. Those who believe in God have an advantage in a way, in that they believe in a driving force in the universe which pervades everything in their life. For those who do not have a God as the central force in their life, and in Buddhism there is no place for an all-powerful creator God, then there needs to be another force which drives them.

I have already described *dhamma-chanda,* the drive and desire for the truth. For Buddhists there is also *vīrya*. We can find all sorts of translations for *vīrya* – effort in pursuit of the good, courage, enthusiasm, heroic perseverance, energetic effort, vigour, determination, delight in doing what is skilful, eagerness, exertion, aspiration, diligence, driving force. 'Sometimes it's said in the Mahāyāna that *vīrya* is, in a way, the foundation of everything. If you've got that then everything follows, but if you don't have that then nothing is possible at all.'[318]

Undoubtedly *vīrya* is a powerful force, a passion and, as we have seen, where a powerful energy is applied transformation will occur. And we need something powerful to deal with our intransigent habits, our nagging thoughts and emotions, our cravings, those recalcitrant aspects of ourselves which don't want to go away; they are so resilient within us all, and we have to utilize something equally, if not more, resilient.

Traditional Buddhist writings are full of expressions of *vīrya*. For example, 'the driving power of purposeful thought propels me,'[319] 'without vigour there is no merit, just as there is no movement without wind';[320] and 'do not be downcast, but marshal all your strength; take heart and be master of yourself!'[321]

By exercising *vīrya* constantly and consistently, we develop confidence in how we are acting, because we experience outcomes that are beneficial to us and those around us. We develop more and more trust and confidence in our path, more and more *śraddhā* [322], confidence in bringing our whole being into the path. This *śraddhā* arises initially through our intuition – something draws us towards these teachings; through our reason – the teachings make sense to us; and through our experience – when we practise them we can see that they work. Faith in what we are doing needs to have a fierce side, a determined aspect. Energy in pursuit of the good, *vīrya,* is what connects *śraddhā* with action, consciously turning our mind away from sensuous longing to something more ultimately satisfying and wholesome.

Taking a mythic approach again, if we are to shake off the influence of Māra, we have to be equally - no, much more - determined and persistent. We have to rally all the resolve and fight that we can muster. He is not easily put off. We have to throw everything at him. But we are fortunate in that we have use of a weapon that cuts through that which binds us. We can employ a double-edged sword, the dual aspect of *vīrya*, of vigilance and passion. These work against the inertia of our minds. The mind that simply reacts to stimuli that make contact with our senses is effectively inert; the mind that responds with mindfulness is active and creative, the opposite to inertia.

The linctus for laziness is *vīrya*. Being bothered. Being bothered to use our mind and heart. If we are not moving forward we are inevitably moving backward, slipping back into our unhelpful habitual tendencies, allowing them to become stronger and more rigid. We all need a spiritual kick up the backside sometimes, a good dose of *vīrya,* to revive our energy and commitment to overcoming that which limits and impairs the promise of what we are capable of. Our being has got to get off of its cozy sofa and do some work. Just wanting to drift along in a snug world of relative contentment, free of challenges, a nice cocoon of well-being and comfortable practice, this will not change our habits. Mind and body are very much connected. Release, purification, energy, expansion, the themes of Part Two of this book, all of these are actions of mind and body.

We also have to be on our guard not to disperse or misuse your energy, it's precious. As I age, I am only too aware of this. I know that I have invested a lot of energy during my life in activities like mindless internet-surfing, boozy parties that I didn't really want to be at, and watching countless shallow TV programmes. Oh my days! However much fruitless energy and time have I dispensed, how much oomph has been drained from me, all through those hopeless pointless cravings!

We frequently squander our valuable energy, our treasured breaks from the daily grind. We diffuse our energies in pastimes which are not at all productive, not at all conducive to our best interests, and often downright harmful to us; we may end up using what energy remains in grumbling and feeling sorry for ourselves. One could question whether much of the time spent on social media is constructive and conducive to our best interests. Energy is an indispensable resource, don't blow it.

Apart from our energy being dissipated or ill-used, it can also get blocked or frustrated, so that it feels as though we don't have the energy needed to set about or complete a task. Lack of energy, or perceived lack of energy, is clearly an impediment to anything in life. At times we feel that we don't have the energy to do what we know is beneficial for us, or to do something that we know we need to do, a walk round the park, for example, or that long put-off phone call to our brother. And yet, lo and behold, a good friend phones, and I can easily find the energy to spend an hour chatting away merrily, laughing and joking, in top form. We have access to energy if we really want it, and if the situation seems attractive enough for us. Funny, isn't it, that many of us always seem to have the energy to watch Netflix.

As stressed in Chapter 6, in the end it is down to you. You can only rely on your own efforts. Desire for what is good, *dhamma-chanda*, only goes so far if you are not prepared to act on the desire. It requires little effort to talk in a general way about the theory and practice of Buddhism, about taking desire as the path to freedom, but such rhetoric on its own is not worth much in the end. We have to empower ourselves in order to overcome the force of our negative habitual tendencies.

This relates to *vīrya*-as-effort as a guiding principle in our personal practice. The Buddhist teaching of the Four Right Efforts describes this quite simply; it is easy to explain the teaching as a gardening metaphor.

First, pull up the weeds that are presently growing (eradicate your unskilful mental states); inhibit new weeds from growing (prevent the arising of unskilful mental states); grow healthy plants (cultivate skilful mental states); and look after healthy plants (maintain skilful mental states). Healthy plants grow better when there are no weeds to choke them. In the same way, healthy urges develop more strongly when unhealthy urges are confronted and weakened. We need to be the vigilant gardener, always on the lookout to nip weeds in the bud before the roots go too deep.

Balanced effort

It is tempting to say that the best protection from our unwholesome urges and itches is always positive effort and striving in pursuit of something higher. But some words of caution here. Striving has negative connotations as well, connotations both of over-exertion and burning oneself out - which are helpful to nobody's well-being - but also of directionless, blinkered, or one-sided endeavour. There is a danger inherent in 'craving to attain non-craving', clutching to a goal at all costs. We must beware of wilfulness, which suggests a determination to do something regardless of whether it is right or wrong, for example, a disregard of the impact of one's actions upon others. Balance and vigilance then are key in our spiritual efforts.

There is a story in the Pali Canon which illustrates this. The monk Soṇa is having trouble with striving in his secluded meditation. The Buddha comes to him with an analogy, pointing out that a lute is not 'well-tuned and easy to play either if its strings are too loose or too tight. In the same way, Soṇa, overly exerted effort leads to restlessness, overly loose effort leads to idleness. Therefore you, Soṇa, should determine the correct effort.'[323]

Many of us lead very stressful lives. We all need some kind of break from our pressured routines now and again, particularly when those routines seem to be meaningless and mind-dulling, or simply routines that are necessary but extremely draining. Some of us live in very demanding circumstances, due to financial, environmental, housing, employment and family pressures, due to societal prejudice, or because we have been displaced from our homes for whatever reasons by circumstances beyond our control. For these circumstances not to drive us crazy, we have to balance out those pressures with contrasting periods of enjoyment when and where we can find them. Sometimes we just absolutely need the space to chill, as a counterbalance to our stressful lives.

Without some space for ourselves, life can overpower us and severely affect our mental well-being. Meditation, as we saw in chapter 7, is a space where we can stop, pause and let go; as our meditation practice develops however it becomes much more than that, a space where we can really find connection and insight.

In fact, *vīrya* is just one of five 'spiritual faculties' which Buddhists are encouraged to develop, and upon which spiritual progress depends. The others are *smṛti* (mindfulness), *śraddhā* (faith, confidence), *prajñā* (wisdom), and *samādhi* (concentration). Concentration and *vīrya* are seen as a pair in contrast and having a controlling effect on each other, the two balanced by mindfulness. An emphasis on immobile contemplation can result in sluggishness, and too much effort can lead to restless agitation. The strength of *vīrya*'s driving nature needs to be tempered by wise ethical vigilance. Remember the definition of *vīrya* as 'effort in pursuit of the good', not simply effort *per se*.

Words like 'should' and 'need to', these only mean what is beneficial to us and others, and are not there to be used as a means to self-loathing and feelings of inadequacy. Balance again, a balance between accepting and non-accepting; accepting that we have limitations at the moment, about what we can do and what we are, but not accepting that we are incapable of change, that those limitations are there for always.

A quality that is sometimes portrayed as a counterbalance to *vīrya* in Buddhism is *kṣānti*, which we can translate as patience, forbearance, tolerance, endurance; on the face of it, these appear to be passive rather than active virtues. Yet in our strong positive desire to deal with our equally strong negative cravings, we need *kṣānti* as well. Patience, yes, because the journey may be a long and uneven one. But forbearance equally, the resolve to put up now with small hardships, minor irritations, for the greater benefits which we can have confidence in and which will follow, further along the line.

I have learnt to put up with chronic back pain for many years. But I have also used it at times to put me in touch with the greater pain that is going on all around the world; my pain is paltry compared to what others have to suffer. Through practice we can learn to put up with much, including the absence of those things which we normally crave, whether they be sunny weather, potato crisps, pornography, Instagramming, shopping for clothes, gaming or whatever creature comforts we depend upon.

It can really seem to hurt when you can't have what you really want, trying to come off a dependence on tobacco, for example. We are almost bound to experience discomfort initially, but we build up resilience this way. Resilience is an inner strength that we can build up by linking it to something greater than our own meagre suffering. By the way, I like that (somewhat British) little ditty 'Whether the weather is cold, or whether the weather is hot, we'll weather the weather whatever the weather, whether we like it or not'. Well, you have to really, don't you?

Bit by bit

So, not daunted by the magnitude of our ideals, not turning back regardless of difficulties, and not blaming others or expecting others to remove our difficulties, we move forward in our quest to move beyond our daily cravings[324]. We have to acknowledge that *vīrya* is a faculty that needs to be developed over time, from moment to moment, from day to day. With the resources we have at our disposal we do what we can. An important aspect of *vīrya* is persistence, persistence in the course of freedom. Here's Śāntideva: 'Therefore leaving everything that is averse to it, I'll labor to increase my perseverance – through cheerful effort, keenness, self-control, through aspiration, firmness, joy, and moderation.'[325] It is through perseverance rather than strength that we can achieve great things.[326]

Initially, a lot of effort may be needed on the path to freedom from our constraining habits; we make headway centimetre by centimetre, although occasionally we may make metre-long leaps. We learn bit by bit to desire not to desire what is not helpful to us. It's not feasible to imagine that we can straightaway transform powerful desires, some of which are instinctual, into pure wholesome energy.

We know that 'the power of virtue is weak, while the forces of darkness are strong.'[327] Nobody is pretending that the path of coming to terms with our deep cravings is an easy one. And sometimes we will feel that we are straying from this path, or tripping over unexpected obstacles on the way. There will be setbacks, as we saw in Chapter 7. However, there is good advice available, 'if you fall down, pick yourself up, carry on, continue to make an effort, never give up, never give in, if you can just practise these two things, remaining constantly aware and always making an effort, then success is assured, you'll get there in the end, perhaps sooner rather than later.'[328]

Persistence is the key then on our journey to open the door to freedom from our problems. We will come to the realization that we can transform our cravings but not entirely banish them. The spiritual path is a constant revisiting and transformation of the emotions that we find difficult. To overcome deep craving we need to be a warrior.

We can be clear about our ideal, but without *vīrya* we have no chance of realising it. Yes, let us want peace and freedom from turmoil for ourselves and the world. But also let us build up our determination and commitment, with others, in pursuing these aims; otherwise these desires may only become hollow hopes. In the world today, the determination that is *vīrya* is what is so needed; whether an individual determination to transform oneself, to rid oneself of one's damaging habits, or a determination with others to transform the world, to sow the seeds of an alternative way of living which is not founded on institutional greed, hatred and delusion. The drive which we need to see the world and all its myriad connections much more clearly means that we need to have trust in *paṭicca-samuppāda*, the interdependence of all phenomena, and also in the law of *karma*, that the positive force of our behaviour of body, speech and mind will have beneficial consequences for us all.

The effort that becomes no effort

Along the path of consistent effort we will eventually encounter forces which seem to have a drive of their own. You may have encountered something resembling an intuitive force before. If you are new to Buddhism - or for those of you who are not but can look back at your first experience of the *dharma* - what made you pick up this or that book, how did you find yourself in a Buddhist centre one day, what drew you to an image of the Buddha?

As we make progress and move forward, our energies may seem to become more free-flowing. In horse-racing terms, as we ride along the steeplechase course which is our life, encountering the many hurdles and surmounting them, we may find that each obstacle on the track gets smaller and so less problematic. The going has become good and, firm-footed, we drive forward, unremittingly, but with a calmed disposition.

The further we can move ourselves away from our cravings, the less their gravitational pull becomes; like drawing away from the tugs and the drags of samsaric earth into a gravitation-free space, which has limitless possibilities, and which is our true fulfilment as an enlightened human being. We may feel that we are making the effort that is no effort. The desire to act skilfully becomes more and more our natural mode of being, up to the point where our actions become virtually desireless actions.

I remember that when I first starting going to a Buddhist centre, I noticed how generous everyone seemed to be, bringing along food and drink to share, making me cups of tea, a regular supplying of biscuits, people offering me some of their lunch, buying me books, offering me their precious time to talk over something. Gradually this became my behaviour as well; generosity is infectious and becomes effortless, unpremeditated, the totally natural way of behaving. It's as though there's 'a power that seems to come from somewhere outside oneself, or at least outside one's present conscious self.'[329]

This becomes like a car which drives itself. 'Think of new drivers who have not yet learned to relax behind the wheel', writes Thubten Yeshe. 'Because they are anxious to do everything correctly they are constantly busy, adjusting their steering, speed, and so forth. The result is a jerky, uncomfortable ride. Instead of being a pleasurable experience, driving becomes a chore. Experienced drivers, on the other hand, are relaxed. Although they remain aware of what is going on, they have learned to let go, and allow the car to drive itself. As a result their ride is smooth and effortless and it sometimes feels as if the car were flying blissfully through the air rather than bouncing noisily along the road!'[330]

We desire with positive intent, resulting in consequences which are subject to the law of *karma* until, because of our deliberate efforts, we become subject to another type of process. This is the process known as *dhamma-niyāma*,[331] the process by which Enlightenment arises, the culmination of a sequence of conditions brought about by our diligent practice. This is a spontaneous force, a momentum, a progressive trend or evolution within human beings. It goes beyond the personal, whereby our individual willing, our self-referencing, is transcended. It is the force that we align ourselves with and which takes us towards freedom. In a commonly used analogy, we have to put all our efforts into raising the sails on the boat journey which is our becoming, so that we can catch the wind of this momentum in our sails, and allow it to drive us along our path. But this may be a long way away yet. In the meantime we open our heart and feel the energy there as a guiding light on our journey.

Reflecting – Chapter 9

Do you feel that you are longing to connect with anything at this moment? Which activities really engage you? How does it feel to be engaged in this way? Do these energies seem positive and healthy, or negative and unhelpful? Do you find willpower a useful strategy for dealing with your cravings? Can you relate to connecting with something 'bigger than yourself'? When you feel yourself craving, notice the energy within your body, somatically – where is it in the body, what does it actually feel like, its strength, its range, its qualities. Try the exercise in this chapter of experiencing the energy of craving and then expanding it outwards. What force drove you to pick up this or other writing about the dharma, or go to a Buddhist Centre for the first time?

Chapter 10:

EXPANDING

When I was a small boy, I became fascinated by acorns. Playing in the local park with my friends in autumn, stopping and bending down when I came across that little tough nut - those that fall early still pale lime green, those that had turned to their mature shiny walnut brown, most sitting pretty in their knobbly cup, some lying alone, others in twin pairs. Many to be taken up by squirrels and buried for later, or be eaten by other passing wildlife. Others to get trodden on and eventually perish. A very few waited patiently till they attained their innate purpose of germination and growth. I enjoyed simply picking them up from the ground, feeling them in my fingers, and examining their beauty, little parcels of strength and durability.

The teacher and poet Maitreyabandhu has talked about taking an acorn and polishing, polishing, polishing it until it is really shiny; this he says represents a 'good life'. The life you lead may be a good and shiny one; you may appear to be self-contained like the acorn, and have everything you need to be quite happy, although the sheen may wear a bit thin sometimes, or perhaps often. A shiny acorn life though is a life of potential unfulfilled. Or you can take an acorn, plant it in the ground, nurture it and see it sprout, flourish and grow into an enormous wonderful oak tree; this is the 'spiritual life'.

We are much more than just a seed, however beautiful that seed may seem. We can expand through our sturdy ego casing, unfold, and grow into a resilient being, finding our true nature. Our tree will soar ever upwards, to higher levels, into rarefied air, away from the pollutants below; we know that there is only restricted growth in the presence of toxins. Where our tree will reach to and what we will find there, we cannot know. Growth is not always constant; our leaves may look as they did a year ago. Or even, with the flux of the seasons, they may seem to wilt and fade. But we can trust that, once the growth is well-established, our renewal is guaranteed.

And, as we are nourished by supportive conditions - our own sun and rain - then our tree becomes nourishment for other living beings, very naturally. Our great boughs give shelter from excessive heat, and protection from damp and cold. Our leaves and blooms provide sustenance, our fruits ripen and drop for the benefit of others. We breathe in harmful gases and exhale the fresh air that sustains fulfilling life.[332] Our tree gives of itself, and others receive and thrive.

When one day, inevitably, as happens even to strong giants, our sap, our energy flows no more, we leave behind for future generations small seeds, small acorns, which carry life forward and grow in their own unique way. Each tree leaves its mark, whether great or small, its impact on all that surrounds it, and is reborn in other living things.

Different ways of being

As we have explored throughout this book, there are different ways of being. We can exist in a 'self-mode'. When we crave for sensual pleasure, for experiential avoidance, or to protect and promote our sense of self, then we desire in the self-mode. The self-mode is inward-regarding, limiting and fundamentally unsatisfying; it is characterised by self-centredness, confusion, dispersed energy, essentially *dukkha*.

Conversely we can grow, like an acorn into a magnificent oak tree, in an 'expansive-mode'. The expansive-mode is other-regarding, outward-looking and ultimately fulfilling; it is characterised by interconnection, clarity, focussed energy, equanimity and calm. When we long for freedom from ingrained unhelpful habits, to fulfil our human potential, and for the well-being of all, then we desire in the expansive-mode. We can either contract and cloud the mind, or open it out and liberate it. We can live with a narrow perspective and a delusional sense of certainty, or release into our possibilities. Our minds have the massive capacity to bring us and others happiness. 'This is our evolution' writes Thubten Yeshe, 'from an ordinary, limited, and deluded person trapped within the shell of a petty ego into a fully evolved, totally conscious being of unlimited compassion and insight.'[333]

This book is about how the spiritual tradition of Buddhism addresses our unhelpful longings and clingings. The spiritual life is a movement. A moving away from one mode of being to another. The movement is from taking to giving. We progress from taking, for ourself, to giving, of ourself. Taking moves us inward, it is movement back on ourself, having, holding on to, maintaining ourself as the centre of things, emphasising and increasing the sense of own importance, indulging ourselves; it is 'small mind'. Giving moves us outward, it is movement away from ourself, reaching outwards, giving of our energy, lessening our self-centredness and self-importance; it is 'big mind'. As Paul Hawken writes 'It is hard to be grasping when we are reaching out.'[334] Your hands cannot do both at the same time. Try it and see. Either your hands are closing in or opening out.

If, in our modern world, consumerism is the principal manifestation of human craving, then its antidote is giving. The opposite of taking for ourselves is giving to others. The practice of consuming is predicated on satisfying ourselves. The practice of giving is predicated on the needs of others. In this sense we can be a force for good in the world rather than being dominated by the force of niggling craving. Our ethical actions are our legacy to the future; either the perfume of a life lived with kindness, or the reek of selfishness.

Beyond self-interest

When we begin to expand beyond our own self-interest, we discover miraculously that we have patience, patience towards whatever cravings arise. They become less important in our lives. We are no longer overwhelmed by them. In short, we become less self-obsessed.

When we start to care for others as much as ourselves, when the well-being of others is as important, or even more important, than our own self-cherishing, our sense of self diminishes to the extent that we crave less and less for ourselves. What we desire is the well-being of all sentient beings. As we let go of unhelpful, unhealthy emotions, the positive emotion of warmth towards our brothers and sisters on this planet begins to fill us.

When we expand out of the armour that surrounds our tiny self, we can move beyond self-cherishing, beyond self-conceit, to the cherishing of all beings (including, naturally, ourselves). Maitreyabandhu sums up this movement succinctly. 'Actually the spiritual life is a simple matter.... All we need to do is take a step away from selfishness towards selflessness – there is nothing besides this.' [335]

When we are no longer so full of ourselves, we can eventually relax. As we soften our sense of self we open up, we develop an attitude that is more spacious, more compassionate, melting the barriers that we erect between ourselves and others. The realization of how we and all phenomena are interconnected dissolves the false boundaries and false identities that we are stuck with. My and your happiness and well-being are not separate, they are co-dependent.

When we can begin to see that what we conceive as a stable ego is not some kind of physical entity, but rather a mental attitude, in fact 'just a very weak thread of waking consciousness artificially holding together a large bundle of disparate materials'[336] or 'a transitory assemblage of evanescent parts',[337] our self-centredness, our desire to please this idea called 'self' starts to disintegrate. We have already looked at this dissolution of the idea of the self in Chapter 8.

Whether it's when we're nervous about giving a talk in front of an audience, having a conversation with friends (or ourselves), arguing with a partner, pondering a weighty problem, or whether we are treading a spiritual path and seeking total liberation from *dukkha,* we need to get ourselves out of the way. It is essentially our ego that craves unskilfully. We can move from identifying with ourselves to identifying with everything, with no separation between. We realise that we don't need to have a strong identity, a badge that defines us. This is how we could interpret what Bob Dylan meant when he sang, 'Mama take this badge off of me, I can't use it anymore'. [338]

The poet and visionary William Blake wrote, 'Nought loves another as itself nor venerates another so.'[339] This may be the nature with which we were born, but it need not always be so. When I look back at some of the really magic moments of my life, I find that my awareness of my self has momentarily faded away – time spent in concord with my loved ones, my family and friends; lost in a Himalayan sunset; deep in a meditation; snorkelling and communing with fish in the Red Sea; absorbed in playing music with a band; experiencing joy at the blossoming of my garden in spring; communicating the *dharma.*

Our attempts to satisfy ourselves through craving for sensual pleasure and our continual self-referencing are so limiting and profoundly frustrating. There is no reasonable justification for giving ourselves preferential treatment. Here is how the poet Rilke expresses this idea: *'know as well the need to not be: let that ground of all that changes bring you to completion now. To all that has run its course, and to the vast unsayable numbers of beings abounding in Nature, add yourself gladly, and cancel the cost.'*[340]

In the previous chapter I mentioned the devotional rituals or *pūjā* which form part of the practice of many Buddhists. One *pūjā* derived from the

Bodhicaryāvatāra finishes with what I find sublimely beautiful verses, the 'transference of merits and self-surrender', in which we offer up ourselves symbolically, as well as the positive energy gained from our skilful actions, for the benefit of all beings. In that same vein, I generally finish my meditations with a line from the *Bodhicaryāvatāra*, 'With my whole being, I offer myself as a servant to the world.'[341]

Deeds of loving kindness

Every small act of kindness chips away at the edifice of selfishness, constructed not of solid bricks and mortar, but of the cotton wool of deluded desiring. This is the movement from I to we. With loving kindness, not only will we be able to chase away our own headaches but also the headaches of other people.[342] I love how this is captured by the Japanese Zen Buddhist poet Ryōkan:

> *Sporting and sporting*
> *As I pass through this floating world*
> *Finding myself here,*
> *Is it not good*
> *To dispel the bad dreams of others?*

This movement away from our self-centred craving and attachment is central to the Buddhist path. The key elements of this path are often summarised as the cultivation of wisdom and compassion. In the same way that wisdom can be seen as an expansion of awareness, of mindfulness, compassion can be seen as an expansion of loving kindness, of emotional engagement. The psychologist Paul Gilbert has defined compassion as 'behaviour that aims to nurture, look after, teach, guide, mentor, soothe, protect, offer feelings of acceptance and belonging – in order to benefit another person.'[343]

Thubten Yeshe has pointed out that acts of compassion have a wise aspect and are not just emotional gestures: 'dedicating yourself to others doesn't mean stripping naked and giving them all your clothes. Dedicating yourself to others is an act of wisdom, not emotion, and derives from discovering how harmful the mind of attachment is…attachment has accumulated in your mind, occupying and polluting it completely.'[344] So through giving of ourselves we loosen our attachments.

Ultimately the Buddhist goal as expressed in the Mahāyāna tradition is the exchange of self and other: 'All those who suffer in the world do so because of their obsession for their own happiness. All those happy in the world are so because of their desire for the happiness of others.'[345] However, if this goal seems way beyond our current mode of being, in the meantime we can love.

Love universal

Love is an antidote to craving. This is *Mettā*, which lies at the very heart of the Buddha's teaching. Self-directed desire becomes desire directed to all. Love for ourselves becomes love for all beings, including ourself. *Mettā* does not require reciprocity, it is unconditional - 'As strongly as a mother, perhaps risking her life, cherishes her child, her only child, develop an unlimited heart for all beings.'[346] *Mettā* is undiscriminating. The usual English translation 'loving kindness' does not do it justice; better the Spanish rendering of *'amor universal'*. Sensual desire is thirst for one's own sake; *Mettā* is thirst for the sake of everybody. 'Love is the real nuclear bomb that destroys all our enemies, because when we love all living beings, we have no enemies,' says the Tibetan teacher Geshe Kelsang Gyatso. But also, where there is real love - selfless, universal, unattached love, there can be no self-directed craving.

Mettā is seeing other people as our fellow human beings, experiencing our interconnection, treating others with loving kindness and empathy, not as objects to satisfy our ignoble, egoistic needs. We may feel ourselves sometimes drowning in an ocean of self-centred passions and thrills; the conversion of our craving-as-energy can be the raft that rescues us from the insubstantiality of 'cheap thrills' and transports us to the enjoyment of purposeful desire.

Mettā is not only a remedy to craving for sensual pleasure and craving for the centrality of our self. Love is also the corrective to the desire for non-existence. In the passage from Thomas Mann's *The Magic Mountain*, referred to in Chapter 4, where a character is lost in a snowstorm and is on the point of ceding to death, it is love that saves him. 'Love stands opposed to death. It is love, not reason, that is stronger than death. Only love, not reason, gives sweet thoughts. And from love and sweetness alone can form come: form and civilisation, friendly, enlightened, beautiful human intercourse.... I will let death have no mastery over my thoughts. For therein lies goodness and love of humankind.'[347] Or, as the psychiatrist M. Scott Peck puts it, in his famous book *The Road Less*

Travelled, love is 'the miraculous force that defies the natural law of entropy.'[348]

So many ways to love

The *Mettā* that draws us out of ourselves and towards others can take many forms. To counter the feeling of being on our own in an agitated world, we can think of how we can contribute to the collective good by acts of generosity, compassionate thoughts, words of kindness and helpfulness, as well as harmonious relationships; the effect of our actions will ripple outwards. For Buddhists, *danā* - giving, generosity - is central to our ethical life and one of the qualities we seek to develop and perfect. It involves, writes the Theravāda teacher Santikaro, 'sharing the gifts, benefits, and resources that have come to us – material, intellectual, artistic, social, spiritual…giving things of value where they are needed and when they will be of benefit.'[349] So not only material things, but also being resourceful in giving our time and energy. To break our attachment to possessiveness, we can practice giving away those things which we feel we would most like to hold onto. The path to happiness and to freedom is paved with generosity.

Gratitude has a transformative power also to break us out of our self-centredness, being grateful for what we have, instead of craving for more or better possessions, relationships, situations. Even though we may be suffering we can still appreciate, be grateful for, and find beauty in, the things that surrounds us. 'We seem to have the wrong default setting for our approvals and satisfactions:' writes Bradford Hatcher, 'these should be set at the minimum levels that are needed for continued existence. Then everything else is a gift.'[350]

And we can also practice being appreciative and taking enjoyment in the positive qualities and good fortune of others. This is the Buddhist quality of *muditā*, sympathetic joy. I have always found that when I look for the good in another person, I coincidentally discover the good in myself. Geshe Kelsang Gyatso writes that 'someone who has learned to rejoice in the good fortune of others experiences only happiness. Seeing another person's beautiful house or attractive partner immediately makes him happy - the fact that they are not his own is irrelevant.'[351]

The Buddhist spiritual path is a social one. When we expand our concern outwards, beyond our own self-centred concerns, what we see is the same fallibility, frailty and vulnerability in others that we experience ourselves. We all suffer, we all crave - crave to be happy in our individual way, sometimes in blinkered, unhelpful ways. When we connect to other people, we see also that they have deep longings, just like us, and we can experience empathy and connection since we, just like them, do foolish things sometimes. We have empathy with all our fellow human beings who find themselves somewhere along the same continuum as ourselves, some with extreme very harmful urges, others with irritating fancies and pinings. We are all along there somewhere and, if not for the grace of the conditions which have shaped our existence, might easily have found ourselves in a much worse state than we currently are; and could still easily find ourselves in the future if our supportive conditions were to alter.

Traleg Kyabgon dispels the myth of Buddhists just being concerned with their own personal self-development. 'In Buddhism,' he writes, 'contrary to what some may believe, following a spiritual path such as is being presented here is not about not having anything to do with people because the world is samsaric and illusory and we have to run away from illusion and attain buddhahood, seeing it as a trans-worldly state disconnected from anything to do with experience. That is not the Buddhist view. The Buddhist view is to create better relationships with oneself, others, and the world. We work towards being an undivided person, and to see and experience the interconnection with others and the world.'[352] We relate to other people not in a utilitarian way, not in terms of what we can get out of them, but rather as human beings with whom we identify.

When I am confronted by the suffering of another human, my mind and body tell me whether I am responding in a self-centred way, which feels constricting and negating, or in a more selfless way, which feels expansive and accepting. The less I am concerned about protecting myself, the more effective I am in my response to the suffering fellow being. The less I crave for a protective wall between her and me, the more I desire her well-being and am ready to help. Self-centredness gets in the way of connection with my fellow beings in the world. This is a great message of the Buddha. Compassion comes from the wisdom of seeing through our obsession with ourselves. Wisdom comes from the compassion that arises naturally when we feel our interconnection with others. Thich Nhat Hanh calls this connection 'interbeing' and he summarizes it beautifully in his poem *Interrelationship*: 'You are me, and I am you. Isn't it obvious that we "inter-are"?'[353]

A deep wish

There is a desire that comes from your depths and makes you feel wholesome. And when you have discovered this profound desire, you can let it direct your life rather than allow yourself to be carried along by the waves of your cravings. As we have seen in this book, Buddhism is not about eliminating desire. It is about fostering a desire, the desire for fulfilment and connection; the desire to be greater than our normal selves. It is about tuning in to our deepest values rather than our deepest unhelpful desires, and being in harmony with those values. And ironically, as we become less, we become more; Ṭhānissaro Bhikkhu of the Thai Forest Buddhist tradition writes, 'Whoever has learned to be more than himself knows that he loses little when he loses himself.'[354]

This deep-seated urge within us to experience ourselves fully and without reservations is uplifting and all-embracing. It is a foretaste, as the psychotherapist and spiritual teacher David Richo explains, of what the Buddha experienced. 'The psyche with all its longings and desires is Buddha alive today and here in us. In our longings, we glimpse our Buddha nature, a realm of love, meaning, freedom, happiness, growth…when we long or desire with an openness to any outcome, a "let it be" attitude, we are free of craving. We have let go of the "must have" energy that is the cause of suffering.'[355] Skilful desires can be seen as the stepping-stones towards Enlightenment.

We may talk of transcendence here. This deep desire is a desire to transcend, to go beyond our own self-interest. If we wish to connect with our full potential in life, we have to look up and reach out, to commit ourselves to something beyond our limited perspective based on our minor selfish longings. In order to grow we need an ideal. An ideal like the Buddha, 'a man beyond the patchwork world of greed.'[356] The boundaries of what can provide us happiness are much larger than our own ego and what immediately protects it. 'Instead of being confined in our own petty reality,' writes Thubten Yeshe, 'we move into the larger sphere of universal concern.'[357] Perhaps most of us live with a narrow concave lens perception of ourselves and the world, whereas a convex lens perception corresponds more to reality.

We may even say that there is a calling to a way of being beyond just releasing our cravings, beyond purifying our cravings, beyond transforming our cravings. Here we can focus not so much on dealing with our cravings, but rather on what lies beyond what we think of as ourselves. 'It's a sort of general spiritual law' said Sangharakshita in a seminar, 'that you can transform your present pain and suffering by being in touch with, and experiencing, a higher spiritual reality.'[358]

We looked in the previous chapter at how we can contact our higher self, some greater purpose in our life. Here we can think more of giving ourselves up to something beyond ourselves, to a force that will carry us forwards to freedom from what bedevils and constrains us. This giving ourselves up to a way of being beyond our current self, to a higher ideal, is self-surrender. Self-surrender involves a deep letting go of clinging. Instead of surrendering to our desires, one can surrender and align ourselves with a greater force.[359] This aspiration and commitment is cultivated through practices of meditation, ritual and, in fact, all Buddhist practices that are based on great compassion and the loosening of the bonds of selfhood.

The heart's release

Being free from deluded craving brings about great joy. As Vessantara has said, the *dharma* is about freedom, about crashing through barriers, and dancing! [360] When we release our cravings, another different type of release arises – the release of the heart. In one of my favourite Buddhist quotes, 'the heart's release by love shines and glows and radiates.'[361] This is bliss that goes beyond anything we can experience through our mundane desires. Just look at the gentle blissful smile of the Buddha.

Sometimes, particularly when I am communicating the *dharma* to others, I can feel amazingly peaceful whilst at the same time experiencing enormous joy and almost boundless energy. At such times I feel delight, the delight that 'my life has borne fruit',[362] not so much happy as feeling incredibly alive. This I believe is just a taster of what it must feel like to experience oneself as pure energy, unmediated by any concepts or views, a glimpse of the enlightened mind. In Tantric terms, ultimately this is desire transmuted into bliss, but also transmuted into wisdom, and 'the penetrating brilliance of this blissful wisdom…cuts like a laser beam through all false projections of this and that and pierces the very heart of reality.'[363] This is the delight that purifies.

When the Buddha-to-be was just a boy, he sat one day in the shade of a rose-apple tree and spontaneously fell into a meditative state of blissfulness, well-being and calm. And it was the recollection of this experience in later life which was the inspiration that provoked a deep state of meditation and led to his eventual enlightenment. Great happiness and freedom from self-centredness go hand in hand. This is 'the liberation of the mind by altruistic joy.'[364]

If we no longer want to be a slave to our habitual cravings, we will need to get in touch with that longing to be free, free of everything that conditions us, free of everything that limits us, free of laziness and inertia, as free and as peaceful as the Buddha. Freedom from, but also freedom towards – towards a higher purpose; this is the longing for life in all its abundant richness, the urge for life's fulfilment. It is the negation of life-negation. As Rilke wrote, 'break free, as if a bouquet of wildflowers had come untied: The upswing of the light ones, the bowing sway of the heavy ones and the delicate ones' timid curve. Everywhere joy in relation and nowhere grasping.'[365]

Instead of craving for non-existence, instead of clinging to the delusory self, instead of grasping after transient phenomena, this is the quest to experience the world as a liberated being. Perfectly free, with perfect clarity and profound connection to all beings – 'wishless, free and wise'[366] and 'freed of delusive hindrance.'[367] And liberation can be our inspiration, as Sangharakshita has suggested, 'the spiritually-minded person thinks in terms of liberation…. In the search for freedom, happiness is a by-product.'[368]

Transforming ourselves, transforming the world

We may lament our lack of political power to modify the world, but we have huge personal power to modify ourselves. We can't refashion the world into how we want it to be, but we can refashion ourselves. When we follow our path to our own liberation from the affliction of craving, we are also contributing to liberation in a more social universal sense. Where there is kindness and awareness in an act, there is a positive evolution in the universe, since all phenomena, including our actions, are interconnected and impact on each other. This, as we have seen, is the Buddhist principle of *paṭicca-samuppāda*.

It may be that spiritual traditions such as Buddhism offer the only real alternative for our fragile unstable world, pervaded as it is by ideologies of acquisition, delusion, protectionism, individualism, ill-will, cynicism, and short-termism - both on an institutional and on a personal level. As I made clear in Chapter 6, I am not dismissing political movements, since they have brought about immense changes in the physical well-being of human beings. But their aim is not to achieve a fundamental change in the workings of our minds - our cravings, anger, hatred and confusion. And, without those changes, the future of humankind does not look bright. In the end, I believe that neither dominant political ideologies, nor science, technology and economics will provide all the answers to the world's problems and to our own individual incompleteness.

A halt to the degradation of our planet depends upon a tempering of self-interest and an over-riding concern for the well-being of us all. These are attitudes of mind. Change within is inextricably linked to change in the world around us. The latter cannot happen without the former. There *is* an alternative, despite what fatalistic narratives and mistruths tell us. Moreover, all of us have the power to contribute to and bring about change. As the Dalai Lama is quoted as joking, 'If you think you are too small to make a difference, try sleeping with a mosquito.' We all wish for peace and harmony in the world, but the Buddhist message is that these can never be achieved unless we firstly develop peace and harmony within our own hearts and minds.

Moving onwards

We have come in our exploration of craving from describing a lack, a thirst, and deluded self-satisfying, to opening up to a longing for freedom and abundance; and from taking in, to giving out. If the Buddhist three-fold classification of *taṇhā* can be summarised as 'to have, to be, and not to be,' then the ultimate slaking of that thirst can be summarised as 'to give, to love, to connect.'

We can broaden out from a self-mode to an expansive mode, from egoistical craving to compassion and a solidarity with life. We may long for the sun to shine, may ache for it. But, if we can allow the sun to shine within our hearts, we would not notice or care whether the phenomenal sun was shining or not. Our potential for radiance is there all the time.

This movement is the one taught by the Buddha, not a path of extremes, neither indulgence nor austerity, neither avoidance nor suppression. It is a path he called the Middle Way, a way of facing up to those urges that make life difficult for us, a way that is accessible to us all. As David Brazier describes this path, it is 'a state of optimum mental health, free of self-defeating views, self-defeating thoughts, self-defeating actions, self-defeating speech, self-defeating modes of livelihood, self-defeating effort, self-defeating memories and self-defeating visions. In particular, our efforts to avoid the reality of affliction and passion are self-defeating.'[369]

The Buddha's final words are there for us to follow – 'with vigilance, strive on'. With compassion and wisdom, we can open our hearts and minds, and drive forward on the path to freeing ourselves, for the benefit of *all* beings in this world. We can dedicate our lives to thirsting for more.

Reflecting – Chapter 10

What is your idea of a 'good life'? To what extent do you already desire in the 'expansive mode'? Close your eyes, and grasp your hands tightly inwards to your chest; now open up the palms of your hands and stretch them away from your body; do this clenching and releasing slowly several times, noticing how it feels; reflect on the wider implications of this experience. To what degree do you feel that you can impact upon the world in a positive way? Reflect upon 'magic moments' you have experienced in your life, and how strong your sense of ego was at that moment. Consider acts of kindness and generosity that you have performed recently; how do they make you feel physically, mentally and emotionally when you bring them to mind? How much do you desire to be free of your unhelpful cravings?

WITH GRATITUDE

Expressing gratitude is a practice that moves us away from simply taking what has been given to us, to giving thanks in return. To that extent it is a movement from self-mode to expansive-mode described in the final chapter of this book.

There are many people to whom I would like to express gratitude here in relation to the writing of this book. To start with, the first two Buddhists I really got to know, Mangala and Jayaka, who guided my beginning along this spiritual path. My *kalyāna mitras*, my spiritual friends, Taradasa and Abhayamati, who have always been there for me. My mentor, role model, principal teacher and preceptor, Ratnaghosha, who gave me my wonderful name and who is a marvel. Those who I consider to be my other main teachers in Triratna – Sangharakshita, of course, the founder of our movement, as well as Padmavajra, Vessantara and, again, Taradasa. I am also so grateful to all my friends in the Cambridge Triratna Sangha who have enthused me in their many different ways.

I would like to express thanks to some of those who suggested particular ideas for this book: Kamalamati, for pointing me towards Silavadin's article on intimate relationships; Kamalanaga, for telling me about Rob Burbea's talks on desire; Arthasiddhi, for directing me to Sangharakshita's comments on Vajrayāna Buddhism being perhaps the most appropriate tradition for Western Buddhists; Amritasara, for using Maitreyabandhu's metaphor about conkers; and Sarvajit for his helpful comments on early chapters of the book.

Special thanks go to Claire Taylor-Jay of Clarion Editing, whose services I originally bid for at a skills auction, and who went on to perform incredibly thorough and detailed developmental editing for me, who recommended the scalpel - without which this book would have been much longer - and who initiated me on a massive cut-and-paste job.

Finally, the warmest gratitude to my family. My children and grandchildren who are a constant inspiration to me, and of whom I am so proud. And my wife, to whom this book is dedicated, and without whom I am not sure where I would be.

REFERENCES

[1] The term *kleśa* is used to describe the disturbing emotions that trouble our minds.

[2] Subhuti, *Mind in Harmony*, Windhorse, 2015, page 124

[3] I came across this word for the first time recently and liked what it conveyed, the idea of a weak desire or inclination that might not be strong enough to lead to action.

[4] In the foreword to Judson Brewer, The Craving Mind: from cigarettes to smartphones to love - why we get hooked and how we can break bad habits, Yale University Press, 2017

[5] Lama Yeshe, *Introduction to Tantra: The Transformation of Desire*, Wisdom, 2014, Kindle edition, location 130

[6] David Brazier, The Feeling Buddha: An Introduction to Buddhism, Robinson, 2001, page 25.

[7] Lama Yeshe 2014, op.cit., Kindle location 725

[8] Wisdom in Buddhism is traditionally acquired in three ways: through listening to the teachings of the Buddha, through reflecting on them, and through meditating and thus embodying them.

[9] Together, Pali and Sanskrit are the languages in which the majority of Buddhist texts originating in India are written. The oldest texts are written in Pali, which is said to be close to the language that the Buddha actually spoke. The Sanskrit equivalent of *taṇhā* is *tṛṣṇā*.

[10] As described by Sangharakshita, *A Survey of Buddhism,* in *Complete Works, Volume 1*, Windhorse, 2018, chapter 1 section XIII

[11] J.P. Donleavy, *The Ginger Man*, Abacus, 1997. Kindle edition, location 1458

[12] Allen Carr, *The Little Book of Quitting*, 'The Second Powerful Influence', Penguin, 1999

[13] David Webster, *The Philosophy of Desire in the Buddhist Pali Canon*, Taylor & Francis, 2005, Kindle edition, location 278

[14] Traleg Kyabgon, *Desire: Why It Matters*, Shogam, 2019, Kindle edition, location 476

[15] For more on Buddhism's five ethical precepts, see Chapters 6 and 8

[16] In Introduction to Anna Lembke, Dopamine Nation: Finding Balance in the Age of Indulgence, Headline, 2023,

[17] Michelle Drouin The age of intimacy famine: when we interact with our phones rather than our loved ones, The Guardian online, 31 January 2022

[18] See for example Rutger Bregman, *Humankind: A Hopeful History*, Bloomsbury, 2020, pages 13-15, for an analysis of the effect of compulsive news browsing.

[19] Thomas Mann, *Tonio Kröger* in *Death in Venice; Tristan; Tonio Kroger*, Penguin Classics, 1990, page 146

[20] Joseph Conrad, *Heart of Darkness*, Penguin Books, 1973, page 108

[21] Stefan Zweig, Twenty-Four Hours in the Life of a Woman, in The Collected Stories of Stefan Zweig, Pushkin Press, 2013, Kindle edition, page 497

[22] The Middle Way in Buddhism is used in different contexts to describe a path between two extremes.

[23] See Johann Hari, *Stolen Focus: Why You Can't Pay* Attention, Bloomsbury, 2023, for more on the phenomena of attention deficiency in the 21st century.

[24] A 'false refuge' is one which that does not give security, does not relieve suffering, and indeed can enhance our troubles. A 'true refuge' relieves suffering and leads to an end to craving, ill-will and delusion. The three true refuges which all Buddhists commit to are the Buddha, the Dharma and the Sangha (the teacher, his teachings, and the community of those who follow his teachings).

[25] Stefan Zweig, *The Collected Novellas of Stefan Zweig*, Puskin Press, 2021, Kindle edition, page 366

[26] Attributed to Bhartrihari, in *Some Unquenchable Desire: Sanskrit Poems of the Buddhist Hermit Bhartrihari*, Shambhala, 2018, Kindle edition, page xvii

[27] The third ethical precept that Buddhists undertake is the training principal to abstain from sexual misconduct.

[28] Alain Badiou in the Foreword to Byung-Chul Han, *The Agony of Ecstasy*, The MIT Press, 2017

[29] Sangharakshita, *Living Ethically*, Windhorse, 2013, page 84

[30] Silavadin, *Intimate Relationships as Buddhist Practice*, Western Buddhist Review, Volume 8, 2022, www.westernbuddhistreview.com.

[31] Rob Burbea, *Eros Unfettered (Part 1)*, 2017, page 49, www.dharmaseed.org/talks/40171

[32] Desmond Morris, *The Naked Ape*, Jonathan Cape, 1967

[33] Subhuti, Remorse and Confession in the Spiritual Community, pdf www.freebuddhistaudio.com

[34] Mark Epstein, Open to Desire: The Truth about What the Buddha Taught, Penguin, 2006, page 5

[35] Arthur Schnitzler, *Dream Story*, Kindle edition, location 1141

[36] *Āditta Sutta* in the *Saḷāyatanavagga* of the *Samyutta Nikāya*, translated by Bhikkhu Bodhi, *The Connected Discourses of the Buddha*, Wisdom, 2000, and in the *Vinaya Mahāvagga*, www.dhammatalks.org. The poet T.S. Eliot, in *The Waste Land*, gave the name *The Fire Sermon* to a section of his great poem that portrayed in particular sexual craving.

[37] Consumerism from a Buddhist viewpoint is explored extensively in Vaddhaka Linn, *The Buddha on Wall Street*, Windhorse, 2015, and Stephanie Kaza, ed., *Hooked! Buddhist Writings on Greed, Desire, Desire, and the Urge to Consume*, Shambhala, 2005

[38] For a very interesting article by a Buddhist on what the internet does to our minds, read *You Are What You Download* in Stephanie Kaza, ed, 2005, op.cit.

[39] David Brazier, The Feeling Buddha: An Introduction to Buddhism, Robinson, 2001, page 77

[40] Dr Anna Lembke, *Dopamine Nation* : Finding Balance in the Age of Indulgence, Headline, 2023

[41] The chapter 'Buddhist Economics' in E.F. Schumacher's groundbreaking book *Small is Beautiful*, Vintage, 1993, develops this idea further.

[42] Subhuti, *Re-imagining the Buddha*, Padmaloka Books, 2012, page 21

[43] Paul Mazur, a leading Wall Street banker working for Lehman Brothers in 1927, from the BBC television documentary series, *The Century of the Self*, by Adam Curtis, 2002

[44] This is an informal rendering of the Buddhist term *saṃsāra*, which is developed more in Chapter 2

[45] See chapters 2 and 9 for more about how *karma* works.

[46] See section on the Four Noble Truths below.

[47] Majjhima Nikaya iii.251, Sutta 141 verse 21, in A Translation of the Majjhima Nikaya 10, Wisdom 1995. Similar descriptions can be found in MahāSatipaṭṭhānasutta, Digha-Nikaya 22 and Digha-Nikaya iii.216 in The Long Discourses of the Buddha translated by Maurice Walshe, Wisdom, 1995; Itivuttaka 58 in The Udana and the Itivuttaka translated by John D. Ireland, Buddhist Publication Society, 2007

[48] Sagaramati, 2001, op cit.

[49] For further reading on the three types of *dukkha*, see for example, Sangharakshita, *Vision and Transformation*, Windhorse, 1999, page 26

[50] Stefan Zweig, *The Collected Novellas of Stefan Zweig*, Kindle edition, page 277

[51] Lama Yeshe, 2014, op. cit., Kindle edition, location 600

[52] Sangharakshita, Seminar on the Dhammapada in A Stream of Stars: Reflections and Aphorisms, Windhorse, 2003, page 39

[53] *Bodhicaryāvatāra 6.45*, translation in Pema Chödrön, *No Time to Lose : A Timely Guide to the Way of the Bodhisattva*, Shambhala, 2006, page 184

[54] *Bodhicaryāvatāra* 4.28, 4.29, my rendering, compiled from other translations.

[55] Sangharakshita, Know Your Mind, in The Complete Works of Sangharakshita, Windhorse, 2023

[56] *Dvayatanupassana Sutta* 4, 3.12, *The Sutta Nipata*, translated by H. Saddhatissa, Routledge, 1995

[57] Bruce Matthews, *Craving and Salvation: A Study in Buddhist Soteriology*, Wilfrid Laurier University Press, 2006, page 76f

[58] Rob Burbea, 2017, op.cit., page 3

[59] Rob Burbea, 2017, op.cit., page 4

[60] This is the Pali term; the Sanskrit is *pratītya-samutpāda*.

[61] Sangharakshita, *A Guide to the Buddhist Path*, Windhorse, 2011, page 77

[62] There are very many detailed and pictorial descriptions of the processes involved in the Wheel of Life in Buddhist literature, for example, in Sangharakshita, 2011, op.cit., page 77ff

[63] Sangharakshita, 2011, op.cit., page 78

[64] Mark Epstein, Open to Desire: The Truth About What the Buddha Taught, Penguin 2006, page 98

[65] This example is suggested by Rob Burbea, 2017, op.cit., page 5

[66] The Sanskrit word *tṛṣṇā* for 'thirst' is usually used in the Wheel of Life, but I have kept the Pali word *taṇhā* in these writings for the sake of consistency. Incidentally, in the Wheel of Life, *taṇhā* is usually represented pictorially as a group of people drinking alcohol; the more they drink, the more they crave.

[67] The traditional interpretation in Buddhism of this link is rebirth, being reborn into a new life of *saṃsāra,* where the cyclic pattern of the *nidāna* chain continually repeats itself. However, I am grateful to the psychologist and Buddhist practitioner Judson Brewer in *The Craving Mind: From Cigarettes to Smartphones to Love—Why We Get Hooked and How We Can Break Bad Habits,* Yale, 2017, Kindle location 767, for this

alternative suggestion for elucidating the *nidana* of 'birth' by talking about memory-forming.

[68] Dvayatanupassana Sutta 13, 3.12, The Sutta Nipata, 1995, op.cit.

[69] Sagaramati, 2001, op. cit.

[70] *Know Your Mind* in Sangharakshita, 2023, op.cit.

[71] Dvayatanupassana Sutta 13, The Sutta Nipata 3.12, 1995, op.cit.

[72] Subhuti, 2015, op.cit., page 62

[73] Sangharakshita, *A Survey of Buddhism,* in *Complete Works, Volume 1*, Windhorse, 2018, chapter 1 section XIII

[74] Traleg Kyabgon, 2019, op.cit., location 1163

[75] Traleg Kyabgon, 2019, op.cit., location 73

[76] Bruce Matthews in *Craving and Salvation* pages 76f gives a fuller description of this misapprehension, and J. Jeffrey Franklin in *The Lotus and the Lion* gives a detailed history of Buddhism's reception in the West.

[77] Mark Epstein, 2005, op.cit., page 3

[78] *Bodhicaryāvatāra* 7.40, translated by Kate Crosby and Andrew Skilton, Oxford, 2008

[79] Subhuti, 2015, op.cit., page 49

[80] Subhuti, 2015, op.cit., page 50

[81] See for example the section The Five Niyāmas in Subhuti, *Revering and Relying upon the Dharma,* at www.thebuddhistcentre.com/triratna/seven-papers-subhuti-sanghrakshita, which describes the different types of conditioned relationships at play in the world.

[82] Doug Smith, *On Craving,* 23 April 2015, www.secularbuddhism.org/on-craving

[83] The Buddhist term *moha* is usually used for the root poison of ignorance or delusion, and it is more or less synonymous with *avijjā* (in Pali *avidya*)

[84] Walpola Rahula, *What the Buddha Taught,* chapter 3, various published editions.

[85] *Know Your Mind* in Sangharakshita, 2023, op.cit., page 171f

[86] Robert Wright, *Why Buddhism is True,* Simon & Schuster, 2018

[87] Sagaramati, 2001, op.cit.

[88] Letter to Annabella Milbanke, 6 September 1813 in *The Byron-Lady Melbourne Correspondence, 1812-1813* Edited by Peter Cochran, at https://petercochran.wordpress.com

[89] There is more on the Buddha's 'noble search' in Chapter 9

[90] Some Unquenchable Desire: Sanskrit Poems of the Buddhist Hermit Bhartrihari, translated by Andrew Schelling, page 12, Shambhala, 2018

[91] Mark Epstein, 2006, op.cit., page 2

[92] *Factory farming is turning this beautiful British river into an open sewer* by George Monbiot https://www.theguardian.com/commentisfree/2022/jun/10/factory-farming-british-river-sewer-wye-chicken-factories?CMP=Share_iOSApp_Other

[93] William James, *The Will to Believe,* quoted in Rutger Bregman, *Humankind,* page 257, Bloomsbury, 2020

[94] David Loy, Money, Sex, War, Karma: Notes For A Buddhist Revolution, Wisdom 2008, page 137

[95] John Clare, *Poems,* Kindle edition, location 2140

[96] Chapter 8 will explore in more detail the concepts of pure and impure.

[97] **Bodhicaryāvatāra** 8.19 in Pema Chodron, No Time to Lose: A Timely Guide to the Way of the Bodhisattva, Shambhala, 2007

[98] Lama Yeshe, 2014, op. cit., Kindle location 720

[99] Thomas Hardy, *Far From the Madding Crowd,* www.digireads.com, Kindle location 304

[100] Rob Burbea, 2017, op.cit., page 69

[101] Jnanaketu, Views and the Yogacara in Dharma Training Course for Mitras: Year Two page 179, www.lulu.com

[102] 'Go, pluck the summer flower, and see how long it lives' *The Vanities of Life* in John Clare, op.cit., Kindle location 2211

[103] Lama Yeshe, 2014, op. cit., Kindle location 449

[104] Mark Epstein, 2006, op.cit., page 98

[105] Robert Wright, op.cit., 2018, location 160

[106] William Shakespeare, *Anthony and Cleopatra*, II.ii.225-245

[107] Robert Zajonc, *Attitudinal Effects of Mere Exposure*, 1968, https://doi.org/10.1037/h0025848

[108] Traleg Kyabgon, 2019, op.cit., location 179

[109] Innate tendencies are governed by the *mano-niyāma* law of conditionality (which was mentioned above in the discussion about evolutionary psychology), and acquired tendencies by the *karma-niyāma* law of conditionality.

[110] Bruce Matthews *Craving and Salvation: A Study in Buddhist Soteriology*, Wilfrid Laurier University Press, 2006, page 67. Matthews describes here in some detail the relationship between unconscious inclinations and craving. See also the description of *store-consciousness* in Chapter 5 of this book.

[111] See for example, Norman Doig, *The Brain That Changes Itself*, Penguin, 2008, page 102ff, in relation to pornography; also Rick Hanson, *Buddha's Brain: The Practical Neuroscience of Happiness, Love, and Wisdom*, New Harbinger, 2009

[112] *Dvedhavitakka Sutta v6*, in *A Translation of the Majjhima Nikaya*, Wisdom, 1995. A *bhikkhu* is a Theravada Buddhist monk. In much of the Pali Canon, the Buddha addresses his teachings to bhikkhus, but his teachings equally apply to all of us.

[113] Prajnaketu, Cyberloka : A Buddhist Guide to Digital Life, Windhorse, 2022

[114] These contrasting views are still with us. 'Eternalism' is how for example traditional Christianity generally views death, i.e. our 'soul'

carries on to either heaven or hell. 'Nihilism' is the modern atheistic, materialistic, scientific view of death.

[115] It is not my intention here to go into detail about the Buddhist doctrine of rebirth. For further reading, I would recommend Nagapriya's book *Exploring Karma and Rebirth*, Windhorse, 2016

[116] Dalai Lama, *The Meaning of Life,* Hopkins, Jeffrey, ed., Wisdom, 1992

[117] Nagapriya, Seeing Like A Buddha: The Four Noble Truths, Kindle edition, location 452

[118] Alan Moore, *Watchmen*, Dc Comics, 2005

[119] From the article *'Is internet addiction a growing problem?'* The Guardian, 25 October 2021

[120] *Suvarṇaprabhāsa Sūtra*, trans. R.E. Emmerick as *The Sutra of Golden Light*, page 12, Pali Text Society, 1979,

[121] Sangharakshita, *The Essential Sangharakshita*, page 621, Wisdom, 2009. Different types of 'oppression' are examined further in the following pages of that book.

[122] See footnote 24

[123] The Sanskrit word *prapañca* means mental chatter, discursive thought, pointless speculation.

[124] Henry James, Portrait of a Lady, 100 Eternal Masterpieces of Literature, Volume 1, Kindle location 358309

[125] Aldous Huxley, *The Doors of Perception*, Classics to Go, Kindle location 415

[126] Rob Burbea, 2017, op.cit., page 8

[127] David Brazier, 2001, op.cit., page 22

[128] Downfall of the Heart in The Collected Stories of Stefan Zweig, Kindle location 7810

[129] Valerie Mason-John (Vimalasara) and Paramabandhu Groves, *Eight Step Recovery: Using the Buddha's Teachings to Overcome Addiction*, Windhorse, 2018, page 49

[130] Pema Chödrön, *Welcoming the Unwelcome*, Shambhala, 2019, Chapter 2

[131] Subhuti, 2015, op.cit., Chapter 11

[132] Subhuti, 2015, op.cit., Chapter 11

[133] Sangharakshita, Sangharakshita: Collected Lectures Vols I and II, Lecture 40, The Analytical Psychology of the Abhidharma, Lokabandhu/Triratna, 2013

[134] *Bodhicaryāvatāra* 7.64, translated by Kate Crosby and Andrew Skilton, Oxford, 2008

[135] Confusion in The Collected Novellas of Stefan Zweig, Kindle page 317

[136] Subhuti, 2015, op.cit., page 176

[137] Compare the use of the acronym for a devil-may-care attitude - YOLO, 'you only live once'

[138] Valerie Mason-John and Paramabandhu Groves, 2018, op.cit., page 1

[139] *Thirsting for More* by the way is not about how to recover from serious drug and alcohol addiction; that however is the subject of Mason-John and Paramabandhu's book.

[140] From *The Long Discourses of the Buddha: A translation of the Digha Nikaya* Wisdom, page 7, as quoted by Gabor Maté in the Foreword to Mason-John and Paramabandhu, 2018, page xxxv op.cit.

[141] Thanks to Judson Brewer, 2017, op.cit., Kindle edition, page 77, for these suggestions.

[142] Bradford Hatcher, *Craving and Aversion as Addiction and Denial: Buddha's Eightfold Path as a Step Program*, www.hermetica.info/Buddha1b.htm, 2013, page 43

[143] Hooked On Games: The Lure And Cost Of Video Games And Internet Addiction by Andrew Doan and Brooke Strickland, FEP International, 2012

[144] *Bodhicaryāvatāra 6.37* translated by Kate Crosby and Andrew Skilton, Oxford, 2008

[145] Pingiya's Praises to the Way to the Beyond 22, The Sutta Nipata, 1995, op.cit.

[146] Veil of Stars in Poems and Short Stories, The Complete Works of Sangharakshita, Vol 25, Windhorse, 2020

[147] Traleg Kyabgon, op.cit, 2019, Kindle location 275

[148] Ron Leifer, *The Happiness Project:* Transforming the Three Poisons that Cause the Suffering We Inflict on Ourselves and Others page 102. Snow Lion, 1997

[149] Sangharakshita: Collected Lectures Vols I and II, Lecture 117, Buddhism and Psychoanalysis, paragraph 6, Lokabandhu/Triratna, 2013

[150] Thomas Mann, *The Magic Mountain,* Kindle location 3791-3793

[151] Thomas Mann, *The Magic Mountain,* Kindle location 8016 – 8019

[152] The Book of Thel in William Blake: Selected Poetry, Penguin, 1998

[153] Udāna 7.4, as translated in The Complete Works of Sangharakshita, Vol 10, Windhorse, 2021

[154] Stephen Batchelor, Living with the Devil: A Meditation on Good and Evil, Riverhead, 2005

[155] Bhadravudhamanavapuccha 3, 5.12, The Sutta Nipata, 1995, op.cit.

[156] Dzigar Kongtrul, The Intelligent Heart: A Guide to the Compassionate Life, Shambala, 2016, page 53

[157] See, for example, *The Narcissism Spectrum Model: A Synthetic View of Narcissistic Personality*, Zlatan Krizan and Anne D. Herlache, Personality and Social Psychology Review, January 2017, https://doi.org/10.1177/1088868316685018

[158] Mark Epstein, *Thoughts without a Thinker: Psychotherapy from a Buddhist Perspective,* page 59, Duckworth, 1997

[159] Byung-Chul Han, *The Agony of Eros,* Kindle location 118

[160] Sangharakshita, *The Complete Works of Sangharakshita, Vol 10,* page 521, Windhorse, 2021

[161] Lionel Shriver, *Should We Stay or Should We Go*, The Borough Press, 2022, Kindle edition, location 3446

[162] Lama Yeshe, 2014, op. cit., Kindle location 775

[163] Ron Leifer, The Happiness Project: *Transforming the Three Poisons that Cause the Suffering We Inflict on Ourselves and Others*, page 101, Snow Lion, 1997

[164] I am grateful to the Zen Buddhist nun Sister Lang Nghiem of the Plum Village Buddhist tradition, founded by Thich Nhat Hanh, for some of the ideas in this chapter, taken from an interview with her at *The Way Out Is In: Understanding How Our Mind Works*, Episode 28, Apple podcast, 22 April 2022

[165] Fredrik Falkenström, A *Buddhist Contribution to the Psychoanalytic Psychology Of Self*, The International Journal of Psychoanalysis Volume 84 Issue 6, 2003, https://doi.org/10.1516/XH6D-2YLY-P2JV-9VRC

[166] Bradford Hatcher, 2013, op.cit.

[167] Śāntideva, *Bodhicaryāvatāra*, 6.93, my rendering

[168] Reginald Ray, *Touching Enlightenment*, page 79/80, Sounds True Adult, 2014

[169] Jnanaketu, Views and the Yogacara, in Dharma Training Course for Mitras, page 177, www.lulu.com

[170] Dalai Lama and Thubten Chodron, *Saṃsāra, Nirvana and Buddha Nature*, page 179, Wisdom, 2019

[171] See Chapter 8 for more on what constitutes the five *skandha*; in Buddhism, what is our 'self-make-up'.

[172] Amoretti, sonnet 75 in *Edmund Spenser, The Shorter Poems*, Penguin, 1999

[173] Valerie Mason-John and Paramabandhu Groves, 2018, op.cit., page 54.

[174] A Translation of the Majjhima Nikaya 82, Wisdom, 1995

[175] Rob Burbea, 2017, op.cit., page 17

[176] Thank you to Sister Lang Nghiem for this metaphor, see footnote 164

[177] Traleg Kyabgon, 2019, op.cit., Kindle location 1292

[178] Subhuti, *A Supra-Personal Force* page 26, www.subhuti.info

[179] Ajahn Sucitto, Turning the Wheel of Truth: Commentary on the Buddha's First Teaching. Shambhala, 2010, Kindle locations 966-979

[180] Robert Wright, 2018, op.cit., page 62

[181] Je Tsongkhapa in the Dalai Lama, *Teachings on Je Tsongkhapa's Three Principal Aspects of the Path*, Library of Tibetan Works and Archives, 2009, verse 3

[182] The Four Reminders are: the preciousness of our human birth, the truth of impermanence, the inevitability of *karma*, and the pervasiveness of *saṃsāra*.

[183] www.wiseattention.org

[184] Sharon Salzberg, *Real Happiness: The Power of Meditation : A 28-Day Program*, Highbridge, 2011

[185] The worldly winds of praise and blame, pleasure and pain, loss and gain, infamy and fame, mentioned in Chapter 4

[186] See Chapter 9 Driving for more on the ignoble and the noble search

[187] Vessantara, Tales of Freedom: Wisdom from the Buddhist Tradition, Windhorse, 2000

[188] Ratnaghosha, *The Five Stages of the Spiritual Life*, page 4, Cambridge Buddhist Centre booklet

[189] London in William Blake: Selected Poetry, Penguin, 1998

[190] Lama Yeshe, 2014, op. cit., Kindle edition, location 1110

[191] *Anguttara Nikaya* 1.58, quoted in Matthews, 2006, op.cit., page 2

[192] Lama Thubten Yeshe, The Essence of Tibetan Buddhism: The Three Principal Aspects of the Path and An Introduction to Tantra, Lama Yeshe Wisdom Archive, 2001

[193] Bhadravudhamanavapuccha 1, 5.12, The Sutta Nipata, 1995, op.cit.

[194] *Know Your Mind* in Sangharakshita, 2023, op.cit.

[195] Kukkuravatika Sutta, in A Translation of the Majjhima Nikaya, 1.390, Wisdom, 1995

[196] The Endlessly Fascinating Cry seminar, in The Complete Works of Sangharakshita, Vol 4, Windhorse 2019

[197] Traleg Kyabgon, 2019, op.cit., location 162

[198] Vimalasara, podcast Sept 2022, www.windhorsepublications.com/podcast

[199] Bradford Hatcher, 2013, op.cit.

[200] David Brazier, 2001, op.cit., page 13

[201] Joseph J. Merz et al, *World scientists' warning: The behavioural crisis driving ecological overshoot*, Sage Journals, https://journals.sagepub.com/doi/10.1177/00368504231201372, September 2023

[202] Danapriya, *It's Not Out There*, Windhorse, 2020

[203] David Brazier, 2001, op.cit., page 14

[204] The Endlessly Fascinating Cry seminar, in The Complete Works of Sangharakshita, Vol 4, Windhorse 2019

[205] Traleg Kyabgon, 2019, op.cit., Kindle location 1082

[206] Lama Yeshe, 2014, op. cit., Kindle location 162

[207] *Uposatha Sutta, Udāna* 5:5 at www.suttafriends.org/sutta/ud5-5

[208] Traleg Kyabgon, 2019, op.cit., location 1082

[209] Anna Lembke, *Dopamine Nation: Finding Balance in the Age of Indulgence*, Headline, 2023

[210] Traleg Kyabgon, 2019, op.cit., location 1440

[211] Lama Yeshe, 2014, op. cit., Kindle location 351

[212] There are other Buddhist responses to craving. For example, there is the teaching of the Six (or sometimes Ten) Perfections, the *pāramitā*, virtues to be cultivated in order to realize awakening. The six perfections are ethical behaviour, generosity, patience, effort or energy

in pursuit of the good, meditative absorption and wisdom. And we could find a *pāramitā* antidote appropriate to each of the three *taṇhā* – perhaps patience or *kṣānti* for *kāma-taṇhā* (the craving for sensual gratification); energy or *vīrya* for *vibhava-taṇhā* (the craving for non-existence); and wisdom or *prajñā* for *bhava-taṇhā* (the craving for existence).

[213] Lama Yeshe, 2014, op. cit., Kindle location 667

[214] Ajahn Munindo translation, *A Dhammapada for Contemplation*, verse 290, Aruna, 2006

[215] Lama Yeshe, 2014, op. cit., Kindle location 695

[216] Referred to, for example, in the *Sariputto Sutta*, Samyutta Nikaya 35.120; *Sukhavihāra Sutta*, Itivuttaka 2.2.13; *Telapatta Jātaka* 96

[217] Lama Yeshe, 2014, op. cit., Kindle location 244

[218] Traleg Kyabgon, 2019, op.cit., Kindle location 1123

[219] Ariyapariyesanā Sutta v34, in A Translation of the Majjhima Nikaya 10, Wisdom, 1995

[220] Subhuti, *A Supra-Personal Force* page 26, www.subhuti.info

[221] Cūḷataṇhāsankhaya Sutta 37.15 in A Translation of the Majjhima Nikaya, Wisdom, 1995. See note 148 for meaning of bhikkhu

[222] Sangharakshita translation, *Dhammapada: The Way of Truth*, verse 401, Windhorse, 2008

[223] Subhuti, *The Bodhisattva Ideal*, page 15, Padmaloka Books, 2018

[224] Lama Surya Das, *Awakening the Buddha Within: Tibetan Wisdom for the Western World*, Random House, 1998

[225] Alagaddupama Sutta in A Translation of the Majjhima Nikaya, Wisdom, 1995

[226] Pema Chödrön, *When Things Fall Apart: Heart Advice for Difficult Times*, Shambhala, 2002

[227] Shunryu Suzuki, *Zen Mind, Beginners Mind*, page128, Shambhala, 1973

[228] Lama Yeshe, 2014, op. cit., Kindle location 703

[229] Sangharakshita, *Living Ethically* page 78, Windhorse, 2009

[230] Russ Harris, *The Happiness Trap: Stop Struggling, Start* Living, Robinson, 2008. The term 'urge surfing' was coined in the 1980s by psychologist Alan Marlatt and Judith Gordon

[231] *The Sutta Nipata*, 1995, op.cit., 36.6

[232] Judson Brewer, 2017, op.cit., page 111

[233] *The Bodhisattva Ideal* page 37, Subhuti, Padmaloka Books, 2019

[234] Refer back to Chapter 5 for more on how we seek to protect our 'self'

[235] Stephanie Kaza, ed, Hooked! Buddhist Writings on Greed, Desire, Desire, and the Urge to Consume, page 84, Shambhala, 2005

[236] Buddhism without negativity bias: Early Buddhism versus Secular Buddhism on dukkha and taṇhā - Josef Mattes, 2018, www.academia.edu

[237] From her song 'Will You Still Love Me Tomorrow?'

[238] Ajitamanavapuccha 3-4 Sutta Nipata 5.1, 1995, op.cit

[239] *Bodhicaryāvatāra* 5.2/5.3, translation by Kate Crosby and Andrew Skilton. Oxford, 1995

[240] Rob Burbea, 2017, op.cit., page 37

[241] For further details, refer back to Chapter 2

[242] For further details, refer back to Chapter 2

[243] See Rob Burbea, *Seeing That Frees*, Troubador, 2014, page 125f, for some exercises on working with *vedanā* and craving

[244] Mason-John and Paramabandhu, 2016, op.cit., page 26

[245] Stephanie Kaza, ed, 2005, op. cit. page 48

[246] Sangharakshita, *Mind - Reactive and Creative*, Windhorse, 2024

[247] Mason-John and Paramabandhu, 2016, op.cit., page 89

[248] Stephen Batchelor, *Buddhism without Beliefs: A Contemporary Guide to Awakening*, Bloomsbury, 1998

[249] King Pasenadi Goes on a Diet (Samyutta Nikāya 3:13) Andrew Olendzki Insight Journal, Fall 2002, Barre Centre for Buddhist Studies

[250] Satipaṭṭhāna Sutta in A Translation of the Majjhima Nikaya 10, Wisdom, 1995

[251] *dhamma* in Pāli, *dharma* in Sanskrit

[252] Thich Nhat Hanh was a Vietnamese monk, teacher and founder of the Plum Village Buddhist tradition. He was nominated for the Nobel Peace Prize by Martin Luther King. This is from his book *The Heart of the Buddha's Teachings: Transforming Suffering into Peace, Joy and Liberation*, Rider, 2021, chapter 6

[253] Traleg Kyabgon, 2019, op.cit., Kindle location 361

[254] The term 'monkey-mind' appears to be a translation of the Chinese word *xīnyuán*, originally a Buddhist term for a mind that is unsettled and grasping, like a monkey leaping from branch to branch

[255] There are many excellent books on the market and apps available on the Internet which teach meditation. I feel though that none of them can match going to a Buddhist centre and learning in-person from an experienced meditation teacher, being able to ask questions and receive feedback.

[256] See for example the Appendix to Kamalashila, *Buddhist Meditation: Tranquillity, Imagination and Insight*, Windhorse, 2012

[257] As described in Mason-John and Paramabandhu, 2018, op.cit., page xxv

[258] Ian McEwan, *Lessons*, Vintage, 2022, Kindle location 6786

[259] Attadanda Sutta 15, 4.15, The Sutta Nipata, 1995, op.cit.

[260] Traleg Kyabgon, 2019, op.cit., location 212

[261] Rob Burbea, 2017, op.cit., pages 35/36

[262] *Dhammapada*, verse 183, translated by Kate Crosby and Andrew Skilton, Oxford 2008

[263] Traleg Kyabgon, 2019, op.cit., location 1484

[264] Lama Thubten Yeshe, Ego, Attachment and Liberation: Overcoming Your Mental Bureaucracy, Kindle location 155

[265] The four *dhyāna* are progressive levels of deep meditation

[266] Lama Yeshe, 2014, op. cit., Kindle location 171

[267] In Pali, *catur-bala*, in Tibetan *thob-bzhi*

[268] Sangharakshita, The Endlessly Fascinating Cry seminar, in The Complete Works of Sangharakshita, Volume 4, Windhorse 2019

[269] Sangharakshita, *Living Ethically*, page 87, Windhorse, 2009

[270] Jack Austin translation, *Dhammapada*, verse 340, The Buddhist Society, 1983

[271] Traleg Kyabgon, 2019, op.cit., Kindle location 1501

[272] Doug Smith, On Craving, www.secularbuddhism.org/on-craving, 23 April 2015

[273] Traleg Kyabgon, 2019, op.cit., Kindle location 494

[274] Geshe Kelsang Gyatso, Modern Buddhism: The Path of Compassion and Wisdom - Volume 2 Tantra, Kindle location 160

[275] *Vimalakīrti Nirdeśa*, Chapter 7. Robert A.F. Thurman translation, *The Holy Teaching of Vimalakīrti*, Pennsylvania State University, 1976

[276] Sangharakshita - Collected Lectures Vols I and II, Kindle location 6737

[277] Sangharakshita - Collected Lectures Vols I and II, Kindle location 6910

[278] *Bāhiya Sutta* in the *Udāna* 1.10, translation in *The Complete Works of Sangharakshita*, Volume 10, Windhorse, 2021

[279] Traleg Kyabgon, 2019, op.cit., location 2719

[280] Reginald Ray, 2014, op.cit., page 81f

[281] *Bodhicaryāvatāra*, see footnote 239

[282] Charles Dickens, *Hard Times*, Kindle edition, location 3093

[283] *The Holy Teaching of Vimalakīrti*, Robert A.F.Thurman translation, !976, op.cit., Chapter 7

[284] Sangharakshita, The Endlessly Fascinating Cry seminar, in The Complete Works of Sangharakshita, Vol 4, Windhorse 2019

[285] *Bodhicaryāvatāra* 4.47, my rendering

[286] Johann Wolfgang Goethe, The Sorrows of Young Werther, in 100 Eternal Masterpieces of Literature, Volume 1, Kindle location 283858

[287] Thank you Vessantara for this image

[288] Judson Brewer, 2017, op.cit., Kindle location 73

[289] Lama Yeshe, 2014, op. cit., Kindle location 617

[290] Lama Yeshe, 2014, op. cit., Kindle location 626

[291] Sagaramati, 2001, op. cit.

[292] Vessantara, 2000, op.cit., page 32

[293] *nibbāna* is Pali for the more commonly recognised Sanskrit word *nirvāṇa*, meaning Enlightenment, awakening, emancipation from, or the extinguishing of, the poisons of craving, hatred and delusion

[294] Traleg Kyabgon, 2019, op.cit., location 73

[295] *Bodhicaryāvatāra* 7.39/40, my rendering

[296] Pingya's Praises of the Way to the Beyond 14, Sutta Nipata, 1995, op.cit

[297] Prajnaketu, 2022, op.cit., page 96

[298] Vajragupta Staunton, *Free Time!* Windhorse, 2019

[299] Plato, *Symposium and Phaedrus*, trans. Benjamin Jowett, Dover Publications, 1993

[300] Robert H. Hopcke, A Guided Tour of the Collected Works of C.G.Jung, Shambhala, 1999, pp.45ff.

[301] Rob Burbea, 2017, op.cit., pages 38/39

[302] Mark Epstein, 2006, op.cit.

[303] See, for example, Vishvapani's biography *Gautama Buddha*, Chapter 2, Quercus, 2011

[304] Sangharakshita, *The Four Foundation Yogas of the Tibetan Buddhist Tantra*, Lecture 60, Lokabandhu/Triratna, 2013, op.cit.

[305] Lama Yeshe, 2014, op. cit., Kindle location 270

[306] Traleg Kyabgon, 2019, op.cit., Kindle location 959

[307] Bradford Hatcher, 2013, op.cit., page 42

[308] Dhivan Thomas Jones, *This Being, That Becomes*, Windhorse, 2011, page 47

[309] Lama Yeshe, 2014, op. cit., Kindle location 320

[310] Sangharakshita has proposed this in *Milarepa and the Art of Discipleship* in *The Complete Works of Sangharakshita*, Volume 18, page 417 (thank you Arthasiddhi for pointing this out to me)

[311] Theravāda, Mahāyāna and Vajrayāna Buddhism, as set out in Chapter 6 Medicating

[312] Lama Yeshe, 2014, op. cit., Kindle location 86

[313] Traleg Kyabgon, 2019, op.cit., Kindle location 951

[314] James Joyce, Portrait of the Artist as a Young Man, in 100 Books You Must Read Before You Die, Kindle location 3555

[315] *The Essential Sangharakshita*, Wisdom, 2009, pages 388/9

[316] Philippe Sands, *East West Street*, W&N, 2017, Kindle location 2133

[317] Bodhicaryāvatāra, Chapter 2

[318] The Endlessly Fascinating Cry seminar, in The Complete Works of Sangharakshita, Vol 4, Windhorse, 2019

[319] Pingya's Praises of the Way to the Beyond 14, Sutta Nipata, 1995, op.ci.t

[320] *Bodhicaryāvatāra* 7.1, translated by Kate Crosby and Andrew Skilton, Oxford, 2008

[321] *Bodhicaryāvatāra* 7.16, translation in Pema Chödrön, *No Time to Lose: A Timely Guide to the Way of the Bodhisattva*, Shambhala, 2006

[322] A Sanskrit word, sometimes translated as 'faith', which literally means 'setting one's heart on something'

[323] *Soṇa Sutta* (AN III.374), as quoted in Justin Whitaker, *Ethics, Meditation, and Wisdom*, page 9, www.academia.edu

[324] For further development of these aspects of *vīrya*, listen to Subhuti, *Mind and Mental Events*, 2001, Talk 8, www.freebuddhistaudio.com/audio/details?num=OM803

[325] *Bodhicaryāvatāra* 7.32, translation in Pema Chödrön, *No Time to Lose: A Timely Guide to the Way of the Bodhisattva*, Shambhala, 2006

[326] A maxim attributed to Dr Samuel Johnson

[327] *Bodhicaryāvatāra* 1.6, my rendering

[328] A Western Buddhist Ordination Ceremony, Lecture 39 in Sangharakshita, Collected Lectures Vols I and II, Lecture 40, The Analytical Psychology of the Abhidharma, Lokabandhu/Triratna, 2013

[329] Sangharakshita, *The Bodhisattva Ideal*, page 143, Windhorse, 1999

[330] Lama Yeshe, 2014, op. cit., Kindle location 1806

[331] This interpretation of *dhamma-niyāma* derives from Sangharakshita, as set out in Subhuti's paper *Revering and Relying on the Dharma*

[332] There is a Buddhist practice, *tonglen,* where in meditation we symbolically breathe into our hearts the dark smoke which is the *dukkha* of all sentient beings, and breathe out white light for the benefit of all

[333] Lama Yeshe, 2014, op. cit., Kindle location 204

[334] Paul Hawken, in the Foreword to Hooked! Buddhist Writings on Greed, Desire, Desire, and the Urge to Consume, page viii, Shambhala, 2005

[335] Maitreyabandhu, *Thicker Than Blood*, page146, Windhorse, 2001

[336] Sangharakshita, *Know Your Mind*, in The Complete Works of Sangharakshita, Volume 17, Windhorse, 2023

[337] Sangharakshita, *A Survey of Buddhism*, page 121, Windhorse, 1987

[338] Bob Dylan, Knocking on Heaven's Door

[339] A Little Boy Lost in William Blake: Selected Poetry, Penguin, 1998

[340] Rainer Maria Rilke, *Sonnets to Orpheus II*, 13, in *A Year with Rilke: Daily Readings from the Best of Rainer Maria Rilke*, poem for January 13, ed Anita Barrow and Joanna Macy, Harper Collins, 2009

[341] *Bodhicaryāvatāra*, 6.125, my rendering

[342] This is my paraphrase of *Bodhicaryāvatāra*, 1.21

[343] Paul Gilbert, *The Compassionate Mind*, page 217, Constable, 2010

[344] Lama Thubten Yeshe, Ego, Attachment and Liberation: Overcoming Your Mental Bureaucracy, 2006. Kindle location 155

[345] *Bodhicaryāvatāra*, 8.129, my rendering

[346] *Karaṇīya Mettā Sutta*, translation by Ratnaprabha, https://thebuddhistcentre.com

[347] Thomas Mann, *The Magic Mountain*, Kindle edition, page 608

[348] M. Scott Peck, *The Road Less Travelled*, Arrow, 1990

[349] Santikaro, Practising Generosity in a Consumer World in Hooked! Buddhist Writings on Greed, Desire, Desire, and the Urge to Consume, page 201, Shambhala, 2005

[350] Bradford Hatcher, 2013, op.cit.

[351] Geshe Kelsang Gyatso, www.azquotes.com/quote/837059

[352] Traleg Kyabgon, 2019, op.cit., location 3039

[353] Call me by My True Names – The Collected Poems of Thich Nhat Hanh, Parallax Press, 2005

[354] Ṭhānissaro Bhikkhu, *Roots of Buddhist Romanticism*, Kindle location 72-73

[355] David Richo, *The Five Longings*, Shambhala 2017, Kindle location 575

[356] Tissametteyyamanavapuccha 3, 5.2, The Sutta Nipata, 1995, op.cit.

[357] Lama Yeshe, 2014, op. cit., Kindle location 784

[358] The Endlessly Fascinating Cry seminar, in The Complete Works of Sangharakshita, Vol 4, Windhorse, 2019,

[359] In Buddhism, this is the *bodhicitta*, the highest motivation and inspiration, the drive to be fully awakened and free.

[360] From an unpublished talk Vessantara gave at Adhisthana Retreat Centre 2021

[361] Mettā Bhāvanā Sutta, *Itivuttaka* 27, in The Udana and the Itivuttaka translated by John D. Ireland, Buddhist Publication Society, 2007

[362] *Bodhicaryāvatāra*, 3.25, rendering by Padmavajra

[363] Lama Yeshe, 2014, op. cit., Kindle location 470

[364] Saṃyutta Nikāya 46.54, translated by Bhikkhu Bodhi, The Connected Discourses of the Buddha, Wisdom, 2000

[365] Rainer Maria Rilke, *Uncollected Poems* in *A Year with Rilke: Daily Readings from the Best of Rainer Maria Rilke*, poem for January 2, ed Anita Barrow and Joanna Macy, Harper Collins, 2009

[366] Bhadravudhamanavapuccha 1, 5.12, The Sutta Nipata, 1995, op.cit.

[367] From The Heart Sutra translated by Philip Kapleau, in Puja: The Triratna Book of Buddhist Devotional Texts, Windhorse, 2022

[368] From Seminar on the Precious Garland, in Sangharakshita, A Stream of Stars: Reflections and Aphorisms, Windhorse, 2003

[369] David Brazier, 2001, op.cit., page 36

About the Author

Kuladipa is a teacher of Buddhism and meditation at the Cambridge Buddhist Centre. He is an ordained member of the Triratna Buddhist Order. He first encountered Buddhism as a teenager in the 1960s and travelled overland to India at that time with a view to finding a 'guru' who would be his guide. During the ensuing years he kept up his interest in Buddhism, but without taking up a regular practice. For many years he worked as a schoolteacher and took up meditation as a means of coping with the stress of the job.

But it was only at a time of deep pain in his later life that he rediscovered what had impassioned him as a teenager and committed himself wholly to following the Buddhist path.

Printed in Great Britain
by Amazon